Working with Children and Adolescents

Working with Children and Adolescents

An Evidence-Based Approach to Risk and Resilience

Edited by
M. Elena Garralda
and Martine Flament

Book Series of the International Association for
Child and Adolescent Psychiatry and Allied Professions

JASON ARONSON
Lanham • Boulder • New York • Toronto • Oxford

Published in the United States of America
by Jason Aronson
An imprint of Rowman & Littlefield Publishers, Inc.

A wholly owned subsidiary of
The Rowman & Littlefield Publishing Group, Inc.
4501 Forbes Boulevard, Suite 200, Lanham, Maryland 20706
www.rowmanlittlefield.com

PO Box 317
Oxford
OX2 9RU, UK

British Library Cataloguing in Publication Information Available

Library of Congress Cataloging-in-Publication Data

Working with children and adolescents : an evidence-based approach to risk and
resilience / edited by M. Elena Garralda and Martine Flament.
    p. cm.
Includes index.
ISBN-13: 978-0-7657-0443-6 (cloth : alk. paper)
ISBN-10: 0-7657-0443-9 (cloth : alk. paper)
    1. Child psychopathology—Risk factors. 2. Adolescent psychopathology—Risk
factors. 3. Resilience (Personality trait). 4. Evidence-based psychiatry. I. Garralda,
M. Elena. II. Flament, Martine.

RJ499.W65 2006
618.92'89—dc22   2006003536

Printed in the United States of America

$\circledcirc^{TM}$ The paper used in this publication meets the minimum requirements of American
National Standard for Information Sciences—Permanence of Paper for Printed Library
Materials, ANSI/NISO Z39.48-1992.

Contents

Preface

Myron Belfer, President of IACAPAP

As child psychiatry has advanced, the concepts that guide the field increasingly reflect the level of evidence to support specific interventions. The International Association for Child and Adolescent Psychiatry and Allied Professions (IACAPAP) has as a primary mission the dissemination of new knowledge and best practices. While child psychiatry is not always associated with the research and clinical application of risk and resilience findings, risk and resilience are concepts that form the very basis of child psychiatry and child mental health historically and to the present day. The mission for child mental health professionals is to first try to maintain children on a trajectory for healthy mental development but at the same time be mindful of the risks for psychopathology and recognize the pathology early enough to intervene effectively to prevent maladaptive consequences.

It is a tradition for IACAPAP to publish a monograph in conjunction with its congresses. The monographs have addressed themes over the years that reflect contemporary concerns. This monograph follows in the tradition and provides authoritative contributions on the latest evidence related to risk and resilience. The chapters take the reader from the most basic biological understandings to the appreciation of the complex interactions between culture and context leading to the manifestation of healthy adaptation or psychopathology in the child and adolescent. The challenge is to use this sound evidence to influence practice and program implementation. It is also hoped that providing this evidence will help to convince a broader audience of the need to support child mental health initiatives and create policy to provide for sustained effective interventions to reduce risk and enhance resilience in all children.

This IACAPAP monograph is the most recent in a series of monographs dating from the 1970s. The volumes have been produced by a series of dedicated editors—Colette Chiland, E. James Anthony, Cyrille Koupernik, Pierre Ferrari, J. Gerald Young—who with the current editors, Elena Garralda and Martine Flament, have devoted themselves to the education of all of us.

Editorial Introduction

M. Elena Garralda

The International Association for Child and Adolescent Psychiatry and Allied Professions (IACAPAP) aims to disseminate emerging knowledge and good clinical practice in the area of child and adolescent mental health worldwide. It organizes international scientific meetings and world regional meetings on individual topics.

This volume marks the celebration of the 2006 World IACAPAP Congress in Melbourne, Australia. The last two books edited by IACAPAP addressed brain/culture and development and pathways to care for child and adolescent mental health problems. The present volume focuses on risk and resilience factors.

Over recent years there has been an altogether impressive increase in our knowledge of child and adolescent mental health problems and of factors and situations that contribute to the development of psychiatric disorders. The search for ever better delineated etiological and maintaining factors will not cease, as it offers the best potential for prevention and it can guide the search for efficacious treatments.

This volume outlines up-to-date, empirically derived knowledge on risk and resilience factors for child and adolescent psychopathology, through chapters written by worldwide experts in their field. In setting up this project, the book series coeditor Martine Flament and I have aimed to ensure that key relevant aspects are covered and reflect the multifactorial etiology of child and adolescent psychiatric disorders, within two main themes: risk factors deeply rooted in biological processes and those stemming from the wider psychosocial environment or context for healthy child and adolescent mental development and functioning. We have also been mindful to invite an international authorship in line with the scope of IACAPAP.

The contributions represent expert views supported by empirical evidence. They do not attempt to cover the field exhaustively, as would textbooks of child psychiatry. Instead authors illustrate new advances through examples of selected disorders, critically appraising the existing evidence, underlining areas where this is lacking, and highlighting the relevance of findings for psychopathology as seen in clinical practice. They emphasize resilience factors conceptualized as both the absence of risk and the presence of factors that have in them a protective effect.

A volume such as this with a fixed publication date and a limited production time relies on the authority and positive cooperation of contributors for its success. Authors have been remarkably efficient at producing definitive work on a tight schedule. If the time pressure has resulted in some technical anomalies such as lack of total uniformity in the presentation of references, this has to be seen in the light of the—by necessity—inescapable deadlines. We would like to believe that the quality of the presentations far outweighs any such inconvenience.

The biological risk factor chapters cover genetics and hypothalamic-pituitary-adrenal axis influences. Psychosocial ones address the influence of abnormal parenting through child abuse and neglect, traumatic events such as exposure to war and violence, as well as school influences. The following paragraphs abstract some aspects of the contents.

The field of genetics is currently witnessing the most spectacular advances and this may have the most far-reaching implications for future practice. The chapter by Johannes Hebebrand and colleagues provides an authoritative, well-informed update on the field globally and as applied to child psychopathology. Following an overview of the current status of knowledge on the human genome, the genetics of Rett syndrome are discussed. As the first DSM-IV axis I disorder mostly attributed to mutations within a single gene, it provides the authors with an opportunity to discuss the molecular analysis of a psychiatric disorder, one that may contribute to our understanding of the pathways involved in the development of pervasive developmental disorders. The authors predict that in the next decade we may well witness the identification of several predisposing gene variants with small effect sizes. They describe the use of specific techniques, including linkage analysis, the candidate gene approach, and linkage disequilibrium matching, and discuss findings on schizophrenia, dyslexia, and Tourette's disorder. They caution nevertheless against potential pitfalls inherent in the genetic analysis of complex disorders. They critically discuss recent findings on the genetics of aggression and conduct disorder using gene-environment techniques and point out that a predisposing genotype by no means inevitably entails the development of any given disorder.

The chapter by Ian Goodyer addresses comprehensively and scholarly the wealth of information on the increasingly productive field of hypothalamic-pituitary-adrenal (HPA) axis function in relation to the mental health of both adults and children. He highlights the fact that certain steroids are manufactured in the brain and play a key role in brain development and plasticity, and he points to alterations in levels of the adrenal steroids cortisol and related compounds such as DHEA having important implications for general cognitive function and emotional regulation. A special methodological advantage for research in this area is the use of comparatively easily available salivary cortisol measures. Cortisol responsiveness to developmental and interactive events is already apparent in infants, and associations have been reported with negative life events and mood disorders. It is intriguing that whereas cortisol hyposecretion is linked to post-traumatic stress disorder, child maltreatment is associated with cortisol hypersecretion in some studies and with hyposecretion in others. This may reflect genetic variations in the behaviorally sensitive neural pathways implicated in response to adversity. There is experimental work indicating that children with conduct disorder can exhibit cortisol hyporeactivity to stress. There may moreover be long-term effects of adverse experiences in early childhood on adolescent HPA axis function, possibly reflecting increased vulnerability to psychopathology. Overall the chapter illustrates a specific line of biological inquiry that is helping to tease out possible mechanisms modulating emotional responses and psychopathology in childhood.

Parenting exerts a crucial influence on children's mental health. Thomas G. O'Connor and Stephen B. C. Scott review the literature selectively and highlight risk and protective factors. They describe theories accounting for the links between parent-child relationships and child outcomes, with a special emphasis on social learning and attachment theories, but they also point out the importance of descriptions of parenting styles. Methods to study parenting and general frameworks for interpreting the results of the literature are covered, and the chapter illustrates links between parent-child relationship quality and child outcomes using key findings on aggression and delinquency, depression and anxiety, cognitive ability and achievement, social competence and peer relationships, and general health and biological development. The authors consider challenges to causal claims implied or made explicit in the research and discuss intervention studies and their practical implications. It can be concluded that there is continuing support from both clinical experience and empirical research that one of the best predictors of children's well-being, perhaps especially for those living in high-risk settings, is a positive and supportive parent-child relationship.

In addressing the important environmental issue of child abuse, Ernesto Caffo and colleagues point out that research in this area seems to have peaked.

This is a particularly good time therefore to take stock and revisit definitions and prevalence of extended notions of abuse, including emotional abuse. The authors outline and discuss critically and fully current knowledge on risk factors, both intrinsic and extrinsic to the child and family, and consequences of different types of abuse for the child's development and mental health. However, they also consider resilience and protective factors, starting from the fact that about a fifth to nearly half of adults with a history of sexual abuse in childhood fail to report adverse psychosocial consequences. There is now evidence that cognitive behavioral treatment can be of benefit to children who have been sexually and physically abused, and secondary school-based prevention programs focusing on teaching children how to resist and report abuse to trusted adults can also be effective. Nevertheless, the authors emphasize work aimed at preventing child abuse. This involves early identification of families at risk and efforts to support families and strengthen parenting. Home-visitation prevention programs in particular have been evaluated; they can be beneficial and their effects sustained at long-term follow-up. The ingredients of a successful program are detailed in the review.

Understanding factors that promote resilience is given most prominence in the chapter by Raija-Leena Punamäki on children exposed to conditions of war and military violence. She considers the interface between sociopolitical realities and the cognitive and emotional processes that enhance resilience, the preconditions that make resilience possible, and the multilevel and complex mechanisms and developmental processes by which children become competent, families secure, and societies supportive, especially at times of profound challenge. This involves discussing issues such as the threshold effect model for resulting psychological distress, as opposed to the simple dose effect model, which assumes that a high dosage of traumatic exposure invariably leads to psychological distress. Coping effectiveness is seen to depend on the controllability, acuteness, and severity of trauma; on the goodness of fit between coping strategies and environmental demands, whereby some coping strategies are helpful in certain circumstances but not others; and on the ability understand and explain the reasons for the trauma and related hardships. She notes that active participation in political struggle among some war-traumatized children and adolescents may in fact enhance social affiliation, feeling of control, venting of feelings, and purposeful activity. The ability of secure attachments to protect against the effects of trauma is discussed critically, as an assumption needing qualification since attachment style may be protective depending on the nature of the stress. Nevertheless, "the illusion of private safety seems to be the secret of resilient development" and resilience possible when children show accurate and age-salient emotional recognition, discrimination, and interpretations linked to emotional regulation. The chapter highlights a developmental approach that emphasizes child agency in making sense of and reacting to environmental stresses and the multilevel nature of mechanisms linking child development and adversities.

A different type of environmental influence is addressed by Amira Seif el Din in the chapter on school influences on child and adolescent mental health. Clearly school is a major influence for children's mental health across the world. The author makes the case for a mental health program being part of a comprehensive school health program, as this is potentially accessible to most children. In some countries school mental health programs may be the best opportunity to access children with a variety of psychiatric problems, including emotional disorders and tendency to suicide: school programs using cognitive behavioral techniques have been tested successfully for depressive disorders and school can be made into a source of relief for anxiety and isolation in adolescents in states of hopelessness. School involvement can be crucial in children with somatoform disorders, school anxiety, and absence, and school-based prevention and treatment efforts can be effective for children with post-traumatic stress disorder or those at risk for trauma. School-based interventions have become increasingly common and can have an important impact on antisocial behavior such as bullying. They can make an active effort to promote school attendance, educate around adolescent risk-taking behaviors, and promote the development of broader life skills in children and adolescents, all of which may help promote mental health and resilience.

We trust that this volume will help highlight and focus some of the important advances in knowledge and practice to be presented and discussed at the forthcoming IACAPAP Congress in Melbourne, assist in the prevention of child and adolescent psychiatric disorders worldwide, and help bring attention to it.

Chapter One

Identifying Genes Underlying Child and Adolescent Psychiatric Disorders

Johannes Hebebrand, Kathrin Reichwald,
Benno Graf Schimmelmann, and Anke Hinney

Over the past two decades child and adolescent psychiatric disorders have become a fascinating research field, which has attracted clinicians and scientists alike. Psychiatry as a whole has greatly benefited from the introduction of novel technologies and methodology to clinically oriented research, such as neuroimaging, molecular genetics, and molecular biology.

Developmental aspects represent a key feature of child and adolescent psychiatry. Our research efforts span the range from infancy to early adulthood. As clinicians, we frequently marvel about the pace of development during this age period; we frequently find ourselves attracted to patients of a specific age range who (luckily for us) have a somewhat more restricted number of disorders; in addition, the symptoms of any given disorder are more uniform for a specific developmental stage than across all of childhood and adolescence. As researchers we continually grapple with the impossibility of competently dealing with the complexity of these developmental issues. We realize that we are merely scratching the surface of the processes underlying normal and aberrant development. Nevertheless, at times we should take the opportunity to stand back and review what our scratching has uncovered.

The genetics of child and adolescent psychiatric disorders is a research field with a most ambitious goal. In essence, we have embarked on a voyage to elucidate causative factors underlying the disorders our patients have. Because many of these disorders must be viewed in the context of development, this endeavor also leads to the identification of genes involved in normal development of the brain and its function.

Genetics has previously concentrated on providing heritability estimates for diverse disorders. Family, twin, and adoption studies have yielded estimates as to what extent genetic and environmental factors and gene environment interactions account for a specific phenotype. Thus genetics by

1

necessity also addresses environmental factors, rendering our endeavor all the more ambitious.

OBESITY EXEMPLIFIES THE INTERACTION OF GENETIC AND ENVIRONMENTAL INFLUENCES

Obesity is a complex disorder that nicely illustrates how genetic and environmental factors act in concert. Clearly, the recent obesity epidemic can be explained only by environmental and social changes with a direct or indirect impact on energy intake and expenditure; our gene pool cannot have changed to a substantial degree during the past thirty years. However, according to the thrifty genotype hypothesis (originally postulated for type 2 diabetes mellitus), gene variants entailing a higher chance of survival during periods of famine have accumulated during vertebrate evolution (Neel, 1962), thus presumably explaining why many humans carry a substantial number of alleles (gene variants) predisposing them to overweight. The recent and unprecedented environmental and social changes promoting both increased energy intake and decreased energy expenditure render such individuals prone to the development of overweight and obesity. Presumably, a large number of genes (>100)—only very few of which are currently known—are involved in the predisposition to obesity. When and via which mechanisms environmental factors lead to the manifestation of overweight in an obesity-prone individual is influenced by the respective genotype; *genotype* used in this sense implies the combined effect of all gene variants with an impact on metabolic and behavioral phenotypes affecting body weight.

Seemingly paradoxically, twin and adoption studies have repeatedly shown that the shared environment has only a negligible effect on body weight adjusted for height (body mass index, or BMI; kg/m^2); e.g., the BMI of young adult adoptees is correlated with that of their biological parents but not with the BMI of their adoptive parents (Stunkard et al., 1986). According to this and several other formal genetic studies, variance of BMI is almost totally explained by nonshared environment (Hebebrand et al., 2001). Is the common environment indeed unimportant?

Quite obviously, the answer is no; a prerequisite for the development of overweight is an abundance of food. The average BMI of a population changes dramatically upon transition of a developing nation into an industrialized country. Because the environment in industrialized societies has become so similar, children and perhaps even more so adolescents are almost uniformly exposed to the same environmental risk factors. They are basically all able to choose from a large variety of tasty, relatively inexpensive, and readily available foods and to pursue sedentary activities, including watching television, which in itself potentially contributes to uniform habits and tastes. The importance of the non-shared environment for the development of obesity presumably only applies in light of a shared environment that in essence shows little variation between individuals living in the same society. Despite the evident importance of an obesogenic (or nonobesogenic) environment, heritability estimates for the quantitative phenotype BMI typically range from 0.4 to 0.7 (Hebebrand et al., 2001, 2003), indicating that 40–70% of the variance of BMI is accounted for by genetic factors. It is again important to realize that these heritability estimates have typically been calculated in industrialized societies.

HERITABILITY OF BEHAVIORAL TRAITS AND DEVELOPMENTAL MILESTONES

For many behavioral traits and developmental milestones, heritability estimates based on categorical or dimensional (quantitative) data similarly indicate that overall approximately half of the variance is explained by genetic factors, the other half by the environment (tables 1.1 and 1.2). For many of these traits, the nonshared environment has also been found to be of greater relevance than shared environment. For most psychiatric disorders, which are usually assessed categorically, genetic factors have also been shown to play an important role (table 1.3).

Table 1.1. Selected Heritability Estimates of Personality Dimensions

| | | Heritability Estimates | | |
	Assessments	Female	Male	Reference
Extraversion	EPQ-R	57%	57%	Keller et al., 2005
Neuroticism	EPQ-R	54%	49%	"
Lie	EPQ-R	44%	35%	"
Psychoticism	EPQ-R	39%	43%	"
Harm avoidance	TCI	53%	57%	Keller et al., 2005
Novelty seeking	TCI	55%	55%	"
Reward depending	TCI	56%	51%	"
Persistence	TCI	55%	55%	"
The "Big Five"				
Extraversion	NEO-PI-R	53%		Jang et al., 1996
Neuroticism	NEO-PI-R	41%		"
Openness	NEO-PI-R	61%		"
Agreeableness	NEO-PI-R	41%		"
Conscientiousness	NEO-PI-R	44%		"

Note: EPQ-R = Eysenck Personality Questionnaire (Eysenck et al., 1985); TCI = Temperament and Character Inventory (Cloninger et al., 1991); NEO-PI-R = NEO Personality Inventory (Costa and McCrae, 1990).

Table 1.2.   Heritability Estimates of Selected Behaviors and Developmental Milestones

	Assessments	Heritability Estimates		Reference
Behaviors				
Dieting	EAT	42%		Rutherford et al., 1993
Body dissatisfaction	EDI	52%		"
Drive for thinness	EDI	44%		"
Disinhibition of eating	TFEQ	40%		Steinle et al., 2002
Restrained eating	TFEQ	28%		"
Hunger	TFEQ	28%		"
Obsessive compulsive behavior	CBCL	45–58%		Hudziak et al., 2004
Developmental Milestones				
Motor development	Crawling, sitting, standing, walking	90%		Goetghebuer et al., 2003
	Crawling, sitting, walking	22–33%		Peter et al., 1999
	Standing	0%		"
		Female	*Male*	
Expressive language vocabulary	MCD-I-R	8%	20%	Van Hulle et al. 2004
Two-word-combination-use	MCD-I-R	28%	10%	"

Note: EAT = Eating Attitudes Test (Garner et al., 1982); EDI = Eating Disorder Inventory (Garner et al., 1983); MCD-I-R = MacArthur Communicative Development Inventories-Short Form (Fenson et al., 1993); CBCL = Child Behavior Checklist (Achenbach, 1991); TFEQ = Three Factor Eating Questionnaire (Stunkard and Messick, 1985).

Table 1.3.   Heritability Estimates of Selected Psychiatric Disorders

Disorder	Heritability Estimates	Reference
PDD	90%	Santangelo and Tsatsanis, 2005
Enuresis	67–70%	Von Gontard et al., 2001
Conduct disorder	53%	Gelhorn et al., 2005
OCD	47%	Clifford et al., 1984
Anxiety disorders	30–40%	Eley et al., 2003
ADHD	60–80%	Heiser et al., 2004
Anorexia nervosa	48–88%	Hinney et al., 2004
Bulimia nervosa	28–83%	Hinney et al., 2004
Schizophrenia	73–90%	Sullivan et al., 2003
Bipolar disorder	60–85%	Smoller and Finn, 2003
Major depression	31–42%	Sullivan et al., 2000

Note: OCD = obsessive compulsive disorder; PDD = pervasive developmental disorders (including autistic disorder, Asperger disorder, disintegrative disorder, and PDD not otherwise specified); ADHD = attention-deficit/hyperactivity disorder.

PLAN FOR THIS CHAPTER

In the following we first present a brief overview of the current status of our knowledge of the human genome. We proceed by taking a look at Rett syndrome, the first (and for the future potentially the only) *Diagnostic and Statistical Manual of Mental Disorder* (DSM-IV) axis I disorder that in the majority of cases has been found to be due to mutations within a single gene. Fascinatingly, the molecular analysis of this disorder is beginning to contribute to our understanding of pathways involved in pervasive developmental disorders in general. The molecular genetic analysis of complex child and adolescent psychiatric disorders will profit from the introduction of new technology; in the upcoming decade we will witness the elucidation of several gene variants that predispose to such disorders. The effect size of most of these gene variants is likely to be small. We conclude by pointing out that we as child and adolescent psychiatrists have a responsibility to critically reflect novel genetic findings. We need to be aware of potential pitfalls inherent to the genetic analysis of complex disorders; it is also important that we realize that a predisposing genotype by no means entails an inevitable fate. For readers new to the genetics of child and adolescent psychiatric disorders, introductory guides to the language of molecular genetics (Eley and Craig, 2005) and the statistics of molecular genetics (Eley and Rijsdijk, 2005) have recently been published.

THE HUMAN GENOME

Formerly, psychiatric genetics was a research area mainly for psychiatrists with an interest in formal genetics who were additionally knowledgeable in basic statistics. Pioneer work pertaining to twin and family studies was performed in Germany in the 1920s and early 1930s. However, the Nazi era led to the complete eradication of solid scientific research in this field in Germany. Several German clinicians and scientists succumbed to the Nazi propaganda, and some even fueled it by supplying a pseudoscientific basis for eugenics and "racial hygiene." The eugenic movement was not limited to Germany; after World War II eugenics for several more years remained a research field in diverse countries.

Today sophisticated technology and advanced bioinformatical and biostatistical approaches are being used to elucidate the molecular basis of diverse human disorders and phenotypes. The completion of the Human Genome Project (HGP) launched in the late 1980s in the United States (National Research Council, 1988) has provided the basis for a much more rapid discovery of novel candidate genes for complex disorders. The first comprehensive analysis of the human draft sequences was published in February 2001 by the International Human Genome Sequencing Consortium (IHGSC) in *Nature* (IHGSC, 2001) and the private enterprise Celera Genomics (CG) in *Science* (Venter et al., 2001). The complete sequences of human chromosomes 22 (Dunham et al., 1999) and 21 (Chromosome 21 mapping and sequencing consortium, 2000) had become available shortly prior to this date. In spite of the different sequencing approaches taken, both draft assemblies covered comparable portions of the human genome (IHGSC: 92%; CG: 88%; Aach et al., 2001; Li et al., 2003; Istrail et al., 2004). Most striking was the small number of estimated human genes. Also, it became apparent that only approximately 1.5% of the human genome contains coding information. About 50% is composed of repetitive elements. Hence human complexity is based on diversity and finely tuned interaction of gene products such as RNA and proteins rather than gene numbers. Consistent with this, approximately 50% of human protein coding genes exhibit alternative splicing (Mironov et al., 1999; Brett et al., 2000; Modrek et al., 2002), creating a proteome of more than 90,000 proteins (Harrison et al., 2002), and gene expression is regulated by the complex interaction of a wide variety of transcription factors (Fickett and Wasserman, 2000; Stamm, 2002).

COMPLETION OF THE HUMAN DNA SEQUENCE

In April 2003, in the 50th-anniversary year of the discovery of the double-helical structure of DNA (Watson and Crick, 1953), the human DNA sequence was virtually completely elucidated. It represents approximately 99% of the euchromatic portion of the human genome (2.85 gigabases) with 99.999% accuracy (IHGSC, 2004). Only 341 gaps were left in the finished sequence, of which 308 (euchromatic gaps) are associated with segmental duplications that cannot be resolved with current technology.

Of main interest is the identification of all genes and a comprehensive genome annotation. Currently, 24,194 genes (including 1,978 pseudogenes, which are not transcribed) listed in the human gene catalogue (Ensemble Release 29.35b). The total number of protein coding genes is estimated at 20,000–25,000, which is consistent with data from cross-species comparisons (Mouse Genome Sequencing Consortium, 2002; Roest Crollius et al., 2000). The finished sequence also provides the basis for the identification of potentially all genes causing or predisposing to disease as well as genetic variations affecting individual responses to medication and environmental factors. To detect variation in a DNA region of interest (e.g., a candidate gene) in individuals with a specific disorder, the respective regions are commonly resequenced.

INTERSPECIES COMPARISON OF GENOMES

Interspecies comparison will be essential to identify regulatory regions and functional motifs, and so sequencing of many prokaryotic as well as eukaryotic organisms, including mammals (mouse, rat, cat, chimpanzee, cow, dog), is completed or well under way. Comparison of highly accurate genome sequences also enables the study of genome evolution, i.e., lineage-specific gene birth (Sabeti et al., 2002; Pavlicek et al., 2004; Emes et al., 2004; Nahon, 2003). Chimpanzee is the closest relative to humans, having DNA sequences 98% identical to each other. Of special medical interest is the high proportion of recent segmental duplications (Bailey et al., 2002) and inversions (Feuk et al., 2005) in the human genome. Those regions are prone to rearrangements or deletions resulting in phenotypic effects and can now be reliably analyzed (Mehan et al., 2004; Cheung et al., 2003).

HAPMAP PROJECT

The challenge of future genomics research is "to translate genomic information into health benefits" (Collins et al., 2003). For example, to systematically identify all genetic variations in the human population, the International HapMap Project was initiated in 2002 (www.hapmap.org/index.html.en). Populations with African, Asian, and European ancestry are studied to identify and catalogue genetic similarities and differences in humans. Genotyping a subset of these in the three populations generates an invaluable resource for the discovery of genes related to complex disorders.

HUMAN EPIGENOME PROJECT

Another international project aimed at better understanding disease state is the Human Epigenome Project (www.epigenome.org/). Its aim is to identify, catalogue, and study genomewide DNA methylation patterns. DNA methylation is a natural modification of the nucleotide cytosine by which gene expression is controlled. It is tissue specific, and changes over time and in response to environmental factors. So DNA methylation represents a direct link between environment and an individual's state. Epigenetic differences between monozygotic twins potentially account for phenotypical variation despite an identical genome at the DNA level. Although twins have been found to be epigenetically indistinguishable during the early years of life, older monozygotic twins exhibited remarkable differences in their overall content and genomic distribution of 5-methylcytosine DNA and histone acetylation, affecting their gene-expression portrait (Fraga et al., 2005). These findings indicate how an appreciation of epigenetics is currently missing from our understanding of how different phenotypes can originate from the same genotype.

There are many more projects, e.g., the international Human Brain Proteome Project, which is concerned with the brain proteome in health, aging, and neuropsychiatric disorders (www.hbpp.org/5602.html) and the ENCODE project aimed at identifying all functional elements in the human genome (www.genome.gov/10005107), both launched in 2003. Together with these and future initiatives, the HGP demonstrates the immense power lying in coordinated efforts to provide the foundation of biological and biomedical research at a new, more global, but at the same time intertwined level.

RETT SYNDROME

Recent insights (reviewed in Weaving et al., 2005) into the molecular mechanisms underlying Rett syndrome (RS) serve to illustrate these aspects. RS constitutes both a DSM-IV (American Psychiatric Association, 1994) and ICD-10 (WHO, 1992) diagnosis within the category of pervasive developmental disorders. Rett (1966) was the first to delineate the features of this serious neuropsychiatric disorder in three females; seventeen years later Hagberg et al. (1983) reported on thirty-five females with "progressive autism, loss of purposeful hand movements, ataxia, and acquired microcephaly," which represent the cardinal symptoms of the disorder.

METHYL-CPG BINDING PROTEIN 2 GENE

In 1999 different mutations in the methyl-CpG binding protein 2 gene (*MECP2*; human genes are commonly abbreviated in italic capital letters) were detected in females with RS (Amir et al., 1999). This discovery marked a turning point in psychiatric genetics: For the first time an official axis I child and adolescent psychiatric disorder was found to be due to mutations within a single gene in the majority of cases. Of classical RS patients, 90–95% have one of several *MECP2* mutations; the remaining 5–10% could have as yet undetected mutations in regulatory regions of *MECP2*. However, locus heterogeneity must also be considered in RS patients without detectable *MECP2* mutations: Mutations in the X-linked cyclin-dependent kinase-like 5 gene (*CDLK5*), which possibly belongs to the same pathway as *MECP2* because of overlapping expression patterns during synaptogenesis and neural maturation, were recently detected in patients with severe neurodevelopmental retardation and infantile spasms and the early onset seizure variant of RS (Mari et al., 2005; Weaving et al., 2004; Tao et al., 2004).

Despite most other child and adolescent psychiatric disorders being likely due to the joint influence of several predisposing gene variants (oligogenic or polygenic inheritance) and environmental risk factors (if several predisposing genes in combination with environmental factors cause a complex disorder, we speak of a multifactorial etiology or somewhat incorrectly of multifactorial "inheritance"), a closer look at RS is warranted to illustrate the rapid progression of developmentally oriented research once a molecular basis of an early onset psychiatric disorder has been elucidated. At the same time the complexity of the relationship between *MECP2* mutations, their biological consequences, and clinical findings provides an example of the implications of molecular variation at just a single gene locus. Finally, we refer to some findings in RS that also apply to autism in order to illustrate how the elucidation of monogenic model disorders can potentially cast light on the etiology of genetically complex disorders.

MECP2 AND THE RETT SYNDROME PHENOTYPE

The X-chromosomal location (Xq28) of *MECP2* helps to explain why mostly only females are affected. In males, *MECP2* mutations, which lead to classical RS in females, entail a much more severe and thus not readily comparable clinical phenotype, which usually involves encephalopathy, motor abnormalities, and respiratory dysfunction; death mostly occurs prior to age two. In RS females, the severity of the disorder is variable even if the same mutation is present. This presumably largely reflects differences in X inactivation: In females, one of the two X chromosomes (excluding the pseudoautosomal region) is randomly inactivated in all cells during early embryogenesis. If the proportion of neurons with an active X chromosome encompassing the *MECP2* mutation is high, the RS phenotype is more severe and vice versa. Recent evidence suggests that *MECP2* mutations entail a growth disadvantage at the cellular level (Weaving et al., 2005), potentially resulting in skewing of X inactivation; the proportion of cells with an inactivated X chromosome harboring the mutation is greater, thus entailing a less severe phenotype as would have been the case upon random inactivation. The type of mutation also seemingly influences the severity of the phenotype: missense mutations resulting in the exchange of a single amino acid result in a milder clinical symptomatology than nonsense mutations that entail a complete loss of function of MeCP2.

MECP2 is subject to alternative splicing (that is, different processing of the mRNA results in proteins of different sizes with partially identical domains). The B isoform has the highest expression in the brain, and mutations specific to the exons encoding this isoform are sufficient to cause RS. The respective protein, MeCP2, is 486 amino acids in size and includes four functional domains, one of which is the methyl-CpG binding domain (MBD). This protein domain binds exclusively to symmetrically methylated CpGs located in the upstream region of many genes; binding of MeCP2 to methylated CpGs has an influence on the transcription rate of such a gene. Variability in the phenotype is also due to the localization of a mutation; thus mutations in the methyl binding domain often lead to a more severe phenotype than those in the other domains.

FUNCTIONAL IMPLICATIONS OF *MECP2* MUTATIONS

It was initially proposed that the gene product of *MECP2* is a global repressor of the transcription of genes involved in brain development. Put simplistically, the expression of many genes in the central nervous system occurs only transiently during development; if due to a nonfunctional MeCP2 the expression of such genes continues after the developmental period during which they should have been silenced or "turned off," neuropsychiatric symptoms ensue. Such a mechanism could explain why RS symptoms first set in after an initially normal early development of six–eighteen months. Subsequent research mainly based on a series of elegant animal studies has, however, revealed that MeCP2 is most likely not a global repressor. Instead MeCP2 seemingly influences the transcription of specific genes.

If *Mecp2* (only the first letter of murine genes is capitalized) is completely knocked out in male mice, a mild RS-like phenotype ensues (female mice remain healthy into adulthood). A conditional knockout of *Mecp2* in the postnatal neurons of restricted regions in the brain leads to a similar although delayed neuronal phenotype, suggesting that the gene plays a role in postmitotic neurons. Transgenic expression of *Mecp2* in *Mecp2* knockout mice results in the rescue of the RS phenotype (Luikenhuis et al., 2004), further suggesting that RS symptoms are exclusively caused by a neuronal MeCP2 deficiency. MeCP2 may regulate the transcription of activity-dependent genes in neuronal cells (Martinowich et al., 2003), which is important in synapse development and neuronal plasticity. In Xenopus MeCP2 was found to inhibit the expression of the gene xHairy2a, which in turn promotes primary neurogenesis (Stancheva et al., 2003). In mammals MeCP2 possibly specifically binds to the promoter of the gene coding for the brain-derived neurotrophic factor

(BDNF; Martinowich et al., 2003; Chen et al., 2003; Klose et al., 2005), thereby repressing *BDNF* transcription in resting neuronal cells. Future research will potentially reveal which RS symptoms are related to the absence of the repression of specific genes due to the loss of function of MeCP2 in RS. For example, the frequent feeding problems in those afflicted with RS might be related to the persistent expression of BDNF, which aside from being involved in the regulation of neural survival, development, function, and plasticity in the brain also has an influence on feeding behavior and weight regulation (Hashimoto et al., 2005).

Transgenic and knockout mice models and comparative sequence analysis (Reichwald et al., 2000) have helped considerably to elucidate the function of MeCP2, assess the effect of specific mutations on the phenotype, and enable the identification of evolutionary conserved regions. Recently, abnormalities in social interaction and home-cage behavior were identified in mice in which a mutation similar to common RS-causing alleles had been introduced (Moretti et al., 2005). The resultant phenotype was reminiscent of the sleep/wake dysfunction and autistic features of RS patients.

A BROADER ROLE OF MECP2 IN NEURODEVELOPMENTAL DISORDERS?

The fact that autism is one of the key features of RS has led to a series of studies that aimed at assessing the role of *MECP2* and related genes in autistic disorder and mental retardation. MECP2, MBD1, MBD2, MBD3, and MBD4 comprise a nuclear protein family sharing the MBD and are related to transcriptional repression. Mutations in *MECP2* have infrequently been detected in patients with autistic features; mutations in the other genes have not systematically been found to play a role in the etiology of autistic disorder (Li et al., 2005). Defined genetic diseases (other than rare *MECP2*-related disorders) that have consistently been associated with autism include fragile X, tuberous sclerosis, Angelman syndrome, duplication of 15q11–q13, Down syndrome, San Filippo syndrome, phenylketonuria, Smith-Magenis syndrome, 22q13 deletion, adenylosuccinate lyase deficiency, Cohen syndrome, and Smith-Lemli-Opitz syndrome (Cohen et al., 2005). However, all of these disorders in total account for less than 10% of all cases of autistic disorders (Muhle et al., 2004). Nevertheless, in genetic studies of autism attempts should be made to exclude individuals with these monogenic and chromosomal disorders in order to obtain a sample of "idiopathic" autism.

In recent studies, significant differences in MeCP2 expression (quantitative immunoblots) were detected between brain samples of individuals with related neurodevelopmental disorders, including autism, pervasive developmental disorder, Prader-Willi and Angelman syndromes, and age-matched controls (Samaco et al., 2004, 2005). Hence the elucidation of the molecular mechanisms underlying RS has led to the theory that multiple pathways regulate the complex developmental expression of *MECP2* and are not only defective in RS but also in other autism-spectrum disorders. We have thus come a long way within a mere six years since the first discovery of *MECP2* mutations as a cause of RS.

IDENTIFICATION OF DISEASE
GENES IN COMPLEX DISORDERS

In contrast to RS most psychiatric disorders are complex, implying that they are not monogenic and thus do not conform to Mendelian patterns of segregation; such disorders result from the combined effects of a limited (oligogenic) up to a large (polygenic) number of gene variants and their interaction with the environment. Accordingly, each gene variant (subsequently also referred to as an allele; the term *allele* is also more generally used to define one of two or more variants of a particular DNA segment) has only a minor to minimal effect on the development of the respective phenotype or disorder. Typically, the effect size of a particular allele or genotype is indicated via the relative risk. (Because, with the exception of the X and Y chromosomes in males, all chromosomes occur in pairs in cells with a diploid genome, humans have two copies of every gene. In this context *genotype* refers to both alleles. Typically, the genotype relative risk is presented for heterozygotes and homozygotes for the predisposing allele; it is set to 1 in individuals homozygous for the wild-type allele.) For most of the alleles that have more or less unequivocally been shown to predispose to a particular psychiatric phenotype, the relative risks are well below 2. Such low relative risks imply that (1) the variant in itself is by no means sufficient to explain the disorder of an affected individual and (2) many individuals without the respective disorder harbor the same allele (or genotype).

In general terms, three approaches—namely genetic linkage analysis, candidate gene approach, and linkage disequilibrium matching—frequently in combination, are most commonly used to identify genes involved in the etiology of complex (psychiatric) disorders.

Genetic Linkage Analysis

DNA sequences at specific loci are inherited together as a consequence of their physical proximity on a single chromosome. The closer the loci are to each other at the DNA level, the lower the probability that they will be separated during meiosis, and hence the greater the probability that they will be inherited together. By analyzing genetic meiotic recombination frequencies between specific loci, genetic linkage analysis can be used to localize susceptibility genes within a framework map of genetic markers with known positions in the genome. Genome scans have typically been based on 350 to 1,000 microsatellite markers spaced rather evenly throughout the genome with marker distances of about 3 to 10 centiMorgan (cM; Morton, 1998).

It should be pointed out that the detection of linkage merely marks the first step required for identification of the relevant gene. Fine mapping with additional markers is frequently performed in an attempt to narrow the chromosomal region that initially can span a large region of a chromosome encompassing up to several hundreds of genes. Both linkage disequilibrium mapping and the candidate gene approach, both explained later, are subsequently used. This process of gene identification within a linkage peak represents a true bottleneck; despite large-scale efforts progress has typically been slow. The advent of more sophisticated technology, including high throughput genotyping, will speed up this crucial step.

Because a priori hypotheses as to functional candidate genes that could influence the phenotype are not required, genes (and pathways) can be identified via linkage analysis that had previously not been implicated in the respective disorder (such as *NOD2* in Crohn's disease: Hugot et al., 2001; Ogura et al., 2001). In addition, no a priori assumptions about mode of inheritance, frequency of the disease allele in the general population, and penetrance are required; such analyses are also termed *nonparametric* or *model-free*. For parametric linkage analyses these parameters must be estimated. If, however, these estimates are strongly misspecified, both false positive and false negative results can ensue.

Whereas linkage studies only a decade ago mainly focused on large, multiply affected families based on the (potentially incorrect) assumption that a single or only a small number of disease genes segregate in each of these families, more recent linkage studies have analyzed sibling pairs and small nuclear families (Risch, 2000). Pairs of siblings affected with the same disorder or concordant for the same phenotype are presumed to share susceptibility genes inherited from the same parent.

Linkage is commonly based on the identity by descent (IBD) of marker alleles in pairs of affected relatives such as affected sib pairs. If a specific marker is not linked to a disease locus, the IBD score in sib pairs is on average 1, which corresponds to the expected rate of allele sharing (50%) between sibs: two sibs can share 0, 1, or both parental alleles, the a priori probabilities of which are 25%, 50%, and 25%, respectively. The significance of an observed deviation from this expected distribution is often given as the logarithm of the odds (LOD) scores (Morton, 1995).

It is a matter of debate as to what LOD score actually constitutes a significant result for a complex disorder. Lander and Kruglyak (1995) have proposed that for nonparametric studies (in the following, the respective values for parametric studies are shown in parentheses) LOD scores greater than or equal to 3.6 (3.3) and between 2.2 (1.9) and 3.6 (3.3) indicate definite and suggestive evidence of linkage, respectively; accordingly, LOD scores less than 2.2 (1.9) are not even suggestive of linkage. LOD scores greater than or equal to 3.6 are only infrequently observed in genome scans for complex disorders; the probability of detecting such a high LOD score increases with the number of available relative pairs (Altmuller et al., 2001). Some researchers prefer to use p values instead of LOD scores, particularly for nonparametric studies to delineate evidence ($p \le 2.2 \times 10^{-5}$) and suggestive evidence for linkage ($p \le 7.4 \times 10^{-4}$).

Genome Scans in Child Psychiatric Disorders

Genome scans have been performed for several disorders relevant in child and adolescent psychiatry; of early onset disorders, the most scans have been completed for autism. A recent meta-analysis of genome scans for autism revealed common loci on chromosomes 7, 17, and 10 (table 1.4). One genome scan was described for each of the eating disorders anorexia (AN) and bulimia nervosa (BN; see table 1.4). For AN, the initial results revealed low LOD scores that did not even meet the criterion for suggestive linkage; however, a LOD score of 3.46 (suggestive linkage) was obtained in a post hoc analysis based on sib pairs with the restricting type only. Linkage to chromosome 13 regions was identified for enuresis nocturna in seventeen families (Eiberg et al., 1995). The results of a genome scan for Tourette's disorder (The Tourette Syndrome Association International Consortium for Genetics, 1999) were disappointing because all LOD scores were less than the cutoff value of 2.2 for suggestive evidence of linkage. Of the four genome scans performed in attention-deficit/hyperactivity disorder (ADHD), linkage to chromosome 5p is a robust finding (Ogdie et al., 2005; Hebebrand et al., 2005; table 1.5). Assuming dominant inheritance, in a post hoc analysis a maximal LOD score of 4.96 was reported in this region; the chromosome 5p linkage results were substantially better for the quantitative DSM-IV symptom-based than for the categorical analysis. Finally, a major difference was observed upon comparing LOD scores based on symptoms of hyperactivity/impulsivity versus attention deficit, with the latter being much higher (Hebebrand et al., 2005).

Table 1.4. Linkage Results of Genome Wide Scans for Psychiatric Disorders of Childhood for Single Studies and a Meta-Analysis

Autism and Autism-Spectrum Disorders[1]

Chromosome	Position	Average Rank p value
7q22–q32[2]	bin 7.5	10^{-5}
17p11.2–q12[3]	bin 17.2	0.0010[4]
10p12–q11.1[3]	bin 10.2	0.0022[4]

Anorexia Nervosa[5-7]

Chromosome	Position	LOD[8]	NPL
4	78.5 cM		1.80[5]
1p36.3–34.3	210 cM	3.46[6,9]	
1p33–36	72 cM		3.91[7,12]
2	114 cM	2.22[6,10]	
13	26 cM	2.50[6,11]	

Bulimia Nervosa[13]

Chromosome	Position	MLS
10p	44 cM	2.92
10p	24 cM	2.70
14q	62 cM	1.97

Gilles de la Tourette Syndrome[14]

Chromosome	Location	MLS
4q	145.98 cM[15]	2.38
8p	26.43 cM[15]	2.09

Enuresis nocturna[16]

Chromosome	Location	Z Score
13q13–q14.3	43.7 cM[17]	3.55
13q13–q14.3	40.4 cM[17]	2.67

Note: bin = region comprising approximately 30 cM, so that bin 7.5 is the fifth bin of chromosome 7; LOD = logarithm of odds; MLS = maximum likelihood score; NPL = nonparametric linkage; cM = centiMorgan; [1]Trikalinos et al., 2005 = Meta-analysis of nine genome scans on autism and autism-spectrum disorders comprising [2]712(autism) and [3]343(autism-spectrum disorders) affected sib-pairs; [4]suggestive evidence; [5]Grice et al., 2002; [6]Devlin et al., 2002; [7]Bergen et al., 2003; [8]results were obtained for a number of co-variates; [9]eating disorders inventory-2 = drive-for-thinness (EDI-DT) and obsessionality; [10]only obsessionality; [11]only EDI-DT; [12]NPL score for 37 families with at least one affected relative pair concordant for a DSM-IV diagnosis of anorexia nervosa, restricting subtype (American Psychiatric Association, 1994); [13]Bulik et al., 2003.

MLS = maximum likelihood score; cM = centiMorgan; [14]The Tourette Syndrome Association International Consortium for Genetics, 1999; [15]location according to the Marshfield genetic map; [16]Eiberg et al., 1995; [17]location according to the Genethon genetic map.

Table 1.5. Overlap of Linkage Results of Genome Scans for Attention-Deficit/Hyperactivity Disorder (ADHD)

Chr.	Bakker et al., 2003		Fisher et al., 2002		Arcos-Burgos et al., 2004 / Ogdie et al., 2003, 2004		Hebebrand et al., 2005	
	Location	MLS[c]	Location	MLS[c]	Location	NPL[d]	Location	LOD
5p	69 cM	1.43[a]	59 cM	2.55	5p13.3[a]	nr	17 cM	2.59
6q	166 cM	1.19[b]	89 cM	3.30	nr	nr	75 cM	0.58
7p	70 cM	3.04[b]	nr	nr	nr	nr	88 cM	0.92
8	nr	nr	nr	nr	67 cM	1.9	8 cM	1.29
9q	137 cM	2.05[b]	nr	nr	nr	nr	104 cM	0.68
11q	nr	nr	133 cM	1.27	113 cM	4.0	95 cM	0.41
12q	nr	nr	165 cM	1.09	nr	nr	166 cM	2.10
17p	nr	nr	46 cM	3.63	12 cM	1.42	1 cM	1.39

Note: Chr = Chromosome; MLS = maximum likelihood score, nr = not reported, [a]broad diagnostic criteria, [b]narrow diagnostic criteria, [c]calculated with Mapmaker/sibs, [d]two-point, estimated with Simwalk2, [e]"other nominal regions exhibiting concordance among different analyses were detected at chromosomes 5p13.3" (Arcos-Burgos et al., 2004).

The Limitations of Linkage Studies

It is important to understand the major limitations of conventional genome-wide linkage scans. Because genetic heterogeneity—different genes are operative in different families—applies to a complex disorder, both the sample size and the effect sizes of the underlying genes are of crucial importance. For example, a genome scan based on one hundred sib pairs allows detection of definite linkage only if the underlying disease gene is operative in several of these families and the effect size is large (Morton, 1998). Increasing the sample size will potentially allow detection of linkage regions harboring infrequent major genes (i.e., gene variants with a major effect) or more common genes with lower effect sizes (oligogenes). Genes with a minor effect (polygenes) escape detection unless thousands of sibships are analyzed (Risch and Merikangas, 1996; Plomin, 2005). This is due to the probability being only minimally elevated higher than the expected 50% if the same minor gene (among potentially up to several hundreds of other predisposing minor genes operative in the families) is inherited by affected sibs within a sibship.

Currently, there is no consensus as to the extent to which major gene alleles contribute to complex disorders. The identification of major genes detected via linkage studies has been successful in single nonpsychiatric disorders with complex inheritance such as Crohn's disease (Hugot et al., 2001; Ogura et al., 2001) and breast cancer (Miki et al., 1994; Wooster et al., 1995). If, however, the familial loading for a particular disorder is based only on polygenic inheritance, genomewide linkage studies will prove futile (unless thousands of affected sib pairs are indeed analyzed). The sibling relative risk (λ_{sib}; Risch, 1990) potentially provides a clue as to the role of major genes. It is calculated by dividing the rate for a specific disorder observed in sibs of an index patient by the population-based prevalence rate. For ADHD, for example, λ_{sib} is in the range of 5 (Fisher et al., 2002) and thus high enough to base linkage studies on it. This of course holds true only if merely a limited number of genes underlie the λ_{sib}, which accordingly would have a rather strong effect on the phenotype. The available formal genetic studies did not include enough data on more distant types of relationships to be able to estimate how many genes contribute to this λ_{sib}. The concordance rates observed in twin studies suggest that the respective number might indeed not be that large.

Synopsis of Linkage Studies

Genomewide linkage studies of psychiatric disorders have been ongoing for several years; tables 1.4 and 1.5 focus on affected sib-pair studies in selected child and adolescent psychiatric disorders. If one is to attempt to summarize the findings in an overall fashion, the following issues deserve notice: (1) Most studies have been based on a limited number of (~100–300) sib pairs. (2) Only single findings fulfill criteria for significant evidence for linkage; most of the linkage findings at best provide suggestive evidence for linkage. (3) Whereas overlapping of the chromosomal regions identified in different linkage studies of the same disorder does occur, it is frequently not possible to conclude that this overlapping is nonrandom in nature. (4) As of today, only a very limited number of genes have been implicated as underlying a linkage peak in psychiatric disorders (see later discussion). In basically all of these cases, the relative risks of the respective disease alleles have been small, which is somewhat in contrast to expectations; alleles underlying linkage peaks in studies encompassing only a few hundred sib pairs should show a larger effect size. Either other genes located within such a chromosomal region also contribute to the linkage peak or the IBD value for markers within the region was randomly inflated in the original linkage study. (5) It appears possible that the genetic basis for different disorders overlaps. Thus the same chromosomal regions have lit up in genome scans for ADHD and autism. It remains to be determined if indeed particular genes in these regions are involved in both disorders.

Work in Schizophrenia

Recent findings based on linkage studies in schizophrenia seem promising (Owen et al., 2005), although they have not yet been confirmed via a meta-analysis. Currently, the positional candidate genes identified within linkage peaks for which the evidence is considered to be strong are those encoding dysbindin (*DTNBP1*) and neuregulin 1 (*NRG1*). Both schizophrenia and bipolar affective disorder have been shown to link to 13q34, in which D-amino acid oxidase activator (DAOA) was identified as a strong candidate gene for schizophrenia (Chumakov et al., 2002). Persecutory delusions in patients with bipolar illness are associated with DAOA haplotypes (Schulze et al., 2005). The finding that the transcript-encoding regulator of G-protein signaling 4 (RGS4) was decreased in the prefrontal cortex of subjects with schizophrenia led to the identification of *RGS4* as a candidate gene for schizophrenia within a previously identified linkage region on chromosome 1q21–22 (Mirnics et al., 2001). Association of schizophrenia to single nucleotide polymorphisms (SNPs) in *RGS4* has subsequently been reported (Owen et al., 2005).

Work in Dyslexia

Even more recently, two studies identified association and linkage disequilibrium of dyslexia, including multiple reading traits to SNPs in *DCDC2* (Schumacher et al., 2006; Meng et al., 2005). *DCDC2* is located on chromosome 6p, which represents the most consistent linkage finding in dyslexia; accordingly Schumacher et al. and Meng et al. identified the *DCDC2* SNPs via fine mapping of the chromosome 6p linkage peak. The function of *DCDC2* is unknown, but it contains two doublecortin peptide domains. These domains also occur in the X-chromosomal doublecortin gene (*DCX*), which encodes a cytoplasmic protein that directs neuronal migration by regulating the organization and stability of microtubules and is mutated in human X-linked lissencephaly and double cortex syndrome. For both syndromes, the large majority of point mutations cluster within the conserved doublecortin peptide motifs of *DCX*, which are also encoded in *DCDC2*. In analogy, it is conceivable that dyslexia can result from abnormal neuronal migration (Meng et al., 2005).

Candidate Gene Approach

The choice of a specific candidate gene is commonly based on pharmacological, physiological, biochemical, anatomical, or genetic data such as chromosomal localization within a linkage region. In light of the estimated 25,000 human genes and our poor knowledge of the molecular basis of any psychiatric disorder the a priori probability for the involvement of a particular gene is low, unless the underlying hypothesis is well founded. Due to the reliance on merely cases and controls, the ascertainment for a simple association study is as straightforward as the test procedure itself: allele or genotype frequencies for genetic markers or haplotypes are compared between the two groups. A significant difference indicates that the respective allele in itself or genetic variation in close vicinity (linkage disequilibrium) influences the phenotype. One major reason for conflicting results is often the small sample size (Kupper and Palmer, 2002). Meta-analyses can help to assess conflicting studies; table 1.6 depicts positive meta-analyses pertaining to candidate genes for psychiatric disorders. Most of the respective genes were originally selected because they belong to neurotransmitter systems assumed to be involved in psychiatric disorders. Some of the genes seem to be involved in more than one disorder. For example, the serotonin 2A receptor gene has been implicated in both AN and schizophrenia (table 1.6).

Table 1.6.   Selection of Meta-Analyses Pertaining to Positive Candidate Gene
Findings for Psychiatric Disorders

Disease Gene	Genetic Marker	Reference
Anorexia Nervosa		
Serotonin 2_A receptor	A-allele of –1438G > A polymorphism	Gorwood et al., 2003
ADHD		
Dopamine D_4 receptor	7-repeat allele of 48-bp repeat	Faraone et al., 2001
Bipolar Disorder		
Serotonin transporter	Gene-linked polymorphic region (5-HTTLPR)	Cho et al., 2005 Furlong et al., 1998
	Intron 2 variable number of tandem repeats (VNTR)	Cho et al., 2005
Monoamine oxidase A	Microsatellite and RFLP alleles	Rubinsztein et al., 1996
Depression		
Dopamine D_4 receptor	2-repeat allele of 48-bp repeat	Lopez Leon et al., 2005
Serotonin transporter	Gene-linked polymorphic region (5-HTTLPR)	Furlong et al., 1998
Schizophrenia		
Serotonin transporter	STin2 VNTR polymorphism	Fan et al., 2005
Methylenetetrahydrofolate reductase (MTHFR)	TT genotype of 677 C > T polymorphism	Muntjewerff et al., 2005 Lewis et al., 2005
CYP2D6	loss of function alleles (2-allele and 10-allele)	Patsopoulos et al., 2005
Serotonin 2_A receptor	T102C and His452Tyr haplotype	Lerer et al., 200
Dopamine D_2 receptor	Cys-allele of Cys31Ser polymorphism	Glatt et al., 2003 Jonsson et al., 2003a
Dopamine D_3 receptor	Gly/Gly genotype of Ser9Gly polymorphism	Jonsson et al., 2003b Lovlie et al., 2000 Dubertret et al., 1998 Williams et al., 1998 Shaikh et al., 1996
Catechol O-methyltransferase (COMT)	Val-allele of Val158/ 108Met polymorphism	Glatt et al., 2003

GENES IDENTIFIED VIA CHROMOSOMAL ANOMALIES

Role of DISC2 and PDE4B in Schizophrenia

Candidate genes have been identified via individuals with specific psychiatric
disorders who are carriers of a chromosomal anomaly. Disrupted in schizophrenia 1 (DISC1) represents such an example for schizophrenia. DISC1 was

originally detected in Scottish kindred carrying a balanced translocation that disrupts DISC1 and DISC2 (St. Clair et al., 1990; Millar et al., 2000). In the original study (St. Clair et al., 1990) the LOD score (maximum LOD score = 6) had been greatest when the mental disorders were restricted to schizophrenia, schizoaffective disorder, recurrent major depression, and adolescent conduct and emotional disorders. Separate studies revealed linkage of schizophrenia to chromosome 1q42; others identified association to DISC1 (Owen et al., 2005). Recent results indicate that DISC1 is involved in cerebral cortex development and suggest that loss of DISC1 function may underlie neurodevelopmental dysfunction in schizophrenia (Kamiya et al., 2005). A coding, nonsynonymous SNP (Ser704Cys) in DISC1 is associated with schizophrenia and has been shown to correlate with variations in hippocampal size and function during cognitive tasks in normal subjects as well as cognitive variations in aged normal subjects (Callicott et al., 2005; Thomson et al., 2005; Sawa and Snyder, 2005).

Recently Millar et al. (2005) identified a chromosomal translocation in a patient with schizophrenia and a relative with unspecified psychotic disturbance involving the gene encoding phosphodiesterase 4B (*PDE4B*). PDEs inactivate $3',5'$-monophosphate (cAMP), a second messenger implicated in learning, memory, and mood. The translocation leads to a 50% reduction in expression of PDE4B1, one subtype of PDE4B. Binding of PDE4B1 to DISC1 was detected, which was decreased upon augmentation of intracellular cAMP. Thus signaling systems that increase cellular levels of cAMP such as those triggered by neurotransmitters could consequently lead to dissociation of the DISC1-PDE4B1 complex and as a consequence to increased phosphodiesterase activity. The involvement of PDE4B in schizophrenia is tantalizing in light of its role in affective and cognitive function (Sawa and Snyder, 2005).

SLITRKR1 and Tourette's Disorder

Abelson et al. (2005) identified a patient with Tourette's disorder (TD) and ADHD, who carried a de novo chromosome 13 inversion. Based on this individual, Slit and Trk-like family member 1 gene (*SLITRK1*), which is one of three genes located within 500 kilobases of the two breakpoints, was considered as a candidate gene for TD. SLITRK1 was subsequently screened in 174 patients with TD. A subject with TD and ADHD possessed a frameshift mutation; two unrelated patients with TD and obsessive-compulsive symptoms had an identical noncoding variant. Both this variant and the frameshift mutation were absent in 4,926 and 3,600 control chromosomes, respectively. Abelson et al. concluded that SLITRK1 mutations underlie TD in a small subgroup of patients affected with this tic disorder. However, caution is warranted because, in contrast to the 174 TD patients, SLITRK1 was not screened in controls; hence it cannot be excluded that healthy controls might also harbor other infrequent mutations.

Association Studies

In association studies a familial loading is per se not required for classification as a case. However, requirement of such a loading would be expected to increase the probability that genetic factors indeed contribute to the disorder of the respective index patient; studies that require a family history of disease or analyze subgroups of familial cases have been performed in other disorders (e.g., Hovatta et al., 1998). Controls are usually screened for the respective disorder; a positive screen entails exclusion of the proband as a control. Use of controls with a phenotype that quantitatively differs as much as possible from cases can theoretically enhance the probability of detecting genes. Controls should be matched to cases for well-established, strong risk factors (e.g., ethnic group, sex, socioeconomic status, intelligence) to ensure that significant results are not caused by a confounding risk factor, other than the trait of interest, differing between the two groups (Kupper and Palmer, 2002). Such confounders would bias the study if they interact with the considered candidate gene. Overmatching, on the other hand, e.g., for many potential, small risk factors, will lead to substantial loss of efficiency. Matching has to be accounted for in the analysis as well. One of the most important confounders in genetic studies could be ethnicity in ethnically admixed or structured populations (Lander and Schork, 1994). This will cause serious bias if the studied candidate gene differs in allele frequencies between ethnically defined subpopulations. It has been proposed to genotype several markers that are thought to bear no relationship to the disorder of interest in both cases and controls to potentially enable adjustment for systematic genetic differences between cases and controls (Pritchard and Rosenberg, 1999; Devlin et al., 2003).

Family-Based Association Studies

Another popular approach to circumvent the potential confounding effects of case-control studies are family-based association studies, which include family members of the cases to use as (ethnically) matched controls. These can be unaffected sibs or pseudocontrols constructed from nontransmitted parental alleles. Statistical tests for such case-parent trios are the haplotype relative risk (HRR) method (Falk and Rubinstein, 1987), haplotype-based haplotype relative risk (HHRR) method (Terwilliger and Ott, 1992), and the transmission disequilibrium test (TDT; Spielman et al., 1993), which provides a test for both association and linkage. The TDT statistic is based on the comparison of the number of times the allele of interest is transmitted versus nontransmitted by heterozygous parents to an affected child. The ascertainment of parents is usually readily possible in disorders with a childhood onset; however, in ADHD this approach is somewhat complicated by the fact that biological parents of ADHD children have frequently separated (Brown et al., 1998), thus potentially rendering the ascertainment of usually the father particularly difficult or even impossible. The ascertainment of complete trios in ADHD could theoretically imply that the respective index patients (and their families) are not representative of all ADHD patients.

Family-based association studies have certain disadvantages; in particular they are less efficient than case-control studies. Sibs share on average one allele identical by descent, so there is effectively only one allele that can differ instead of two for unrelated cases and controls. Also, sibs tend to be more similar in many possible risk factors that imply overmatching with its associated loss in efficiency. In the trio design, three subjects have to be genotyped to yield information similar to two subjects in the case-control design. And finally, for diseases with a later age of onset, it will be difficult to ascertain parents of cases. Therefore, family-based association studies are more expensive and complex than case-control studies. Future genomewide association studies will potentially be based on tens to hundreds of thousands of SNPs, which ideally should include tag SNPs to identify association to specific haplotype blocks. It has been estimated that 500,000 SNPs are sufficient to cover all haplotype blocks (Bakker et al., 2003).

Polygeny and Heterogeneity

Also it has to be assumed a priori that at least some genes (oligogeny) or even several genes (polygeny) are involved in the development of the respective phenotypes. Almost 8,000 population-based controls (Heid et al., 2005) were required to confirm the result of a meta-analysis (Geller et al., 2004) performed for the V103I variant of the melancortin-4 receptor gene. This variant occurs in approximately 4% of Germans; the variant is associated with a reduced risk of obesity (relative risk of 0.7); carriers on average weigh 1.5 kilograms less than noncarriers; this variant is thus a true example of a polygenetic influence on body weight.

Heterogeneity has to be assumed too in association studies. A special combination of gene variations (alleles) may be relevant in family A whereas a totally different—or to some extent overlapping—combination may be relevant in family B. For this reason, molecular genetic findings have to be interpreted cautiously and are potentially conflicting.

LINKAGE DISEQUILIBRIUM MAPPING

Linkage disequilibrium (LD, or population allelic association) describes the phenomenon whereby two alleles at different loci co-occur more frequently than can be expected by chance. Alleles associated in such a way may reflect fragments of ancestral chromosomes that remain intact despite many meiotic events over multiple generations and therefore appear to be associated even in individuals from different families. The respective DNA stretches are termed *LD blocks*; interindividual variations within these blocks represent different haplotypes. LD extends on average 60 kb from common alleles (Reich et al., 2001). Today LD mapping is commonly used to identify genes with linkage peak regions. In the future LD can be used to directly map a disease gene based on a genomewide approach. For this purpose so-called haplotype-tagging SNPs can be used, which unambiguously identify a haplotype. Although the length of an LD block varies considerably between loci and human populations, the use of haplotype-tagging SNPs would greatly reduce the number of SNPs for a genomewide association study (Kruglyak, 1999).

THE FUTURE AND A WORD OF CAUTION

Genomewide Scans Based on Chip Technology

Currently, the first genomewide scans based on DNA chip technology are being performed; using a very small amount of DNA of a single individual, such a chip enables the simultaneous determination of 10,000 to up to 500,000 genotypes based on SNPs. The future will witness chips capable of detecting up to 1 million SNPs. Whereas the information content gained from genotyping a large number of SNPs can readily surpass that obtained from conventional linkage studies based on 300-1,000 microsatellites, it is hoped that LD mapping will allow genomewide association studies on a case-control basis. This transition to SNP-based technology has been rendered possible by the construction of a map of naturally occurring polymorphisms (International SNP Map Working Group, 2001): 1.4 million unique SNPs were built in an approximately 2-kb-resolution map, placing approximately 2–4 SNPs per human gene. Currently, there are approximately 27 million submitted, 10 million referenced, and 5 million validated SNPs known (www.ncbi.nlm.nih.gov/projects/SNP/snp_summary .cgi). Also, the construction of a haplotype map of the human genome became feasible, again facilitating comprehensive genetic association studies of human disease (Gabriel et al., 2002; Goodstadt and Ponting, 2001). Any two unrelated human beings differ on average at approximately every 1,000th base pair.

Novel and Refined Statistical Methods

In most cases, association approaches have been used for fine mapping or candidate gene analyses. Compared to genetic linkage studies, genomewide association approaches are still rare (e.g., Schaid et al., 2004) as until recently technological constraints posed a major limitation. As a consequence, both the genotyping strategy as well as the development of new, refined statistical methods become more and more important. Concepts like DNA pooling, haplotype-tagging SNPs, the identification of regions with reduced LD, haplotype analyses, staged or data-adaptive study designs—to name a few—have been suggested to improve the efficiency of these studies (e.g., Sham et al., 2002; Schaid et al., 2004; Gu and Rao, 2001). An excellent overview of important issues in the development of statistical methods is given by Terwilliger and Göring (2000) or recently by Freimer and Sabatti (2004). Van Steen et al. (2005) just recently described a groundbreaking method for the analysis of huge amounts of SNP data (10,000 to 1,000,000 SNPs) by simultaneously circumventing the problem of multiple testing. Finally, as association studies have unfortunately yielded a number of contradictory results, attention has to be paid to issues like differences in phenotype definition, study populations, or inadequate sample sizes for the assumed small effects (e.g., Ioannidis et al., 2003). In our opinion, this can only be achieved if investigators cooperate in networks that operate on the basis of appropriate and explicit decision rules. In addition, these networks should commit themselves to the idea of confirmation and replication (Vieland, 2001; Neale and Sham, 2004) instead of publishing premature findings.

Fate of Molecular Genetic Studies in Psychiatric Disorders

In marked contrast to the ongoing revolution in biotechnology, neuroimaging, bioinformatics, and biostatistics, our clinical practice has remained comparatively stable. When and to what extent will the technical revolution influence clinical psychiatry and for that matter our understanding of temperament and personality? Even prior to the identification of the respective "disease genes" we are convinced of the importance of genetic factors in the etiology of psychiatric disorders. We need to be aware that this conviction to a large extent currently rests on the results of family, twin, and adoption studies. And we should be careful to critically reflect on how this conviction influences our clinical practice.

What Can Realistically Be Expected for the Future?

It is our personal belief that the upcoming possibility for performing genomewide association studies based on chip technology will eventually decide the fate of molecular genetic studies in psychiatric disorders. Two extreme scenarios appear possible:

1. Only a limited number of novel genes are unambiguously identified within the next ten years. This finding would imply that the effect sizes of most predisposing alleles are so small that they cannot be picked up using this sophisticated technology. The ultimate step would then be to resequence the whole genome (or at least all known genes) in a substantial number of cases and controls in an attempt to statistically identify those loci in which variations cluster in cases (Margulies et al., 2005). Genomewide resequencing is currently, however, not feasible in a large number of individuals. The accumulating costs for the search for alleles with very small effect sizes will eventually need to be put in perspective to the expected outcome. If only alleles with minute effects (e.g., relative risks <1.1) can be detected, we need to be even more aware that we can really only grasp the genetics of psychiatric disorders by an in-depth analysis of gene–gene and gene–environment interactions, which implies a long-term commitment.

2. The advent of chip technology leads to the identification of at least five novel genes for each analyzed psychiatric disorder. These genetic results are robust, implying that there is a consensus that indeed the respective genes contribute to the etiology of the respective disorder; repeated replications of each single finding are the prerequisite for the attainment of such a consensus. This knowledge will allow us to identify (a) the molecular genetic mechanisms relevant for psychiatric disorders (e.g., variation primarily within regulatory versus coding regions), (b) novel systems and pathways relevant in specific disorders, which may or may not include pharmacological targets, (c) the extent of overlap in the genetic predisposition to different psychiatric disorders (e.g., identification of genetic variation predisposing to both affective disorders and schizophrenia), (d) gene–gene and gene–environment interactions, and (e) developmental relationships between genotype and phenotype.

The Importance of Large Study Samples

The crucial prerequisite for the use of sophisticated molecular technology is that several large and well-characterized samples of patients with a given disorder exist to allow repeated confirmations of a single finding and subsequent meta-analyses. By large, we imply that the respective samples should encompass more than 1,000 cases and an equal number of controls, thus providing sufficient power to detect alleles with a modest to weak effect. Undoubtedly, the need to analyze large samples and to confirm original findings will lead to extensive collaborations that should also address ethnic aspects. Family-based association and linkage studies are also extremely helpful and may represent the only way to identify their involvement in specific situations such as the involvement of imprinted genes in the etiology of a given disorder.

Relevance for Child and Adolescent Psychiatric Practice

As the field of molecular genetics of psychiatric disorders advances, we as child and adolescent psychiatrists need to stay at the forefront of these developments. We have the clinical knowledge, and we raise the clinically relevant questions; of course, to achieve our goals we depend on an interdisciplinary approach also encompassing molecular geneticists and biologists, biostatisticians, and several other specialists. We will profit by extensively integrating these disciplines into our research; a fundamental issue is to establish a sufficient amount of cross talk to ensure that the full potential of this interdisciplinary approach can bear full profit. We as psychiatrists will also be responsible for the integration of novel molecular findings into our clinical routine.

We need to be aware of ethical and societal implications of molecular genetic findings. In order to ensure that we will be able to do just that we need to have training programs that provide us with the capability to grasp the molecular findings and to integrate them into novel research (e.g., analysis of gene–environment interactions) and even more importantly into our daily clinical routine. If a sufficiently large number of predisposing alleles for a given disorder are known, genetic analyses will most likely for the first time provide us with "somatic" parameters useful for diagnostic purposes, prediction of the clinical course of a disorder, and its treatment. We will learn that the elucidation of the molecular puzzle of psychiatric disorders has the potential to alter our current phenomenological basis for the definition of neuropsychiatric disorders.

Despite these exciting potential implications of the discovery of predisposing alleles, we nevertheless should remain critical. Due to the necessity to reach a diagnosis via explicit diagnostic criteria, we as psychiatrists have become extremely critical of our own research work; with good reason we have come to expect a solid diagnostic procedure based on standard criteria. We would recommend that this critical approach is extended to the field of psychiatric genetics, where at times novel results are uncritically taken for granted. There is no easy solution to this problem. Again, a thorough training in psychiatric genetics can help us to better understand the limitations of novel findings. We also believe that a truly interdisciplinary approach offers protection. Clinicians, biostatisticians, and molecular geneticists must have a thorough understanding of each other's work. We need scientists who can bridge the communication barrier.

Caveats Inherent to Genetic Studies of Psychiatric Disorders

Some of the caveats inherent to genetic studies of psychiatric disorders are illustrated by the following two examples.

Bipolar Illness and Red-Green Color Blindness

Bipolar illness was first suggested to be linked to red-green color blindness in the 1960s (Reich et al., 1969). Subsequently, linkage was also detected to G6PD polymorphisms and markers in close vicinity to the locus for red-green color blindness on the long arm of chromosome X. A steadily increasing number of studies of a limited number of research groups supported the initial linkage findings. Publications appeared in prestigious journals, including *Archives of General Psychiatry*, *Lancet*, and *Nature*; evidence in favor of a locus on the X chromosome underlying a subfraction of all types of bipolar illness appeared unequivocal despite single groups being unable to confirm the findings.

The major hypothesis underlying these linkage studies was that an X-linked dominant mode of inheritance accounts for this particular subgroup of bipolar disorder. However, a closer look at the published pedigrees revealed that seemingly mostly only females had reproduced; as expected for X-linked dominant disorders half the sons and daughters were affected. However, in all published pedigrees, affected males were either without children or their children had not reached the manifestation age of bipolar illness. An X-linked dominant mode of inheritance, which is exceedingly rare in monogenic disorders, is characterized by affected males transmitting the relevant mutation to all daughters but none of their sons. Exactly these characteristic segregation patterns were thus lacking in all of the X-linkage studies (Hebebrand, 1992); in addition, systematic deviations of expected parameters were detected (Hebebrand and Hennighausen, 1992). After publication of this critical appraisal, X-linkage studies of bipolar illness largely collapsed. The lesson to learn is to critically reflect the underlying assumptions made in (molecular) genetic studies.

"Aggression Gene": The MAO-A Gene and the Importance of Adequate Phenotypic Assessment

Another highly published finding pertains to the "aggression gene." In 1993 Brunner and coworkers (1993a, 1993b) reported on a mutation in the MAO-A gene underlying a phenotype characterized by "borderline mental retardation" and "aggression." This study is widely held to indicate that human aggression can be caused by a mutation in a single gene. It is surprising that this finding has had a great impact on psychiatrists, because the phenotype depicted in the respective publications is anything but straightforward: The mutation carriers were reported to have been involved in voyeurism, exhibitionism, arson, or rape. The affected males were described as "withdrawn and shy, being often without friends." All had shown aggressive outbursts of some sort, usually with little or no provocation. A number of males exhibited sexually aberrant behavior. Aggressive behavior tended to cluster in periods of 1–3 days, during which the affected male would sleep very little and would experience frequent night terrors.

Quite evidently, psychiatric evaluations were not performed, because no attempt was made to classify the symptoms according to a psychiatric classification scheme. The common trait appears to be "aggressive outbursts of some sort," which without further specification could well apply to a substantial minority of the general population. It is unclear whether arson, sexually deviant behavior, and rape were all equated as aggressive behavior. This criticism all the more applies because the investigators deduced the presence of borderline mental retardation in nine males of the pedigree from information compiled thirty years ago by an unaffected family member. The only information provided for those mutation carriers whom the investigators themselves were able to phenotypically assess was as follows: "A typically affected male showed a full-scale IQ of 85." It was not specified how many of the males were psychologically tested and what IQ test was used; a psychiatrist was not a coauthor of the respective papers (for a more detailed critical evaluation of the Brunner et al. studies see Hebebrand and Klug, 1995, and the response of Brunner et al., 1995).

In our opinion, there is no reason for us to be lenient when molecular geneticists report behavioral phenotypes, particularly if they are as complex as aggression or intelligence. Quite to the contrary, we should be very careful to not uncritically take the respective findings at face value.

A Higher Level of Complexity: Gene–Environment Studies

The delineation of the "aggression gene" has paved the way for a more recent sensational finding that pertains to a genotype–environment interaction, only few of which have been studied in psychiatry. MAO-A alleles can be classified as leading to low or high activity of its gene product; a study published in *Science* in 2003 (Caspi et al., 2002), which was purportedly independently confirmed (Foley et al., 2004), showed that the MAO-A genotype is relevant for the development of conduct disorders only in those children with a positive history of maltreatment. More specifically, maltreated children with a genotype conferring low levels of MAO-A were less likely to develop conduct disorders.

Why should these findings, as exciting as they are, not be taken at face value? Critical issues include the following:

1. The recent history of psychiatric genetics has demonstrated that solid molecular genetic findings in complex disorders are as yet scarce. There is no a priori evidence to indicate that a switch to gene–environment interactions will make the elucidation of predisposing alleles easier. The effect sizes of particular alleles are likely to be similarly small.

2. The delineation of a single specific hypothesis pertaining to a gene–environment interaction implies that just this one out of very many different possible ones is tested; both the gene and the environmental condition must be selected. If, however, different gene–environment interactions are tested, the effects of multiple testing need to be considered. Did Caspi et al. (2002) test just one hypothesis? If so, why?

3. In this context, the quality of the underlying hypothesis needs to be assessed. The involvement of the MAO-A gene in conduct disorders to a considerable extent rests on the aforementioned study of Brunner and coworkers (1993a, 1993b), which in psychiatric terms was not satisfactory.

4. Confirmatory studies in gene–environment studies become almost impossible if the original assessment procedure for the relevant environmental factor is not employed in subsequent studies. Foley et al. (2004), who used different variables to construct a maltreatment index than Caspi et al. (2002), elegantly discuss this problem by speculating that their own positive molecular genetic results suggest that the measures used by the two different groups are "intercorrelated and they may indicate an overlapping set of environmental risks." A direct comparison of the variables assessed in the two studies is not too convincing to make this circular reasoning plausible. To the contrary, it seems probable that the two distinct sets of variables used to construct the maltreatment indexes tap different environmental and genetic factors; the extent of overlapping is subject to debate.

5. Finally, as Foley and coworkers (2004) note, most of the power to detect the interaction stemmed from the extremes of the distribution. Only 15 and 5 subjects out of a total of 514 were ranked to be in the second-highest and highest, respectively, level of exposure to childhood adversity. The genotypes of these 20 subjects in total accounted for the significant effect of the genotype–environment interaction. In our opinion, this small number must be viewed critically; additional attempts to confirm the original finding in sufficiently large samples are clearly warranted.

CONCLUSION

The complexity of the issues at hand requires that psychiatrists apply all their knowledge to adequately conduct genetic studies and to assess novel genetic findings. We believe that the elucidation of genes involved in psychiatric disorders has a tremendous potential to advance our understanding of their etiologies. In order to reach this goal we nevertheless should refrain from taking novel findings for real, unless we subject them to a rigorous assessment and have repeatedly confirmed them.

REFERENCES

Aach, J., M.L. Bulyk, G.M. Church, J. Comander, A. Derti, and J. Shendure, "Computational comparison of two draft sequences of the human genome," *Nature* 409 (February 2001): 856–859.

Abelson, J.F., K.Y. Kwan, B.J. O'Roak, D.Y. Baek, A.A. Stillman, T.M. Morgan, C.A. Mathews, D.L. Pauls, M.R. Rasin, M. Gunel, N.R. Davis, A.G. Ercan-Sencicek, D.H. Guez, J.A. Spertus, J.F. Leckman, L.S. Dure, R. Kurlan, H.S. Singer, D.L. Gilbert, A. Farhi, A. Louvi, R.P. Lifton, N. Sestan, and M.W. State, "Sequence variants in SLITRK1 are associated with Tourette's syndrome," *Science* 310 (October 2005): 317–320.

Achenbach, T.M., *Manual for the Child Behavior Checklist/4-18 and 1991 Profile*, (Burlington, VT: University of Vermont, Department of Psychiatry, 1991).

Altmuller, J., L.J. Palmer, G. Fischer, H. Scherb, and M.Wjst, "Genomewide scans of complex human diseases: True linkage is hard to find," *American Journal of Human Genetics* 69 (November 2001): 936–950.

American Psychiatric Association, *Diagnostic and Statistical Manual of Mental Disorders* 4th ed. (Washington, DC: American Psychiatric Association, 1994).

Amir, R.E., I.B. Van den Veyver, M. Wan, C.Q. Tran, U. Francke, and H.Y. Zoghbi, "Rett syndrome is caused by mutations in X-linked MECP2, encoding methyl-CpG-binding protein 2," *Nature Genetics* 23 (October 1999): 185–188.

Arcos-Burgos, M., F.X. Castellanos, D. Pineda, F. Lopera, J.D. Palacio, L.G. Palacio, J.L. Rapoport, K. Berg, J.E. Bailey-Wilson, and M. Muenke, "Attention-deficit/hyperactivity disorder in a population isolate: Linkage to loci at 4q13.2, 5q33.3, 11q22, and 17p11," *American Journal of Human Genetics* 75 (December 2004): 998–1014.

Bailey, J.A., Z. Gu, R.A. Clark, K. Reinert, R.V. Samonte, S. Schwartz, M.D. Adams, E.W. Myers, P.W. Li, and E.E. Eichler, "Recent segmental duplications in the human genome," *Science* 297 (August 2002): 1003–1007.

Bakker, S.C., E.M. van der Meulen, J.K. Buitelaar, L.A. Sandkuijl, D.L. Pauls, A.J. Monsuur, R. van 't Slot, R.B. Minderaa, W.B. Gunning, P.L. Pearson, and R.J. Sinke, "A whole-genome scan in 164 Dutch sib pairs with attention-deficit/hyperactivity disorder: Suggestive evidence for linkage on chromosomes 7p and 15q," *American Journal of Human Genetics* 72 (May 2003): 1251–1260.

Bergen, A.W., M.B. van den Bree, M. Yeager, R. Welch, J.K. Ganjei, K. Haque, S. Bacanu, W.H. Berrettini, D.E. Grice, D. Goldman, C.M. Bulik, K. Klump, M. Fichter, K. Halmi, A. Kaplan, M. Strober, J. Treasure, B. Woodside, and W.H. Kaye, "Candidate genes for anorexia nervosa in the 1p33-36 linkage region: Serotonin 1D and delta opioid receptor loci exhibit significant association to anorexia nervosa," *Molecular Psychiatry* 8 (August 2003): 397–406.

Brett, D., J. Hanke, G. Lehmann, S. Haase, S. Delbruck, S. Krueger, J. Reich, and P. Bork, "EST comparison indicates 38% of human mRNAs contain possible alternative splice forms," *FEBS Letter* 474 (May 2000): 83–86.

Brown, R.T., and J.N. Pacini, "Perceived family functioning, marital status, and depression in parents of boys with attention deficit disorder," *Journal of Learning Disabilities* 22 (1998): 581–587.

Brunner, H.G., "Monoamine oxidase and behaviour," *Annals Medicine* 27 (August 1995): 431–432.

Brunner, H.G., M.R. Nelen, P. van Zandvoort, N.G. Abeling, A.H. van Gennip, E.C. Wolters, M.A. Kuiper, H.H. Ropers, and B.A. van Oost, "X-linked borderline mental retardation with prominent behavioral disturbance: Phenotype, genetic localization, and evidence for disturbed monoamine metabolism," *American Journal of Human Genetics* 52 (June 1993a): 1032–1039.

Brunner, H.G., M. Nelen, X.O. Breakefield, H.H. Ropers, and B.A. van Oost, "Abnormal behavior associated with a point mutation in the structural gene for monoamine oxidase A," *Science* 262 (October 1993b): 578–80.

Bulik, C.M., B. Devlin, S.A. Bacanu, L. Thornton, K.L. Klump, M.M. Fichter, K.A. Halmi, A.S. Kaplan, M. Strober, D.B. Woodside, A.W. Bergen, J.K. Ganjei, S. Crow, J. Mitchell, A. Rotondo, M. Mauri, G. Cassano, P. Keel, W.H. Berrettini, and W.H. Kaye, "Significant linkage on chromosome 10p in families with bulimia nervosa," *American Journal of Human Genetics* 72 (January 2003): 200–207.

Callicott, J.H., R.E. Straub, L. Pezawas, M.F. Egan, V.S. Mattay, A.R. Hariri, B.A. Verchinski, A. Meyer-Lindenberg, R. Balkissoon, B. Kolachana, T.E. Goldberg, and D.R. Weinberger, "Variation in DISC1 affects hippocampal structure and function and increases risk for schizophrenia," *Proceedings of the National Academy of Sciences USA* 102 (June 2005): 8627–8632.

Caspi, A., J. McClay, T.E. Moffitt, J. Mill, J. Martin, I.W. Craig, A. Taylor, and R. Poulton, "Role of genotype in the cycle of violence in maltreated children," *Science* 297 (August 2002): 851–854.

Chen, W.G., Q. Chang, Y. Lin, A. Meissner, A.E. West, E.C. Griffith, R. Jaenisch, and M.E. Greenberg, "Depression of BDNF transcription involves calcium-dependent phosphorylation of MeCP2," *Science* 302 (October 2003): 885–889.

Cheung, J., X. Estivill, R. Khaja, J.R. MacDonald, K. Lau, L.C. Tsui, and S.W. Scherer, "Genome-wide detection of segmental duplications and potential assembly errors in the human genome sequence," *Genome Biology* 4 (2003): R25. (Epub March 17 2003.)

Cho, H.J., I. Meira-Lima, Q. Cordeiro, L. Michelon, P. Sham, H. Vallada, and D.A. Collier, "Population-based and family-based studies on the serotonin transporter gene polymorphisms and bipolar disorder: A systematic review and meta-analysis," *Molecular Psychiatry* 10 (August 2005): 771–781.

Chromosome 21 mapping and sequencing consortium, "The DNA sequence of human chromosome 21," *Nature* 405 (May 2000): 311–319.

Chumakov, I., M. Blumenfeld, O. Guerassimenko, L. Cavarec, M. Palicio, H. Abderrahim, L. Bougueleret, C. Barry, H. Tanaka, P. La Rosa, A. Puech, N. Tahri, A. Cohen-Akenine, S. Delabrosse, S. Lissarrague, F.P. Picard, K. Maurice, L. Essioux, P. Millasseau, P. Grel, V. Debailleul, A.M. Simon, D. Caterina, I. Dufaure, K. Malekzadeh, M. Belova, J.J. Luan, M. Bouillot, J.L. Sambucy, G. Primas, M. Saumier, N. Boubkiri, S. Martin-Saumier, M. Nasroune, H. Peixoto, A. Delaye, V. Pinchot, M. Bastucci, S. Guillou, M. Chevillon, R. Sainz-Fuertes, S. Meguenni, J. Aurich-Costa, D. Cherif, A. Gimalac, C. Van Duijn, D. Gauvreau, G. Ouellette, I. Fortier, J. Raelson, T. Sherbatich, N. Riazanskaia, E. Rogaev, P. Raeymaekers, J. Aerssens, F. Konings, W. Luyten, F. Macciardi, P.C. Sham, R.E. Straub, D.R. Weinberger, N. Cohen, and D. Cohen, "Genetic and physiological data implicating the new human gene G72 and the gene for D-amino acid oxidase in schizophrenia," *Proceedings of the National Academy of Sciences USA* 99 (October 2002): 13675–13680.

Clifford, C.A., R.M. Murray, and D.W. Fulker, "Genetic and environmental influences on obsessional traits and symptoms," *Psychological Medicine* 14 (November 1984): 791–800.

Cloninger, C.R., T.R. Przybeck, and D.M. Svrakic, "The tridimensional personality questionnaire: U.S. normative data. *Psychological Replication* 69 (December 1991): 1047–1057.

Cohen, D., N. Pichard, S. Tordjman, C. Baumann, L. Burglen, E. Excoffier, G. Lazar, P. Mazet, C. Pinquier, A. Verloes, and D. Heron, "Specific genetic disorders and autism: Clinical contribution towards their identification," *Journal of Autismus and Developmental Disorders* 35 (February 2005): 103–116.

Collins, F.S., E.D. Green, A.E. Guttmacher, and M.S. Guyer, "A vision for the future of genomics research," *Nature* 422 (April 2003): 835–847.

Costa, P.T., and R.R. McCrae, "Personality disorders and the five-factor model of personality," *Journal of Personality Disorders* 4 (1990): 362–371.

De Bakker, P.I., R. Yelensky, I. Pe'er, S.B. Gabriel, M.J. Daly, and D. Altshuler, "Efficiency and power in genetic association studies," *Nature Genetics* 37 (November 2005): 1217–1223.

Devlin, B., S.A. Bacanu, K.L. Klump, C.M. Bulik, M.M. Fichter, K.A. Halmi, A.S. Kaplan, M. Strober, J. Treasure, D.B. Woodside, W.H. Berrettini, and W.H. Kaye, "Linkage analysis of anorexia nervosa incorporating behavioral covariates," *Human Molecular Genetics* 11 (March 2002): 689–696.

Devlin, B., K. Roeder, and L. Wasserman, "Analysis of multilocus models of association," *Genetic Epidemiology* 25 (July 2003): 36–47.

Dubertret, C., P. Gorwood, J. Ades, J. Feingold, J.C. Schwartz, and P. Sokoloff, "Meta-analysis of DRD3 gene and schizophrenia: Ethnic heterogeneity and significant association in Caucasians," *American Journal of Medical Genetics* 81 (July 1998): 318–322.

Dunham, I., N. Shimizu, B.A. Roe, S. Chissoe, A.R. Hunt, J.E. Collins, R. Bruskiewich, D.M. Beare, M. Clamp, L.J. Smink, R. Ainscough, J.P. Almeida, A. Babbage, C. Bagguley, J. Bailey, K. Barlow, K.N. Bates, O. Beasley, C.P. Bird, S. Blakey, A.M. Bridgeman, D. Buck, J. Burgess, W.D. Burrill, and K.P. O'Brien, "The DNA sequence of human chromosome 22," *Nature* 402 (December 1999): 489–495.

Eiberg, H., I. Berendt, and J. Mohr, "Assignment of dominant inherited nocturnal enuresis (ENUR1) to chromosome 13q," *Nature Genetics* 10 (July 1995): 354–356.

Eley, T.C., D. Bolton, T.G. O'Connor, S. Perrin, P. Smith, and R. Plomin, "A twin study of anxiety-related behaviors in pre-school children," *Journal of Child Psychology and Psychiatry* 44 (October 2003): 945–960.

Eley, T.C., and I.W. Craig, "Introductory guide to the language of molecular genetics," *Journal of Child Psychology and Psychiatry* 46 (October 2005): 1039–1041.

Eley, T.C., and F. Rijsdijk, "Introductory guide to the statistics of molecular genetics," *Journal of Child Psychology and Psychiatry* 46 (October 2005): 1042–1044.

Emes, R.D., M.C. Riley, C.M. Laukaitis, L. Goodstadt, R.C. Karn, and C.P. Ponting, "Comparative evolutionary genomics of androgen-binding protein genes," *Genome Research* 14 (August 2004): 1516–1529.

Eysenck, H.J., S.B.G. Eysenck, and P. Barret, "A revised version of the Psychoticism Scale," *Personality Indicator Differences* 76 (July 1985): 21–29.

Falk, C.T., and P. Rubinstein, "Haplotype relative risks: An easy reliable way to construct a proper control sample for risk calculations," *Annals of Human Genetics* 51 (1987): 227–233.

Fan, J.B., and P. Sklar, "Meta-analysis reveals association between serotonin transporter gene STin2 VNTR polymorphism and schizophrenia," *Molecular Psychiatry* 10 (October 2005): 891.

Faraone, S.V., A.E. Doyle, E. Mick, and J. Biederman, "Meta-analysis of the association between the 7-repeat allele of the dopamine D(4) receptor gene and attention deficit hyperactivity disorder," *American Journal of Psychiatry* 158 (July 2001): 1052–1057.

Fenson, L., P.S. Dale, and J.S. Reznick, *MacArthur Communicative Development Inventories* (San Diego, CA: Singular Publishing Group, 1993).

Feuk L., J.R. Macdonald, T. Tang, A.R. Carson, M. Li, G. Rao, R. Khaja, and S.W. Scherer, "Discovery of human inversion polymorphisms by comparative analysis of human and chimpanzee DNA sequence assemblies," *Public Library of Science Genetics* 1 (October 2005): e56.

Fickett, J.W., and W.W. Wasserman, "Discovery and modeling of transcriptional regulatory regions," *Current Opinion Biotechnology* 11 (February 2000): 19–24.

Fisher, S.E., C. Francks, J.T. McCracken, J.J. McGough, A.J. Marlow, I.L. MacPhie, D.F. Newbury, L.R. Crawford, C.G. Palmer, J.A. Woodward, M. Del'Homme, D.P. Cantwell, S.F. Nelson, A.P. Monaco, and S.L. Smalley, "A genomewide scan for loci involved in attention-deficit/hyperactivity disorder," *American Journal of Human Genetics* 70 (May 2002): 1183–1196.

Foley, D.L., L.J. Eaves, B. Wormley, J.L. Silberg, H.H. Maes, J. Kuhn, and B. Riley, "Childhood adversity, monoamine oxidase a genotype, and risk for conduct disorder," *Archives of General Psychiatry* 61 (July 2004): 738–744.

Fraga, M.F., E. Ballestar, M.F. Paz, S. Ropero, F. Setien, M.L. Ballestar, D. Heine-Suner, J.C. Cigudosa, M. Urioste, J. Benitez, M. Boix-Chornet, A. Sanchez-Aguilera, C. Ling, E. Carlsson, P. Poulsen, A. Vaag, Z. Stephan, T.D. Spector, Y.Z. Wu, C. Plass, and M. Esteller, "Epigenetic differences arise during the lifetime of monozygotic twins," *Proceedings of the National Academy of Sciences USA* 102 (July 2005): 10604–10609.

Freimer, N., and C. Sabatti, "The use of pedigree, sib-pair and association studies of common diseases for genetic mapping and epidemiology," *Nature Genetics* 36 (October 2004): 1045–1051.

Furlong, R.A., L. Ho, C. Walsh, J.S. Rubinsztein, S. Jain, E.S. Paykel, D.F. Easton, and D.C. Rubinsztein, "Analysis and meta-analysis of two serotonin transporter gene polymorphisms in bipolar and unipolar affective disorders," *American Journal of Medical Genetics* 81 (February 1998): 58–63.

Gabriel, S.B., S.F. Schaffner, H. Nguyen, J.M. Moore, J. Roy, B. Blumenstiel, J. Higgins, M. DeFelice, A. Lochner, M. Faggart, S.N. Liu-Cordero, C. Rotimi, A. Adeyemo, R. Cooper, R. Ward, E.S. Lander, M.J. Daly, and D. Altshuler, "The structure of haplotype blocks in the human genome," *Science* 296 (June 2002): 2225–2229.

Garner, D.M., M.P. Olmsted, Y. Bohr, and P.E. Garfinkel, "The eating attitudes test: Psychometric features and clinical correlates," *Psychological Medicine* 12 (November 1982): 871–878.

Garner, D.M., M.P. Olmsted, and J. Polivy, "Development and validation of a multidimensional eating disorder inventory for anorexia nervosa and bulimia," *International Journal of Eating Disorders* 2 (1983): 15–34.

Gelhorn, H.L., M.C. Stallings, S.E. Young, R.P. Corley, S.H. Rhee, and J.K. Hewitt, "Genetic and environmental influences of conduct disorder: Symptom, domain and full-scale analyses," *Journal of Child Psychology and Psychiatry* (June 2005): 580–591.

Geller, F., K. Reichwald, A. Dempfle, T. Illig, C. Vollmert, S. Herpertz, W. Siffert, M. Platzer, C. Hess, T. Gudermann, H. Biebermann, H.E. Wichmann, H. Schafer, A. Hinney, and J. Hebebrand, "Melanocortin-4 receptor gene variant I103 is negatively associated with obesity," *American Journal of Human Genetics* 74 (March 2004): 572–581.

Glatt, S.J., S.V. Faraone, and M.T. Tsuang, "Association between a functional catechol O-methyltransferase gene polymorphism and schizophrenia: Meta-analysis of case-control and family-based studies," *American Journal of Psychiatry* 160 (March 2003): 469–476.

Glatt, S.J., S.V. Faraone, and M.T. Tsuang, "Meta-analysis identifies an association between the dopamine D2 receptor gene and schizophrenia," *Molecular Psychiatry* 8 (November 2003): 911–915.

Goetghebuer, T., M.O. Ota, B. Kebbeh, M. John, D. Jackson-Sillah, J. Vekemans, A. Marchant, M. Newport, and H.A. Weiss, "Delay in motor development of twins in Africa: A prospective cohort study," *Twin Research* 6 (August 2003): 279–284.

Goodstadt, L., and C.P. Ponting, "Sequence variation and disease in the wake of the draft human genome," *Human Molecular Genetics* 10 (October 2001): 2209–2214.

Gorwood, P., A. Kipman, and C. Foulon, "The human genetics of anorexia nervosa," *European Journal of Pharmacology* 480 (November 2003): 163–170.

Grice, D.E., K.A. Halmi, M.M. Fichter, M. Strober, D.B. Woodside, J.T. Treasure, A.S. Kaplan, P.J. Magistretti, D. Goldman, C.M. Bulik, W.H. Kaye, and W.H. Berrettini, "Evidence for a susceptibility gene for anorexia nervosa on chromosome 1," *American Journal of Human Genetics* 70 (March 2002): 787–792.

Gu, C., and D.C. Rao, "Optimum study designs," *Advances in Genetics* 42 (2001): 439–457.

Hagberg, B., J. Aicardi, K. Dias, and O. Ramos, "A progressive syndrome of autism, dementia, ataxia, and loss of purposeful hand use in girls: Rett's syndrome: Report of 35 cases," *Annals of Neurology* 14 (October 1983): 471–479.

Harrison, P.M., A. Kumar, N. Lang, M. Snyder, and M. Gerstein, "A question of size: The eukaryotic proteome and the problems in defining it," *Nucleic Acids Research* 30 (March 2002): 1083–1090.

Hashimoto, K., H. Koizumi, M. Nakazato, E. Shimizu, and M. Iyo, "Role of brain-derived neurotrophic factor in eating disorders: Recent findings and its pathophysiological implications," *Progression Neuropsychopharmacology Biological Psychiatry* 29 (May 2005): 499–504.

Hebebrand, J., "A critical appraisal of X-linked bipolar illness. Evidence for the assumed mode of inheritance is lacking," *British Journal of Psychiatry* 160 (January 1992): 7–11.

Hebebrand, J., and K. Hennighausen, "A critical analysis of data presented in eight studies favouring X-linkage of bipolar illness with special emphasis on formal genetic aspects," *Human Genetics* 90 (November 1992): 289–293.

Hebebrand, J., and B. Klug, "Specification of the phenotype required for men with monoamine oxidase type A deficiency," *Human Genetics* 96 (September 1995): 372–376.

Hebebrand, J., C. Sommerlad, F. Geller, T. Gorg, and A. Hinney, "The genetics of obesity: Practical implications" *International Journal of Obesity and Related Metabolic Disorders* 25 (May 2001): S10–18.

Hebebrand, J., S. Friedel, N. Schauble, F. Geller, and A. Hinney, "Perspectives: Molecular genetic research in human obesity," *Obesity Review* 4 (August 2003): 139–146.

Hebebrand, J., A. Dempfle, K. Saar, H. Thiele, B. Herpertz-Dahlmann, M. Linder, H. Kiefl, H. Remschmidt, U. Hemminger, A. Warnke, U. Knolker, P. Heiser, S. Friedel, A. Hinney, H. Schafer, P. Nurnberg, and K. Konrad, "A genome-wide scan for attention-deficit/hyperactivity disorder in 155 German sib-pairs," *Molecular Psychiatry* 11 (October 2005) (Epub ahead of print).

Heid, I.M., C. Vollmert, A. Hinney, A. Doring, F. Geller, H. Lowel, H.E. Wichmann, T. Illig, J. Hebebrand, and F. Kronenberg; KORA Group, "Association of the 103I MC4R allele with decreased body mass in 7937 participants of two population-based surveys," *Journal of Medical Genetics* 42 (April 2005): e21.

Heiser, P., S. Friedel, A. Dempfle, K. Konrad, J. Smidt, J. Grabarkiewicz, B. Herpertz-Dahlmann, H. Remschmidt, and J. Hebebrand, "Molecular genetic aspects of attention-deficit/hyperactivity disorder," *Neuroscience and Biobehavioral Reviews* 28 (October 2004): 625–641.

Hinney, A., S. Friedel, H. Remschmidt, and J. Hebebrand, "Genetic risk factors in eating disorders," *American Journal of Pharmacogenomics* 4 (April 2004): 209–223.

Hovatta, I., D. Lichtermann, H. Juvonen, J. Suvisaari, J.D. Terwilliger, R. Arajarvi, M.L. Kokko-Sahin, J. Ekelund, J. Lonnqvist, and L. Peltonen, "Linkage analysis of putative schizophrenia gene candidate regions on chromosomes 3p, 5q, 6p, 8p, 20p and 22q in a population-based sampled Finnish family set," *Molecular Psychiatry* 3 (September 1998): 452–457.

Hudziak, J.J., C.E. Van Beijsterveldt, R.R. Althoff, C. Stanger, D.C. Rettew, E.C. Nelson, R.D. Todd, M. Bartels, and D.I. Boomsma, "Genetic and environmental contributions to the Child Behavior Checklist Obsessive-Compulsive Scale: A cross-cultural twin study," *Archives of General Psychiatry* 61 (June 2004): 608–616.

Hugot, J.P., M. Chamaillard, H. Zouali, S Lesage, J.P. Cezard, J. Belaiche, S. Almer, C. Tysk, C.A. O'Morain, M. Gassull, V. Binder, Y. Finkel, A. Cortot, R. Modigliani, P. Laurent-Puig, C. Gower-Rousseau, J. Macry, J.F. Colombel, M. Sahbatou, and G. Thomas, "Association of NOD2 leucine-rich repeat variants with susceptibility to Crohn's disease," *Nature* 411 (May 2001): 599–603.

IHGSC (International Human Genome Sequencing Consortium), "Initial sequencing and analysis of the human genome," *Nature* 409 (February 2001): 860–921.

IHGSC (International Human Genome Sequencing Consortium), "Finishing the euchromatic sequence of the human genome," *Nature* 431 (October 2004): 931–945.

International SNP Map Working Group, "A map of human genome sequence variation containing 1.42 million single nucleotide polymorphisms," *Nature* 409 (February 2001): 928–933.

Ioannidis, J.P., T.A. Trikalinos, E.E. Ntzani, and D.G. Contopoulos-Ioannidis, "Genetic associations in large versus small studies: An empirical assessment," *Lancet* 361 (February 2003): 567–571.

Istrail, S., G.G. Sutton, L. Florea, A.L. Halpern, C.M. Mobarry, R. Lippert, B. Walenz, H. Shatkay, I. Dew, J.R. Miller, M.J. Flanigan, N.J. Edwards, R. Bolanos, D. Fasulo, B.V. Halldorsson, S. Hannenhalli, R. Turner, S. Yooseph, F. Lu, D.R. Nusskern, B.C. Shue, X.H. Zheng, F. Zhong, A.L. Delcher, D.H. Huson, S.A. Kravitz, L. Mouchard, K. Reinert, K.A. Remington, A.G. Clark, M.S. Waterman, E.E. Eichler, M.D. Adams, M.W. Hunkapiller, E.W. Myers, and J.C. Venter, "Whole-genome shotgun assembly and comparison of human genome assemblies," *Proceedings of the National Academy of Sciences USA* 101 (February 2004): 1916–1921.

Jang, K.L., W.J. Livesley, and P.A. Vernon, "Heritability of the big five personality dimensions and their facets: A twin study," *Journal of Personality* 64 (September 1996): 577–591.

Jonsson, E.G., L. Flyckt, E. Burgert, M.A. Crocq, K. Forslund, M. Mattila-Evenden, G. Rylander, M. Asberg, V.L. Nimgaonkar, G. Edman, L. Bjerkenstedt, F.A. Wiesel, and G.C. Sedvall, "Dopamine D3 receptor gene Ser9Gly variant and schizophrenia: Association study and meta-analysis," *Psychiatric Genetics* 13 (March 2003a): 1–12.

Jonsson, E.G., A. Sillen, M. Vares, B. Ekholm, L. Terenius, and G.C. Sedvall, "Dopamine D2 receptor gene Ser311Cys variant and schizophrenia: Association study and meta-analysis," *American Journal of Medical Genetics Part B Neuropsychiatric Genetics* 119 (May 2003b): 28–34.

Kamiya, A., K.I. Kubo, T. Tomoda, M. Takaki, R. Youn, Y. Ozeki, N. Sawamura, U. Park, C. Kudo, M. Okawa, C.A. Ross, M.E. Hatten, K. Nakajima, and A. Sawa, "A schizophrenia-associated mutation of DISC1 perturbs cerebral cortex development," *Nature Cell Biology* 7 (December 2005): 1067–1078.

Keller, M.C., W.L. Coventry, A.C. Heath, and N.G. Martin, "Widespread evidence for non-additive genetic variation in Cloninger's and Eysenck's personality dimensions using a twin plus sibling design," *Behavior Genetics* (November 2005): 707–721.

Klose, R.J., S.A. Sarraf, L. Schmiedeberg, S.M. McDermott, I. Stancheva, and A.P. Bird, "DNA binding selectivity of MeCP2 due to a requirement for A/T sequences adjacent to methyl-CpG," *Molecular Cell* 19 (September 2005): 667–678.

Kruglyak, L., "Prospects for whole-genome linkage disequilibrium mapping of common disease genes," *Nature Genetics* 22 (June 1999): 139–144.

Kupper, L.L., and L.J. Palmer, "Matching," in: Elston, R.C., Olson, J. and Palmer, L.J., ed., *Biostatistical Genetics and Genetic Epidemiology* (Chichester: Wiley, 2002) 518–523.

Lander, E., and L. Kruglyak, "Genetic dissection of complex traits: guidelines for interpreting and reporting linkage results," *Nature Genetics* 11 (November 1995): 241–247.

Lander, E., and N. Schork, "Genetic dissection of complex traits," *Science* 265 (September 1994): 2037–2048.

Lerer, B., R.H. Segman, E.C. Tan, V.S. Basile, R. Cavallaro, H.N. Aschauer, R. Strous, S.A. Chong, U. Heresco-Levy, M. Verga, J. Scharfetter, H.Y. Meltzer, J.L. Kennedy, and F. Macciardi, "Combined analysis of 635 patients confirms an age-related association of the serotonin 2A receptor gene with tardive dyskinesia and specificity for the non-orofacial subtype," *International Journal Neuropsychopharmacology* 8 (September 2005): 411–425.

Lewis, S.J., S. Zammit, D. Gunnell, and G.D. Smith, "A meta-analysis of the MTHFR C677T polymorphism and schizophrenia risk," *American Journal of Medical Genetics, Part B Neuropsychiatric Genetics* 135 (May 2005): 2–4.

Li, H., T. Yamagata, M. Mori, A. Yasuhara, and M.Y. Momoi, "Mutation analysis of methyl-CpG binding protein family genes in autistic patients," *Brain Development* 27 (August 2005): 321–325.

Li, S., G. Cutler, J.J. Liu, T. Hoey, L. Chen, P.G. Schultz, J. Liao, and X.B. Ling, "A comparative analysis of HGSC and Celera human genome assemblies and gene sets," *Bioinformatics* 19 (September 2003): 1597–1605.

Lopez Leon, S., E.A Croes, F.A. Sayed-Tabatabaei, S. Claes, C. Van Broeckhoven, and C.M. van Duijn, "The dopamine D4 receptor gene 48-base-pair-repeat polymorphism and mood disorders: A meta-analysis," *Biological Psychiatry* 57 (May 2005): 999–1003.

Lovlie, R., A.K. Daly, R. Blennerhassett, N. Ferrier, and V.M. Steen, "Homozygosity for the Gly-9 variant of the dopamine D3 receptor and risk for tardive dyskinesia in schizophrenic patients," *International Journal of Neuropsychopharmacology* 3 (March 2000): 61–65.

Luikenhuis, S., E. Giacometti, C.F. Beard, and R. Jaenisch, "Expression of MeCP2 in postmitotic neurons rescues Rett syndrome in mice," *Proceedings of the National Academy of Sciences* 101 (April 2004): 6033–6038.

Margulies, M., M. Egholm, W.E. Altman, S. Attiya, J.S. Bader, L.A. Bemben, J. Berka, M.S. Braverman, Y.J. Chen, Z. Chen, S.B. Dewell, L. Du, J.M. Fierro, X.V. Gomes, B.C. Godwin, W. He, S. Helgesen, C.H. Ho, G.P. Irzyk, S.C. Jando, M.L. Alenquer, T.P. Jarvie, K.B. Jirage, J.B. Kim, J.R. Knight, J.R. Lanza, J.H. Leamon, S.M. Lefkowitz, M. Lei, J. Li, K.L. Lohman, H. Lu, V.B. Makhijani, K.E. McDade, M.P. McKenna, E.W. Myers, E. Nickerson, J.R. Nobile, R. Plant, B.P. Puc, M.T. Ronan, G.T. Roth, G.J. Sarkis, J.F. Simons, J.W. Simpson, M. Srinivasan, K.R. Tartaro, A. Tomasz, K.A. Vogt, G.A. Volkmer, S.H. Wang, Y. Wang, M.P. Weiner, P. Yu, R.F. Begley, and J.M. Rothberg, "Genome sequencing in microfabricated high-density picolitre reactors," *Nature* 437 (September 2005): 376–380.

Mari, F., S. Azimonti, I. Bertani, F. Bolognese, E. Colombo, R. Caselli, E. Scala, I. Longo, S. Grosso, C. Pescucci, F. Ariani, G. Hayek, P. Balestri, A. Bergo, G. Badaracco, M. Zappella, V. Broccoli, A. Renieri, C. Kilstrup-Nielsen, and N. Landsberger, "CDKL5 belongs to the same molecular pathway of MeCP2 and it is responsible for the early-onset seizure variant of Rett syndrome.," *Human Molecular Genetics* (July 2005): 1935–1946.

Martinowich, K., D. Hattori, H. Wu, S. Fouse, F. He, Y. Hu, G. Fan, and Y.E. Sun, "DNA methylation-related chromatin remodeling in activity-dependent BDNF gene regulation," *Science* 302 (October 2003): 890–893.

Mehan, M.R., N.B. Freimer, and R.A. Ophoff, "A genome-wide survey of segmental duplications that mediate common human genetic variation of chromosomal architecture," *Human Genomics* 1 (August 2004): 335–344.

Meng, H., S.D. Smith, K. Hager, M. Held, J. Liu, R.K. Olson, B.F. Pennington, J.C. DeFries, J. Gelernter, T. O'Reilly-Pol, S. Somlo, P. Skudlarski, S.E. Shaywitz, B.A. Shaywitz, K. Marchione, Y. Wang, M. Paramasivam, J.J. LoTurco, G.P. Page, and J.R. Gruen, "DCDC2 is associated with reading disability and modulates neuronal development in the brain," *Proceedings of the National Academy of Sciences USA* 102 (November 2005): 17053–17058.

Miki, Y., J. Swensen, D. Shattuck-Eidens, P.A. Futreal, K. Harshman, S. Tavtigian, Q. Liu, C. Cochran, L.M. Bennett, and W. Ding, "A strong candidate for the breast and ovarian cancer susceptibility gene BRCA1," *Science* 266 (October 1994): 66–71.

Millar, J.K., J.C. Wilson-Annan, S. Anderson, S. Christie, M.S. Taylor, C.A. Semple, R.S. Devon, D.M. Clair, W.J. Muir, D.H. Blackwood, and D.J. Porteous, "Disruption of two novel genes by a translocation co-segregating with schizophrenia," *Human Molecular Genetics* 9 (May 2000): 1415–1423.

Millar, J.K., B.S. Pickard, S. Mackie, R. James, S. Christie, S.R. Buchanan, M.P. Malloy, J.E. Chubb, E. Huston, G.S. Baillie, P.A. Thomson, E.V. Hill, N.J. Brandon, J.C. Rain, L.M. Camargo, P.J. Whiting, M.D. Housley, D.H. Blackwood, W.J. Muir, and D.J. Porteous, "DISC1 and PDE4B are interacting genetic factors in schizophrenia that regulate cAMP signaling," *Science* 310 (November 2005): 1187–1191.

Mirnics, K., F.A. Middleton, G.D. Stanwood, D.A. Lewis, and P. Levitt, "Disease-specific changes in regulator of G-protein signaling 4 (RGS4) expression in schizophrenia," *Molecular Psychiatry* 6 (May 2001): 293–301.

Mironov, A.A., J.W. Fickett, and M.S. Gelfand, "Frequent alternative splicing of human genes," *Genome Research* 9 (December 1999): 1288–1293.

Modrek, B., and C. Lee, "A genomic view of alternative splicing," *Nature Genetics* 30 (January 2002): 13–19.

Moretti, P., J.A. Bouwknecht, R. Teague, R. Paylor, and H.Y. Zoghbi, "Abnormalities of social interactions and home-cage behavior in a mouse model of Rett syndrome," *Human Molecular Genetics* 14 (January 2005): 205–220.

Morton, N.E., "Meta-analysis in complex diseases," *Clinical Expert Allergy* 25 (1995): S110–112.

Morton, N.E., "Significance levels in complex inheritance," *American Journal of Human Genetics* 62 (1998): 690–697.

Mouse Genome Sequencing Consortium, "Initial sequencing and comparative analysis of the mouse genome," *Nature* 420 (December 2002): 520–562.

Muhle, R., S.V. Trentacoste, and I. Rapin, "The genetics of autism," *Pediatrics* 113 (May 2004): e472–486.

Muntjewerff, J.W., R.S. Kahn, H.J. Blom, and M. Heijer, "Homocysteine, methyl-enetetrahydrofolate reductase and risk of schizophrenia: A meta-analysis," *Molecular Psychiatry* 20 (September 2005) (Epub ahead of print).

Nahon, J.L., "Birth of 'human-specific' genes during primate evolution," *Genetica* 118 (July 2003): 193–208.

National Research Council, *Mapping and Sequencing the Human Genome* (National Academy Press, Washington DC, 1988), www.hugo-international.org.

Neale, B.M., and P.C. Sham, "The future of association studies: Gene-based analysis and replication," *American Journal of Human Genetics* 75 (September 2004): 353–362.

Neel, J.V., "Diabetes mellitus: A thrifty genotype rendered detrimental by progress?" *American Journal of Human Genetics* 14 (1962): 353–362.

Ogdie, M.N., I.L. Macphie, S.L Minassian, M. Yang, S.E. Fisher, C. Francks, R.M. Cantor, J.T. McCracken, J.J. McGough, S.F. Nelson, A.P. Monaco, and S.L. Smalley, "A genome-wide scan for attention-deficit/hyperactivity disorder in an extended sample: Suggestive linkage on 17p11," *American Journal of Human Genetics* 72 (May 2003): 1268–1279.

Ogdie, M.N., S.E. Fisher, M. Yang, J. Ishii, C. Francks, S.K. Loo, R.M. Cantor, J.T. McCracken, J.J. McGough, S.L. Smalley, and S.F. Nelson, "Attention deficit hyperactivity disorder: Fine mapping supports linkage to 5p13, 6q12, 16p13, and 17p11," *American Journal of Human Genetics* 75 (October 2004): 661–668.

Ogdie, M.N., S.C. Bakker, S.E. Fisher, C. Francks, M.H. Yang, R.M. Cantor, S.K. Loo, E. van der Meulen, P. Pearson, J. Buitelaar, A. Monaco, S.F. Nelson, R.J. Sinke, and S.L. Smalley, "Pooled genome-wide linkage data on 424 ADHD ASPs suggests genetic heterogeneity and a common risk locus at 5p13," *Molecular Psychiatry* (October 2005) (Epub ahead of print).

Ogura, Y., D.K. Bonen, N. Inohara, D.L. Nicolae, F.F. Chen, R. Ramos, H. Britton, T. Moran, R. Karaliuskas, R.H. Duerr, J.P. Achkar, S.R. Brant, T.M. Bayless, B.S. Kirschner, S.B. Hanauer, G. Nunez, and J.H. Cho, "A frameshift mutation in NOD2 associated with susceptibility to Crohn's disease," *Nature* 411 (May 2001): 603–606.

Owen, M.J., N. Craddock, and M.C. O'Donovan, "Schizophrenia: Genes at last?" *Trends Genetics* 21 (September 2005): 518–525.

Patsopoulos, N.A., E.E. Ntzani, E. Zintzaras, J.P. Ioannidis, "CYP2D6 polymorphisms and the risk of tardive dyskinesia in schizophrenia: A meta-analysis," *Pharmacogenetic Genomics* 15 (March 2005): 151–158.

Pavlicek, A., V.N. Noskov, N. Kouprina, J.C. Barrett, J. Jurka, and V. Larionov, "Evolution of the tumor suppressor BRCA1 locus in primates: Implications for cancer predisposition," *Human Molecular Genetics* 13 (November 2004): 2737–2751.

Peter, I., M. Vainder, and G. Livshits, "Genetic analysis of motor milestones attainment in early childhood," *Twin Research* 2 (March 1999): 1–9.

Plomin, R., "Finding genes in child psychology and psychiatry: When are we going to be there?" *The Journal of Child Psychology and Psychiatry* 46 (October 2005): 1030–1038.

Pritchard, J.K., and N.A. Rosenberg, "Use of unlinked genetic markers to detect population stratification in association studies," *American Journal of Human Genetics* 65 (1999): 220–228.

Reich, T., P.J. Clayton, and G. Winokur, "Family history studies: V. The genetics of mania," *American Journal of Psychiatry* 125 (April 1969): 1358–1369.

Reich, D.E., M. Cargill, S. Bolk, J. Ireland, P.C. Sabeti, D.J. Richter, T. Lavery, R. Kouyoumjian, S.F. Farhadian, R. Ward, and E.S. Lander, "Linkage disequilibrium in the human genome," *Nature* 411 (May 2001): 199–204.

Reichwald, K., J. Thiesen, T. Wiehe, J. Weitzel, W.H. Stratling, P. Kioschis, A. Poustka, A. Rosenthal, and M. Platzer, "Comparative sequence analysis of the *MECP2*-locus in human and mouse reveals new transcribed regions," *Mammalian Genome* 11 (March 2000): 182–190.

Rett, A., "On a unusual brain atrophy syndrome in hyperammonemia in childhood," *Wien Medizinische Wochenschrift* 116 (September 1966): 723–726. German.

Risch, N., "Linkage strategies for genetically complex traits. III. The effect of marker polymorphism on analysis of affected relative pairs," *American Journal of Human Genetics* 46 (February 1990): 242–253.

Risch, N.J., "Searching for genetic determinants in the new millennium," *Nature* 405 (June 2000): 847–856.

Risch, N., and K. Merikangas, "The future of genetic studies of complex human diseases," *Science* 273 (September 1996): 1516–1517.

Roest Crollius, H., O. Jaillon, A. Bernot, C. Dasilva, L. Bouneau, C. Fischer, C. Fizames, P. Wincker, P. Brottier, F. Quetier, W. Saurin, and J. Weissenbach, "Estimate of human gene number provided by genome-wide analysis using Tetraodon nigroviridis DNA sequence," *Nature Genetics* 25 (June 2000): 235–238.

Rubinsztein, D.C., J. Leggo, S. Goodburn, C. Walsh, S. Jain, and E.S. Paykel, "Genetic association between monoamine oxidase A microsatellite and RFLP alleles and bipolar affective disorder: Analysis and meta-analysis," *Human Molecular Genetics* 5 (June 1996): 779–782.

Rutherford, J., P. McGuffin, R.J. Katz, and R.M. Murray, "Genetic influences on eating attitudes in a normal female twin pair population," *Psychological Medicine* 23 (May 1993): 425–436.

Sabeti, P.C., D.E. Reich, J.M. Higgins, H.Z. Levine, D.J. Richter, S.F. Schaffner, S.B. Gabriel, J.V. Platko, N.J. Patterson, G.J. McDonald, H.C. Ackerman, S.J. Campbell, D. Altshuler, R. Cooper, D. Kwiatkowski, R. Ward, and E.S. Lander, "Detecting recent positive selection in the human genome from haplotype structure," *Nature* 419 (October 2002): 832–827.

Samaco, R.C., R.P. Nagarajan, D. Braunschweig, and J.M. LaSalle, "Multiple pathways regulate MeCP2 expression in normal brain development and exhibit defects in autism-spectrum disorders," *Human Molecular Genetics* 13 (March 2004): 629–639.

Samaco, R.C., A. Hogart, and J.M. LaSalle, "Epigenetic overlap in autism-spectrum neurodevelopmental disorders: MECP2 deficiency causes reduced expression of UBE3A and GABRB3," *Human Molecular Genetics* 14 (February 2005): 483–492.

Santangelo, S.L., and K. Tsatsanis, "What is known about autism: Genes, brain, and behavior," *American Journal of Pharmacogenomics* 5 (2005): 71–92.

Sawa, A., and S.H. Snyder, "Genetics. Two genes link two distinct psychoses," *Science* 310 (November 2005): 1128–1129.

Schaid, D.J., J.C. Guenther, G.B. Christensen, S. Hebbring, C. Rosenow, C.A. Hilker, S.K. McDonnell, J.M. Cunningham, S.L. Slager, M.L. Blute, and S.N. Thibodeau, "Comparison of microsatellites versus single-nucleotide polymorphisms in a genome linkage screen for prostate cancer-susceptibility loci," *American Journal of Human Genetics* 75 (December 2004): 948–965.

Schulze, T.G., S. Ohlraun, P.M. Czerski, J. Schumacher, L. Kassem, M. Deschner, M. Gross, M. Tullius, V. Heidmann, S. Kovalenko, R.A. Jamra, T. Becker, A. Leszczynska-Rodziewicz, J. Hauser, T. Illig, N. Klopp, S. Wellek, S. Cichon, F.A. Henn, F.J. McMahon, W. Maier, P. Propping, M.M. Nothen, and M. Rietschel, "Genotype-phenotype studies in bipolar disorder showing association between the DAOA/G30 locus and persecutory delusions: A first step toward a molecular genetic classification of psychiatric phenotypes," *American Journal of Psychiatry* 162 (November 2005): 2101–2108.

Schumacher, J., H. Anthoni, F. Dahdouh, I.R. König, A.M. Hillmer, N. Kluck, M. Manthey, E. Plume, A. Warnke, H. Remschmidt, J. Hülsmann, S. Cichon, S.M. Lindgren, P. Propping, M. Zucchelli, A. Ziegler, M. Peyrard-Janvid, G. Schulte-Körne, M.M. Nöthen, and J. Kere, "Strong genetic evidence of DCDC2 as a susceptibility gene for dyslexia," *American Journal of Human Genetics* 78 (January 2006): 52–62.

Shaikh, S., D.A. Collier, P.C. Sham, D. Ball, K. Aitchison, H. Vallada, I. Smith, M. Gill, and R.W. Kerwin, "Allelic association between a Ser-9-Gly polymorphism in the dopamine D3 receptor gene and schizophrenia," *Human Genetics* 97 (June 1996): 714–719.

Sham, P., J.S. Bader, I. Craig, M. O'Donovan, and M. Owen, "DNA pooling: A tool for large-scale association studies," *Nature Review Genetics* 3 (November 2002): 862–871.

Smoller, J.W., and C.T. Finn, "Family, twin, and adoption studies of bipolar disorder," *American Journal of Medical Genetics, Part C, Seminar of Medical Genetics* 123 (November 2003): 48–58.

Spielman, R.S., R.E. McGinnis, and W.J. Ewens, "Transmission test for linkage disequilibrium: The insulin gene region and insulin-dependent diabetes mellitus (IDDM)," *American Journal of Human Genetics* 52 (March 1993): 506–516.

St. Clair, D., D. Blackwood, W. Muir, A. Carothers, M. Walker, G. Spowart, C. Gosden, and H.J. Evans, "Association within a family of a balanced autosomal translocation with major mental illness," *Lancet* 336 (July 1990): 13–16.

Stamm S., "Signals and their transduction pathways regulating alternative splicing: A new dimension of the human genome," *Human Molecular Genetics* 11 (October 2002): 2409–2416.

Stancheva, I., A.L. Collins, I.B. Van den Veyver, H. Zoghbi, and R.R. Meehan, "A mutant form of MeCP2 protein associated with human Rett syndrome cannot be displaced from methylated DNA by notch in Xenopus embryos," *Molecular Cell* 12 (August 2003): 425–435.

Steinle, N.I., W.C. Hsueh, S. Snitker, T.I. Pollin, H. Sakul, P.L. St. Jean, C.J. Bell, B.D. Mitchell, and A.R. Shuldiner, "Eating behavior in the old order Amish: Heritability analysis and a genome-wide linkage analysis," *American Journal of Clinical Nutrition* 75 (June 2002): 1098–1106.

Stunkard, A.J., and S. Messick, "The three-factor eating questionnaire to measure dietary restraint, disinhibition and hunger," *Journal of Psychosomatic Research* 29 (1985): 71–83.

Stunkard, A.J., T.I. Sorensen, C. Hanis, T.W. Teasdale, R. Chakraborty, W.J. Schull, and F. Schulsinger, "An adoption study of human obesity," *New England Journal of Medicine* 314 (January 1986): 193–198.

Sullivan, P.F., M.C. Neale, and K.S. Kendler, "Genetic epidemiology of major depression: Review and meta-analysis, *American Journal of Psychiatry* (October 2000): 1552–1562.

Sullivan, P.F., K.S. Kendler, and M. C. Neale, "Schizophrenia as a complex trait: evidence from a meta-analysis of twin studies," *Archives of General Psychiatry* 60 (December 2003): 1187–1192.

Tao, J., H. Van Esch, M. Hagedorn-Greiwe, K. Hoffmann, B. Moser, M. Raynaud, J. Sperner, J.P. Fryns, E. Schwinger, J. Gecz, H.H. Ropers, and V.M. Kalscheuer, "Mutations in the X-linked cyclin-dependent kinase-like 5 (CDKL5/STK9) gene are associated with severe neurodevelopmental retardation," *American Journal of Human Genetics* 75 (December 2004): 1149–1154.

Terwilliger, J.D., and H.H. Göring, "Gene mapping in the 20th and 21st centuries: Statistical methods, data analysis, and experimental design," *Human Biology* 72 (February 2000): 63–132.

Terwilliger, J., and J. Ott, "A haplotype-based 'haplotype relative risk' approach to detecting allelic associations," *Human Heredity* 42 (1992): 337–346.

Thomson, P.A., S.E. Harris, J.M. Starr, L.J. Whalley, D.J. Porteous, and I.J. Deary, "Association between genotype at an exonic SNP in DISC1 and normal cognitive aging," *Neuroscience Letters* 389 (November 2005): 41–45.

The Tourette Syndrome Association International Consortium for Genetics, "A complete genome screen in sib pairs affected by Gilles de la Tourette syndrome," *American Journal of Human Genetics* 65 (November 1999): 1428–1436.

Trikalinos, T.A., A. Karvouni, E. Zintzaras, T. Ylisaukko-Oja, L. Peltonen, I. Jarvela, and J.P. Ioannidis, "A heterogeneity-based genome search meta-analysis for autism-spectrum disorders," *Molecular Psychiatry* 27 (September 2005) (Epub ahead of print).

Van Steen, K., M.B. McQueen, A. Herbert, B. Raby, H. Lyon, D.L. Demeo, A. Murphy, J. Su, S. Datta, C. Rosenow, M. Christman, E.K. Silverman, N.M. Laird, S.T. Weiss, and C. Lange, "Genomic screening and replication using the same data set in family-based association testing," *Nature Genetics* 37 (July 2005): 683–691.

Van Hulle, C.A., H.H. Goldsmith, and K.S. Lemery, "Genetic, environmental, and gender effects on individual differences in toddler expressive language," *Journal of Speech Language Hearing Research* 47 (August 2004): 904–912.

Venter, J.C., M.D. Adams, E.W. Myers, P.W. Li, R.J. Mural, G.G. Sutton, H.O. Smith, M. Yandell, C.A. Evans, R.A. Holt, J.D. Gocayne, P. Amanatides, R.M. Ballew, D.H. Huson, J.R. Wortman, Q. Zhang, C.D. Kodira, X.H. Zheng, L. Chen, M. Skupski, G. Subramanian, P.D. Thomas, J. Zhang, G.L. Gabor Miklos, et al., "The sequence of the human genome," *Science* 291 (February 2001): 1304–1351.

Vieland, V.J., "The replication requirement," *Nature Genetics* 29 (November 2001): 244–245.

Von Gontard, A., H. Schaumburg, E. Hollmann, H. Eiberg, and S. Rittig, "The genetics of enuresis: A review," *Journal of Urology* 166 (December 2001): 2438–2443.

Watson, J.D., and F.H. Crick, "Molecular structure of nucleic acids: A structure for deoxyribose nucleic acid," *Nature* 171 (April 1953): 737–738.

Weaving, L.S., J. Christodoulou, S.L. Williamson, K.L. Friend, O.L. McKenzie, H. Archer, J. Evans, A. Clarke, G.J. Pelka, P.P. Tam, C. Watson, H. Lahooti, C.J. Ellaway, B Bennetts, H. Leonard, and J. Gecz, "Mutations of CDKL5 cause a severe neurodevelopmental disorder with infantile spasms and mental retardation," *American Journal of Human Genetics* 75 (December 2004): 1079–1093.

Weaving, L.S., C.J. Ellaway, J. Gecz, and J. Christodoulou, "Rett syndrome: Clinical review and genetic update," *Journal of Medical Genetics* 42 (January 2005): 1–7.

WHO, *The ICD-10 classification of mental and behavioural disorders* (Geneva: World Health Organization, 1992).

Williams, J., G. Spurlock, P. Holmans, R. Mant, K. Murphy, L. Jones, A. Cardno, P. Asherson, D. Blackwood, W. Muir, K. Meszaros, H. Aschauer, J. Mallet, C. Laurent, P. Pekkarinen, J. Seppala, C.N. Stefanis, G.N. Papadimitriou, F. Macciardi, M. Verga, C. Pato, H. Azevedo, M.A. Crocq, H. Gurling, M.J. Owen, et al., "A meta-analysis and transmission disequilibrium study of association between the dopamine D3 receptor gene and schizophrenia," *Molecular Psychiatry* 3 (March 1998): 141–149.

Wooster, R., G. Bignell, J. Lancaster, S. Swift, S. Seal, J. Mangion, N. Collins, S. Gregory, C. Gumbs, and G. Micklem, "Identification of the breast cancer susceptibility gene BRCA2," *Nature* 378 (December 1995): 789–792.

Chapter Two

The Hypothalamic-Pituitary-Adrenal Axis: Cortisol, DHEA, and Psychopathology

Ian M. Goodyer

Steroids are an extensive family of chemical agents distributed widely in the brain. They include cortisol, the classical stress hormone, estradiol, testosterone, progesterone—collectively the sex hormones—and aldosterone and dehydroepiandrosterone (DHEA). Cortisol and DHEA are the most implicated in the response to demands from everyday life involving physical or mental activity. Both have a high density in the limbic system but are also found in the cortex. Circulating levels of steroids can be relatively easily measured in the periphery from blood, urine, and saliva. These peripheral levels are correlated with levels in the cerebrospinal and ventricular fluid in the brain (Guazzo et al., 1996).

There is now clear-cut evidence that certain steroids are manufactured in the brain and play a key role in brain development and plasticity (Baulieu and Schumacher, 2004). These include DHEA and its sulfate, DHEA(S). Within the brain these neurosteroids modulate the effects of other transmitters including gamma-aminobutyric acid (GABA) and glutamate. Neurosteroids can therefore alter neuronal excitability throughout the brain very rapidly by binding to receptors for inhibitory or excitatory neurotransmitters at the cell membrane.

Alterations in levels of the adrenal steroids cortisol and DHEA have important implications for general cognitive and emotional function. These psychological effects are brought about through altered sensitivity in receptors in steroid-sensitive areas of the brain, notably the limbic system and their related frontal regions.

CORTISOL, DHEA, AND THE BRAIN

Since the 1980s, it is become increasingly apparent that steroids have key functions in the brain. Cortisol is critically involved in homeostasis and allostatis and is essential for survival when the body has to mobilize metabolic resources following an event, such as acute illness, physical trauma, or social change. In contrast the functions of DHEA are not yet fully understood, but it is involved in three key processes. One is in maintaining healthy blood vessels (vascular integrity; Liu and Dillon, 2002), a second is protecting the brain from deleterious effects of cortisol (Karishma and Herbert, 2002), and the third is facilitating neurogenesis (Karishma and Herbert, 2002; Suzuki et al., 2004). Neuroprotection by DHEA appears important when the levels of cortisol in the brain are high for days. In those circumstances parts of the limbic system (notably the hippocampus) may be damaged. DHEA may act as a neuroprotective agent (Kimonides et al., 1998; Kimonides et al., 1999).

In addition to adrenal steroids having direct effects on brain and mental functions they have interactions with the monoamines. Cortisol in particular has powerful bidirectional effects on serotonin systems in the brain. During development absence of cortisol results in serotonin downregulation and depletion, indicating a potentially important set of relations between these two systems and perhaps a more complex role in the chemical adaptation to social adversity than considered hitherto (Chalmers et al., 1993; Wissink et al., 2000). Similarly, serotonin depletion can modulate the steroid responses to environmental events (Chung et al., 1999).

A great deal is known about the control of cortisol secretion in relation to stressful environments. The hypothalamic-pituitary-adrenal (HPA) axis is the neurochemical system through which the release of cortisol is regulated. There is a negative feedback between the level of circulating cortisol in the periphery and the receptor regulation at the level of the hippocampus in the brain.

Cortisol enters the brain via the blood-brain barrier and attaches to glucocorticoid (GC) receptors therein. These are located in a number of brain regions but are densely packed in the limbic system and in the hippocampus and amygdala in particular. The degree of receptor occupancy acts as a control signal on the whole axis. High occupancy levels increase inhibitory signals to the hypothalamus, diminishing the release of a peptide, corticotrophin releasing factor (CRF), which is the chemical signal going to the pituitary and regulating the release of a second peptide, adreno-cortico-tropin hormone (ACTH). Diminished ACTH response results in the adrenal gland diminishing the release of cortisol. This negative feedback system operates in a loop. Thus as lower cortisol levels enter the brain, occupancy diminishes, CRF is upregulated (due to loss of inhibition from the hippocampus), and the system releases more cortisol. This is a highly dynamic physiological process, as shown in figure 2.1.

The GC receptor shows polymorphic variation whose functional significance remains to be fully determined but appears to be in part controlling in-

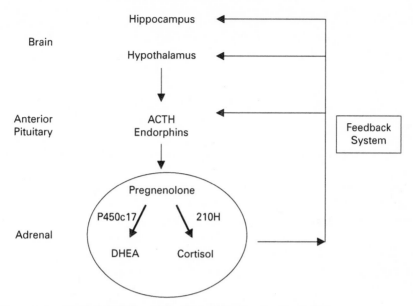

Figure 2.1. Cortisol, DHEA, and the Brain: Negative Feedback System

dividual variations in circulating levels (Rosmond et al., 2000; Rosmond et al., 2001). Allelic variations also occur in the CRF peptide that controls the release of ACTH and hence cortisol. These receptors may be a target for preventing cortisol hypersecretion found in a significant proportion of depressive illnesses (Nemeroff, 2002).

There is some preliminary evidence that if polymorphisms are present in both the GC receptor and the CRF peptide, then cortisol levels will be markedly different depending on the inherited characteristics of these variants (Rosmond et al., 2000; Rosmond et al., 2001; Smoller et al., 2003). Thus there are individual differences in cortisol levels not only due to reactivity to events but also to genetic differences. Furthermore, it is receptor sensitivity that is most likely to determine the impact of high steroid levels on the tissues in the brain and the subsequent physiological and psychological events. It may be that allelic variation leads to differences in receptor sensitivity and therefore variations in response to corticoids (Lu and Cidlowski, 2004).

Thus the genetic structure of the receptor itself may contribute to modulating the risk for individual differences in behavioral response and psychiatric disorder via its sensitivity to circulating cortisol levels. Finally allelic variations of corticotrophin releasing hormone (CRH) may be associated with a very wide variety of behavioral characteristics. These include the psychological process of behavioral inhibition (a measure of impulse control; Smoller et al., 2001) and high body mass index, indicating excess weight gain (Challis et al., 2004). This indicates the complex and manifold functions of large peptide molecules in functional activity within an individual.

HPA AXIS DEVELOPMENT, DYSFUNCTION, AND PSYCHIATRIC DISORDER

In the first nine months of life the HPA axis is rather irregular in its function and cortisol levels fluctuate rather markedly with no discernible pattern or rhythm. Minor perturbations, such as being picked up, feeding, and clothes changing, result in significant alterations in cortisol levels. By twelve months of age there is a marked biobehavioral shift in the HPA axis control of cortisol (Gunnar and Donzella, 2002). Social regulation of the axis is now occurring and a rhythm is clearly established with higher morning levels rising within the first hour after awakening and reaching an apex over the first few hours of the day, followed by a decline over the second half of the day to a nadir in early evening. This diurnal rhythm remains in this form throughout life.

Recent investigations of diurnal rhythm in twins show that the early morning levels are significantly more alike in monozygotic than dizygotic twins, whereas evening levels show no such similarity (Bartels, de Geus, et al., 2003). Other studies have shown genetic influences persist over the 24-hour cycle and may affect the timing of the nadir as well as the apex (Linkowski et al., 1993). This suggests that there is marked genetic control over the switching on of the axis in the morning. Environmental factors exert increasing effects on individual differences in levels as the day proceeds, although genetic factors remain an influence (Bartels, Van den Berg, et al., 2003).

As well as diurnal rhythm, levels show reactivity to events. These episodic movements in levels generally show a rapid rise in the presence of a stimulus regardless of its salience, indicating that this change is related more to surprise or novelty than personal meaning. Levels can remain quite high in relation to the behavioral requirements demanded by the stimulus, for example, to engage in social conversation with a surprise visitor or deal with an unpleasant event such as a car crash. Cortisol levels lower gradually as the consequences of the event pass. In general, levels return to baseline about forty minutes after the cessation of the behavioral response. This rise and fall can occur at any time of the day and appears to be independent of the stage of an individual's diurnal rhythm.

High resilience to external events may be associated with a rapid falling of cortisol levels following exposure to stress or novelty (Davidson, 2004).

Lowering of cortisol in such circumstances may reflect the individual's successful and rapid adaptation to a current demand.

MEASUREMENT OF CIRCULATING ADRENAL STEROIDS

In contrast to indwelling cannulae to obtain blood, or 24-hour urine collections, salivary collection allows repeated sampling of large populations. Salivary levels correlate highly with serum levels ($r = 0.6$–0.9), and the latter also correlate highly with levels in the ventricular CSF ($r = 0.8$; Guazzo et al., 1996). The salivary assays used to measure these steroids are sensitive and specific enough to detect the very low levels present in saliva and alterations in these levels over time.

Cortisol levels in the saliva (and in the CSF) are about 5% of those in the serum (Goodyer et al., 1996), reflecting the free (unbound to plasma protein) fraction (see later discussion). Cortisol and DHEA in the saliva may reflect levels in the CSF (and hence exposure of the brain to these steroids) although there have been no direct studies of the associations between CSF and salivary levels in the same individual. Cortisol is secreted in a pulsatile fashion and this is reflected in the saliva, with a time lag of about fifteen minutes (Kirschbaum and Hellhammer, 1994).

Cortisol shows marked reactivity to the environment, which is reflected in the amplitude of the diurnal rhythm: in the saliva of twelve–eighteen-year-olds, this is about ten-fold from 8 A.M. to 8 P.M. In a study of 234 adolescents the mean ratio of salivary cortisol from 8 A.M. to 8 P.M. was 12.76 (coefficient of variation = 66.8%; Goodyer et al., 2000a). It is therefore important to take sufficient samples, at sufficient time points, to define accurately the form of the diurnal pattern of this steroid. Current findings suggest that less than four samples spread over a 24-hour period is unlikely to provide a reliable index of rhythm, and less than four days of sampling is unlikely to give a valid reflection of mean values.

More studies need to be carried out with adequate numbers of normal and mentally ill subjects across the life span to define the precise parameters of sampling requirements at different ages. Cortisol reacts to stressful events (e.g., Gunnar, 1998), so precautions should be taken to ensure that subjects are in a basal state, unless the response to stress or demand is an intended feature of the study (e.g., during a behavioral challenge task).

Recent studies have shown that levels rise markedly following awakening, with the morning apex obtained approximately 45 minutes to 1 hour later (Pruessner et al., 1997; Pruessner et al., 1999). This intriguing observation has been the subject of intense study recently because of its possible role as a functional marker of risk for psychopathology. Findings are markedly equivocal, with few studies accounting for the effects of a range of factors influencing the liability for both higher and lower cortisol levels over the 45 minutes following awakening (Clow and Thorn, 2004). These include defining when subjects are awake, sampling procedures used to collect cortisol, and the measurement of a number of key moderating factors on cortisol levels. The latter include the degree of stress in the hours prior to awakening, chronic social difficulties, ethnicity, education, social class, age, and level of sleep dysregulation. For example, lower awakening levels have been reported in well adults with a history of early loss experiences in childhood (Meinlschmidt and Heim, 2005), whereas high awakening cortisol has been found in a small sample of well adults compared to those with very low neuroticism scores (Portella et al., 2005).

A further consideration is how the data should be treated. A number of derivations can be obtained that can affect the sampling procedure. For example, by using four samples obtained at the same time of day, it is possible to derive mean group values, compare individual differences in the mean morning awakening apex, or examine the mean maximum secreted level as an index of higher corticoid activity. The precise selection of measurement is necessarily related to the question being investigated. Few studies to date have adequately considered a priori these critical quantitative issues.

There is also a literature using dexamethasone suppression test (DST) as an index of cortisol activity across the life span (Plotsky et al., 1998). DST is an index of feedback sensitivity, not hypersecretion, and compared with cortisol levels has proved a less consistent index of HPA dysregulation. A more powerful challenge is the combined dexamethasone-CRH test (Deuschle et al., 1998; Watson et al., 2002). This has improved sensitivity and specificity and has been shown to identify feedback dysregulation in both patients with acute depression and first-degree relatives at risk for affective disorders.

Pharmacological challenge procedures use drugs (e.g., fenfluramine) to probe the HPA axis or neural systems (e.g., serotonin) that impinge upon it (Park et al., 1996). Abnormal responses to such challenge in the form of blunted hormonal responses in the periphery are interpreted as reflecting dysfunctional neurochemical processes in the brain. These techniques provide valuable information on such systems and have been greatly enhanced through the addition of neuroimaging procedures to delineate alterations in blood flow of the brain regions of interest. Such studies have not examined the relations between levels of adrenal steroids, development, and the onset of subsequent psychopathology. There is no technical reason why a developmental prospective program of research monitoring changes in neurosteroid systems incorporating neuroimaging and challenge tests should not be carried out at different points in the life span. A key issue for such technology-ladened studies is a clear set of a priori hypotheses.

For DHEA, a second major adrenal steroid, the picture is somewhat different. This steroid is also present in the saliva (and CSF) at about 5% of plasma levels, but there is no known plasma binding protein for DHEA, so the source of this relation remains obscure. The diurnal rhythm in saliva (8 A.M. to 8 P.M.) is also much less than for cortisol (about twofold). In adolescents the mean ratio of salivary DHEA from 8 A.M. to 8 P.M. was 2.07 (coefficient of variation = 33.8%). Interestingly, levels vary, with demand being somewhat higher early in depressive illness but becoming increasingly reduced under conditions of chronicity.

The cortisol-DHEA ratio thus changes during the day, from 5–7 in the morning (8 A.M.) to about 2 at 8 P.M. This ratio may be interesting in light of interactions between the two steroids (see later discussion).

DISORDERS OF EMOTION

Cortisol

Studies of the HPA axis in psychiatric patients began some four decades ago with the observation that severely depressed patients showed a sustained elevation of their evening cortisol levels leading to a loss of the expected diurnal rhythm. Such patients showed a sustained high level invariably from around 8 P.M. through to 4 A.M. This observation has been repeated many times, but it is now clear that this dysregulation occurs in no more than about half of depressed patients and perhaps even somewhat fewer (Plotsky et al., 1998). Until relatively recently these evening alterations in HPA axis function were considered to be a consequence of being depressed. Thus the HPA axis dysregulation has been considered an epiphenomenon of acute depressive illness. Two prospective studies have now established that morning cortisol hypersecretion precedes and predicts the onset of major depression in both adult women and adolescents of both sexes (Goodyer et al., 2000b; Harris et al., 2000). There was no difference in evening cortisol levels between those who became depressed over the next twelve months and those who did not. Interestingly, this change in cortisol cannot be accounted for by recent undesirable events or difficulties, so it does not appear to be a reactivity effect to immediate or recent negative social experiences.

A further community study failed to establish a direct association between higher cortisol and depression in adult women but noted a strong link between cortisol levels and an increase in negative life events (Strickland et al., 2002).

Depressed patients with higher cortisol levels are significantly more likely to experience further negative life events than depressed individuals with normal cortisol levels (Goodyer et al., 2003). These depression-dependent negative life events increase the liability for persistent disorder. Thus the pathological process that arises from high cortisol levels in currently depressed patients disturbs some aspects of affective-cognitive function that disrupts interpersonal behavior.

In contrast to depressive conditions we know far less about the HPA axis in anxiety disorders. Post-traumatic stress disorder (PTSD) has been the most extensively studied nondepressive emotional disorder. Cortisol hyposecretion, including blunted awakening levels, are the most commonly found abnormality in patients and the offspring of patients with PTSD (Yehuda et al., 2002; Murphy, 2003; Southwick et al., 2003; Neylan et al., 2005; Yehuda et al., 2005). Cortisol reactivity to subsequent stressful events does not appear to be affected. Cognitive impairments in PTSD patients have been described, generally poor memory function, but the relation to low cortisol remains somewhat equivocal and may be influenced by age, past traumatic experiences, and many of the aforementioned factors that can influence morning cortisol levels (Delahanty et al., 2000; Bremner et al., 2003; Elzinga et al., 2003; Yehuda et al., 2005).

Recent findings correlating GC receptor polymorphisms with cortisol sensitivity in PTSD patients have suggested that a subset of currently ill subjects has a negative correlation between the BclII polymorphism and PTSD symptoms (Bachmann et al., 2005). This is the first psychiatric study to report a putative relationship between genetic variation in receptor subtypes and psychopathology. Further studies on the genetics of the HPA axis as contributing to the risk for psychopathology are clearly warranted.

Although there is some confusion over cognitive impairments in the presence of cortisol hypersecretion, there is increasing evidence that hypersecretion is correlated with disturbances in memory (Newcomer et al., 1999; Lupien et al., 2002). A range of factors may influence this cortisol-memory relationship, including social adversity and a previous history of cortisol hypersecretion (Lupien et al., 2000; Lupien et al., 2001; Lupien and Lepage, 2001; Lupien et al., 2002). It seems highly likely that a key cortisol function in the brains of healthy humans is to modulate learning and memory and perhaps retrieval of information. This modulation process may have its key focus in the limbic system but is likely to exert an influence on general brain state involving many regions, including the prefrontal and orbito-frontal cortex (Mayberry et al., 1999; Drevets, 2003; Seminowicz et al., 2004).

Overall, the neurochemical coding for responses to social events and the subsequent liability for anxiety or depression may be as follows:

1. Occupancy of steroid receptors in the hippocampus and the amygdala triggers a complex cascade of cellular events leading to subjectively altered mood and organization of the appraised experiences.
2. Activation and modulation of these affective processes occur through changes in the level of serotonin (and probably other monoamine systems) in the prefrontal and orbito-frontal cortex.
3. These interrelated physiological changes in the brain, with changes in monoamines as the last chemical step, lead to activation of cognitive controls and behavioral actions.
4. Serotonin-vulnerable individuals will react poorly to the corticoid-driven affective signals arising from deeper in the brain. High cortisol will therefore not be adequately responded to and may lead to abnormal psychological processes and psychiatric disorders.

As yet there are no methodologically sound studies in the community determining how cortisol and serotonin systems interact to cause common anxiety and depressive disorders.

Perhaps there will also be further advances in understanding the neurochemical basis of response to stress and the onset of psychiatric disorders via modern neuroimaging procedures. Combining this technique with functional activation of brain and chemical systems using chemical and psychological challenge has already shown considerable interplay between the limbic and frontal cortex in volunteers and depressed patients (Drevets, 2003; Liotti et al., 2000; Meyer et al., 2001). These studies are only in their first decade and much will be learned rapidly in the near future.

DHEA

DHEA shows a very different developmental history to that of cortisol (Kroboth et al., 1999). Unlike cortisol, concentrations of DHEA and its sulfate, DHEA(S), vary with age (Parker, 1999). DHEA is made by the placenta, so the fetus is exposed to its action: concentrations decline from the first few months of life until five years of age and then rise rapidly from age seven in girls and around nine in boys (this is called adrenarche), until levels reach their peak between ages twenty and thirty. Adrenarche is separable from puberty, since gonadotropins and estrogen have no effect on DHEA levels and the two events are not linked across time. After age 20–30, levels begin to decline in both sexes. By 70–80 years levels are approximately 10% to 20% of a twenty-year-old (Labrie et al., 1997).

Unlike cortisol there is no clear-cut notion of how DHEA is regulated. It is not under the tight control of the HPA axis, however. Thus, although levels can vary somewhat with the rise and fall of cortisol as the adrenal is stimulated to secrete GCs, there are clearly other factors involved. DHEA has been shown to act as an antagonist to cortisol at the level of the GC receptor (Kimonides et al., 1999). There is also evidence that DHEA promotes neurogenesis (Karishma and Herbert, 2002; Suzuki et al., 2004). This ability to promote new neuronal growth if replicated could be a key neural feature of this hormone. Since, as we have seen, high cortisol persisting over days is associated with an increase in depression, DHEA may have neuroprotective effects in the brain, diminishing the liability for cortisol to damage neurons and thereby decreasing the risk for psychopathology.

There is also preliminary evidence that increasing DHEA levels lower cortisol in the periphery, providing further support for an anti-GC effect of DHEA (Kroboth et al., 2003). If this was the action of DHEA, then subjects at risk for psychiatric disorders and showing high cortisol levels would be expected to also show high levels of DHEA.

This was demonstrated in a prospective study of adolescents. Those who subsequently developed major depression over the next twelve months had levels significantly higher than that expected for their age and sex (in well adolescents levels are significantly greater in girls compared with boys) (Goodyer et al., 2000a; Goodyer et al., 2000b). The possibility that this rise is an attempt to offset the increase in cortisol activity is attractive but requires much further investigation before firm conclusions can be drawn. For example, from the adolescent study there is no clear-cut evidence that higher DHEA decreased cortisol in some at-risk youth and thereby lowered the liability for subsequent depression. What is clear is that DHEA is not passively indicating a maturational effect of age but is involved in some active process. The finding requires replication, but DHEA is a promising candidate as a neuroprotective agent at times of acute social adversity.

Interestingly, there is some evidence that while DHEA levels rise during the early phase of a major depression they may then fall if the disorder persists. Two longitudinal studies of depressed patients, one from clinically referred patients and the other from a community-based study, have both shown that higher cortisol-DHEA ratios predict persistent disorder and occur because of declining DHEA levels during the illness (Goodyer et al., 2001; Goodyer et al., 2003). These findings support the notion that DHEA secretion is rather vulnerable to chronic illness effects and that its decline is associated with a poor short-term outcome.

The reasons for this decline in a potentially helpful neurosteroid are not clear. It may reflect the severity of the metabolic strain that a severe mental illness can produce. Similar findings have been noted in critically physically ill patients, where low DHEA levels predict a poor response to treatment and a higher mortality (Beishuizen et al., 2002; Marx et al., 2003). Rising DHEA levels by contrast may reflect increased capacity of the HPA axis system at a time of increased demand (Charney, 2004). Successful DHEA response may be a predictor of a reduction in strain on the individual and perhaps a more rapid recovery. This possibility deserves further investigation in psychiatric disorders.

A further difference from cortisol is the absence of any clear-cut associations with psychological processes. DHEA does not appear to be related to memory or learning nor to (self-report) measures of self-evaluation (Huppert and Van Niekerk, 2001). By contrast, there is now quite good evidence that DHEA enhances positive mood and acts as an antidepressant (Wolkowitz et al., 1999; Hunt et al., 2000; Van Niekerk et al., 2001; Strous et al., 2003; Schmidt et al., 2005). Interestingly, DHEA does not appear to exert effects via testosterone even though it is in the same metabolic pathway of androgen production. Rather it appears to possess direct effects on brain, perhaps via its anti-GC actions in the amygdala and hippocampus, thereby showing a bias for modulating neuroaffective rather than neurocognitive systems.

With the recent discovery of an endothelial receptor for DHEA it may not be too long before we are able to describe the physiology of this compound (Liu and Dillon, 2002). From the psychiatric perspective DHEA potentially looks to be an important modulator of disorder mood states and deserves to be studied in detail as an adjunct to current treatments, particularly in persistent mood disorders.

Much greater precision is required in investigating affective-cognitive-DHEA relations before concluding there is no association between memory, learning, and information retrieval and individual differences in DHEA. Interestingly, compared to cortisol, DHEA shows little or no awakening effect (Hucklebridge et al., 2005). Although DHEA shows a clear diurnal variation with a decline in evening levels there appears to be less sensitivity to daily events, perhaps reflecting the known differences in function between this hormone and cortisol. The specific contribution of genetic influences on levels of circulating DHEA and on brain-based receptor responses is not known.

SPECIFIC SOCIAL ADVERSITIES, STEROIDS, AND MONOAMINES

Infant Stress

Recent research has implicated a role for infant exposure to adverse early experiences in the formation of HPA axis sensitivity. Animal studies have reported a substantial nongenetic effect of adverse maternal rearing practices on the development of chemical coding systems for behavior including HPA axis, hypothalamic and extrahypothalamic CRH, monoaminergic, and GABA-benzodiazepine systems (Kaufman et al., 2000). Loss of maternal care through separation leads to a potential change in the chemical signaling processes between the limbic system and the frontal and prefrontal cortex. Recent findings in rodents have outlined the neurochemical mechanisms that occur via epigenetic programming as a consequence of variations in maternal care style (Weaver et al., 2004). The evidence shows that there are major effects on GC receptor sensitivity in rodent pups, depending on the degree of positive care obtained. This early environmental effect can exert a substantive adverse effect on behavior persistent through to adult rodent life.

The pathological mechanisms result in significantly fewer steroid receptors in the limbic system and lower expression of neurotrophic genes involved in brain growth and function. These dysfunctions occur because in pups exposed to adverse rearing there is methylation of nerve growth factor 1 (NGF1) in the presence of high cortisol, effectively silencing this neurotrophic gene that is a component for activating normal early brain development. Remarkably, the authors showed that in infant rats exposed to poor care it was possible to alter deleterious effects on the brain through demethylation of NGF1 via chemical means, thereby switching on the neurotrophic genes that had been switched off by the higher cortisol levels occurring during the adverse early care events. This led to a restoration of behaviors no different to those of the normally reared pups. Whether the impact of such experiences varies with genetic variation in GC and CRH receptors and shows different effects on steroid levels at different times of the day (or on the 24-hour rhythm as whole) is not known.

Overall, this remarkably clear study provides definitive evidence for a key environmental process on the developmental programming of the HPA axis system in a mammalian model. Prospective studies of human infants can now be carried out delineating both the GC genetic variation and early rearing environment and examining both the HPA axis stability and behavioral patterns of function over time.

A partial advance in this direction can be seen in the results of a recent prospective study of an adolescent cohort followed since birth. Salivary assessment of steroids at thirteen years of age showed significant increases in morning cortisol levels in those exposed to postnatal depression and difficult early maternal experiences compared with those with no such exposure (Halligan et al., 2004). This long-term association remained even when current adolescent depressive symptoms, puberty, and current parental well-being were taken into account. This certainly suggests that early adversities may exert long-term effects on HPA axis function and might indicate one familial pathway that results in an increased vulnerability for psychopathology. Whether the liability for higher cortisol occurred in those with a particular allelic variation in the GC receptor gene is not known.

Furthermore, it is entirely unclear if these early effects on brain systems can be moderated via subsequent positive developmental pathways in the environment (such as good peer relations in the preschool and school years).

It is highly likely that genetic variations in behaviorally sensitive neural pathways are also implicated in responses to adversity. For example, studies on monkeys have shown that offspring who carry the S allele of the serotonin transporter gene and are subject to maternal separation are indeed more likely to show abnormal brain chemistry. These animals have been reported as being more fearful and less prosocial than their mother-reared counterparts with the same genetic makeup (Champoux et al., 2002). This suggests an important gene-environment interaction in early infancy that leads to a vulnerable animal. These findings are complementary to those reported by Caspi and colleagues showing a significant interaction between the same allelic variation and the increased liability for life events predicting the onset of major depression (Caspi et al., 2003). Whether the effects on HPA axis function are related to allelic variations in the serotonin system is not clear. Indeed the potential impact of adversity in early life (or later) in individuals who carry different allelic variations in both serotonin and GC genes is not known.

DEPRIVATION, MALTREATMENT, AND TRAUMATIC EXPERIENCE

As childhood proceeds, two major negative experiences are unfortunately more common than any society would like. First, general deprivation frequently resulting in low emotional stimulation and, second, a poverty of social experiences required for normal cognitive development accompanied by often overlooked poor nutrition. Many studies have demonstrated that these privation experiences are associated with an increase in common emotional and behavioral disorder in the school-age years. Severe chronic privations, such as being brought up in an orphanage since birth, are also associated changes in the sensitivity of the HPA axis with cortisol hypersecretion that are frequently reported (Gunnar et al, 2001). The multiplicity of factors in chronic deprivation prevents any specific associations being made from such studies. Whether social and emotional neglect, poor nutrition, high rates of infection, and poor hygiene act separately or in concert to produce HPA axis abnormalities in the early years of life is not clear.

A second major set of events in childhood to influence the HPA axis is that of child maltreatment. Here the negative experience is focused on physical or sexual abuse of children. Invariably in these studies overt maltreatment is associated with emotionally abusive experiences, such as persistent critical comment, narrow and restricted social opportunities, and a lack of a secure, emotionally consistent confiding relationship. Unfortunately, it has become increasingly apparent that these experiences have significant biological consequences for neural systems and chemical codes for behavior.

Child maltreatment is associated with cortisol hypersecretion in some studies but also with cortisol hyposecretion in others (Gunnar and Donzella, 2002). The latter observation is particularly puzzling but is not confined to maltreatment experiences. As already noted, some patients exposed to severe traumas, including war injuries and road traffic accidents, and diagnosed as suffering from PTSD, also show cortisol hyposecretion. This apparent suppression of HPA axis activity may not arise solely from the recent focal experience but may also be connected either to prior experience or perhaps genetic vulnerabilities for low cortisol activity such as the preliminary finding of a negative correlation between the BclI polymorphism in the GC receptor gene and PTSD symptoms (Bachmann et al., 2005). We do not yet know, but it is clear that we cannot assume that for some individuals very severe trauma has a direct and relatively instant suppressive effect on HPA function (Yehuda et al., 2004).

CONDUCT DISORDERS

There is a small but increasing body of literature suggesting that an entirely different group of behavior disorders also hyposecrete cortisol, even at times of stress. Children, adolescents, and young adults with conduct disorders of rather high severity have been shown to have remarkably suppressed cortisol levels compared with controls (McBurnett et al., 2000; Pajer et al., 2001). These individuals are known to have high levels of chronic psychosocial adversities, but it is not yet clear if the reported low levels of cortisol, suggesting a suppressed HPA axis, are related to a history of adversity, a particular form of adversity, or even no adversity in this group of behavioral disorders. Investigation of cortisol secretory patterns in the community suggests that about 10% of the population at large may have flat cortisol levels over the 24-hour period rather than the more common diurnal variation (Stone et al., 2001). The implications of a flat cortisol level in the population at large in addition to finding this to occur in some individuals with markedly different disorders such as PTSD and severe conduct disorder is a puzzle that requires some considerable sorting out.

For example, the presence of extreme levels of cortisol (high or low) suggests a loss of synchrony or perhaps a blunting between the neurochemical signaling pathways within the brain. Experimental studies on conduct-disordered children that induced frustration showed no increase in cortisol levels relative to age-matched controls who exhibited the predicted rise at the time of stress stimulus (Van Goozen et al., 1998). Interestingly, although cortisol levels remained flat during this emotionally charged challenge test, heart rate also remained flat although the conduct-disordered children reported feeling out of control and angry (Van Goozen et al., 2000). These findings showing dissociation between affective-cognitive and physiological responses following induced frustration suggest a potential loss of synchrony at the neurochemical level.

Repeating these studies using neuroimaging techniques may be able to test if conduct disordered subjects do indeed show a different pattern of neural response to controls. Interestingly, lower heart rate in childhood is associated with higher risk for antisocial personality disorder in adult life (Raine et al., 1997) and behaviorally disordered individuals report fearlessness even when confronted with fearful stimuli (Raine et al., 1998; Blair et al., 2001). There are also reported reductions in the gray matter of the brain in adults diagnosed with psychopathic disorders (Raine et al., 2000).

All these findings support a brain-based etiology to explain responses to social adversity being different in behaviorally disordered individuals over the life span. There are also changes in the serotonin system in severe psychopaths who show low serotonin function correlated with increased impulsivity compared with controls (Dolan et al., 2002). It is possible that the subgroup with low cortisol hyposecretion is made up of those with high traits for psychopathy, which are known to be highly heritable (Viding et al., 2005). These may be the individuals with a reduced serotonin tone in the prefrontal cortex as a consequence of gene-environment interactions arising from early life adversities, methylating NGF1, and lowering cortisol responsivity, but this has yet to be formally tested.

What does this impaired serotonin and increased impulsivity response have to do with low or flat cortisol levels at times of stress? Cortisol is part of the chemical coding pathway that accesses personally salient emotional related memories (episodic memories; Lupien and Lepage, 2001). Low sensitivity to fearfulness may impair the mobilization of a fear response through loss of retrieval of fear-related memories. Such memories may not even be kept in memory by behavior-disordered individuals. This will blunt any signaling processes to cognitive centers in the cortex and serotonin-vulnerable individuals will be at risk for disinhibited, impulsive, nonsocially adaptive behavioral responses following adverse experiences. Low or flat cortisol levels during challenge may indicate a defective affectively driven information processing pathway.

There may also be a developmental connection. The high rate of exposure to chronic adverse life events and difficulties from infancy over the childhood period may suppress or exacerbate the liability for a normal cortisol response to subsequent adversities. Extreme variations in either direction in the cortisol system may induce deleterious changes in monoamine systems in the cortex. The reasons for this may reside in the GC rather than serotonin genes. As described earlier in this chapter the GC receptor gene and the CRH gene possess polymorphisms that influence the regulatory processes controlling the level of circulating cortisol (Rosmond et al., 2000; Rosmond et al., 2001; De-Rijk et al., 2002). These polymorphisms may be functional and alter the response to circulating levels of cortisol at the level of the receptor.

Thus the GC receptor polymorphism may be one gene (of many) determining the liability for up or down regulating the signal from the limbic to the cortical systems following cortisol exposure. It does seem very possible that the level of circulating cortisol varying with experience and the sensitivity of tissue response determined by genetic variation in both cortisol and serotonin systems are working together to effect the most adaptive response to environmental demands. DHEA may be patrolling these interactions in the brain, increasing levels at times of threat to adaptation following high demand from within or without the individual. Developmentally, children and the elderly may be most at risk as capacity for DHEA is low in the former and declining in the latter.

ACKNOWLEDGMENTS

This chapter was completed with funding from the Wellcome Trust and within the MRC Institute for Behavioural and Clinical Neuroscience, Cambridge University.

REFERENCES

Bachmann, A.W., Sedgley, T.L., et al. (2005). Glucocorticoid receptor polymorphisms and post-traumatic stress disorder. *Psychoneuroendocrinology* 30 (3):297–306.

Bartels, M., E.J. de Geus, et al. (2003). Heritability of daytime cortisol levels in children. *Behaviour Genetics* 33:421–433.

Bartels, M., M. Van den Berg, et al. (2003). Heritability of cortisol levels: Review and simultaneous analysis of twin studies. *Psychoneuroendocrinology* 28:121–137.

Baulieu, E.E., and M. Schumacher. (2004). *Neurosteroids: A New Regulatory Function in the Nervous System.* Totowa, NJ: Humana Press.

Beishuizen, A., L.G. Thijs, et al. (2002). Decreased levels of dehydroepiandrosterone sulphate in severe critical illness: A sign of exhausted adrenal reserve? *Critical Care* 6 (5):434–438.

Blair, R.J. (2001). Neurocognitive models of aggression, the antisocial personality disorders, and psychopathy. *J Neurol Neurosurg Psychiatry* 71 (6):727–731.

Bremner, J.D., M. Vythilingam, et al. (2003). Cortisol response to a cognitive stress challenge in posttraumatic stress disorder (PTSD) related to childhood abuse. *Psychoneuroendocrinology* 28 (6):733–750.

Caspi, A., K. Sugden, et al. (2003). Influence of life stress on depression: Moderation by a polymorphism in the 5-HTT gene. *Science* 301 (5631):386–389.

Challis, B.G., J. Luan, et al. (2004). Genetic variation in the corticotrophin-releasing factor receptors: Identification of single-nucleotide polymorphisms and association studies with obesity in UK Caucasians. *International Journal of Obesity and Related Metabolic Disorders* 28:442–446.

Chalmers, D.T., S.P. Kwak, et al. (1993). Corticosteroids regulate brain hippocampal 5-HT1A receptor mRNA expression. *Journal of Neuroscience* 13 (3):914–923.

Champoux, M., A. Bennett, et al. (2002). Serotonin transporter gene polymorphism, differential early rearing, and behavior in rhesus monkey neonates. *Molecular Psychiatry* 7 (10):1058–1063.

Charney, D.S. (2004). Psychobiological mechanisms of resilience and vulnerability: Implications for successful adaptation to extreme stress. *American Journal of Psychiatry* 161 (2):195–216.

Chung, K.K., M. Martinez, et al. (1999). Central serotonin depletion modulates the behavioural, endocrine and physiological responses to repeated social stress and subsequent c-fos expression in the brains of male rats. *Neuroscience* 92 (2):613–625.

Clow, A., L. Thorn, et al. (2004). The awakening cortisol response: Methodological issues and significance. *Stress* 7 (1):29–37.

Davidson, R.J. (2004). Well-being and affective style: Neural substrates and biobehavioural correlates. *Philosophical Transactions of the Royal Society* (London) 359 (1449):1395–1411.

Delahanty, D.L., A.J. Raimonde, et al. (2000). Initial posttraumatic urinary cortisol levels predict subsequent PTSD symptoms in motor vehicle accident victims. *Biological Psychiatry* 48 (9):940–947.

DeRijk, R., M. Schaaf, et al. (2002). Glucocorticoid receptor variants: Clinical implications. *Journal of Steroid Chemistry and Molecular Biology* 81:103–122.

Deuschle, M., U. Schweiger, et al. (1998). The combined dexamethasone/corticotropin-releasing hormone stimulation test is more closely associated with features of diurnal activity of the hypothalamo-pituitary-adrenocortical system than the dexamethasone suppression test. *Biological Psychiatry* 43:762–766.

Dolan, M., W.J. Deakin, et al. (2002). Serotonergic and cognitive impairment in impulsive aggressive personality disordered offenders: Are there implications for treatment? *Psychol Med* 32 (1):105–117.

Drevets, W.C. (2003). Neuroimaging abnormalities in the amygdala in mood disorders. _Annals of the New York Academy of Science_ 985:420–444.

Elzinga, B.M., C.G. Schmahl, et al. (2003). Higher cortisol levels following exposure to traumatic reminders in abuse-related PTSD. _Neuropsychopharmacology_ 28 (9):1656–1665.

Goodyer, I.M., J. Herbert, et al. (1996). Adrenal secretion during major depression in 8 to 16 year olds, I: Altered diurnal rhythms in salivary cortisol and dehydroepiandrosterone (DHEA) at presentation. _Psychological Medicine_ 26:245–256.

Goodyer, I.M., J. Herbert, et al. (2000a). First-episode major depression in adolescents. Affective, cognitive and endocrine characteristics of risk status and predictors of onset. _British Journal of Psychiatry_ 176:142–149.

Goodyer, I.M., J. Herbert, et al. (2000b). Recent life events, cortisol, dehydroepiandrosterone and the onset of major depression in high-risk adolescents. _British Journal of Psychiatry_ 177:499–504.

Goodyer, I.M., J. Herbert, et al. (2003). Psychoendocrine antecedents of persistent first-episode major depression in adolescents: A community-based longitudinal enquiry. _Psychological Medicine_ 33 (4):601–610.

Goodyer, I.M., R.J. Park, et al. (2001). Psychosocial and endocrine features of chronic first-episode major depression in 8–16 year olds. _Biological Psychiatry_ 50 (5):351–357.

Guazzo, E.P., P.J. Kirkpatrick, et al. (1996). Cortisol, dehydroepandrosterone (DHEA), and DHEA sulfate in the cerebrospinal fluid of man: Relation to blood levels and the effects of age. _Journal of Clinical Endocrinology and Metabolism_ 81:3951–3960.

Gunnar, M.R. (1998). Quality of early care and buffering of neuroendocrine stress reactions: Potential effects on the developing human brain. _Preventative Medicine_ 27 (2):208–211.

Gunnar, M. R., S. J. Morison, et al. (2001). Salivary cortisol levels in children adopted from Romanian orphanages. _Dev Psychopathol_ 13 (3):611–628.

Gunnar, M.R. and B. Donzella (2002). Social regulation of the cortisol levels in early human development. _Psychoneuroendocrinology_ 27:199–220.

Halligan, S.L., J. Herbert, et al. (2004). Exposure to postnatal depression predicts elevated cortisol in adolescent offspring. _Biological Psychiatry_ 55 (4):376–381.

Harris, T.O., S. Borsanyi, et al. (2000). Morning cortisol as a risk factor for subsequent major depressive disorder in adult women. _British Journal of Psychiatry_ 177:505–510.

Hucklebridge, F., T. Hussain, et al. (2005). The diurnal patterns of the adrenal steroids cortisol and dehydroepiandrosterone (DHEA) in relation to awakening. _Psychoneuroendocrinology_ 30 (1):51–57.

Hunt, P.J., E.M. Gurnell, et al. (2000). Improvement in mood and fatigue after dehydroepiandrosterone replacement in Addison's disease in a randomized, double blind trial. _Journal of Clinical Endocrinology and Metabolism_ 85 (12):4650–4656.

Huppert, F.A. and J.K. Van Niekerk. (2001). _Dehydroepiandrosterone (DHEA) supplementation for cognitive function_ (Cochrane Review). Cochrane Database System Review 2: CD000304.

Karishma, K.K., J. Herbert (2002). Dehydroepiandrosterone (DHEA) stimulates neurogenesis in the hippocampus of the rat, promotes survival of newly formed neurons and prevents corticosterone-induced suppression. *European Journal of Neuroscience* 16 (3):445–53.

Kaufman, J., P.M. Plotsky, et al. (2000). Effects of early adverse experiences on brain structure and function: Clinical implications. *Biological Psychiatry* 48(8):778–790.

Kimonides, V.G., N.H. Khatibi, et al. (1998). Dehydroepiandrosterone (DHEA) and DHEA-sulfate (DHEAS) protect hippocampal neurons against excitatory amino acid-induced neurotoxicity. *Proceedings of the National Academy of Sciences USA* 95 (4):1852–1857.

Kimonides, V.G., M.G. Spillantini, et al. (1999). Dehydroepiandrosterone antagonizes the neurotoxic effects of corticosterone and translocation of stress-activated protein kinase 3 in hippocampal primary cultures. *Neuroscience* 89 (2):429–436.

Kirschbaum, C., D. Hellhammer. (1994). Salivary cortisol in psychoendocrine research: Recent developments and applications. *Psychoneuroendocrinology* 19:313–333.

Kroboth, P.D., J.A. Amico, et al. (2003). Influence of DHEA administration on 24-hour cortisol concentrations. *Journal of Clinical Psychopharmacology* 23 (1):96–99.

Kroboth, P.D., F.S. Salek, et al. (1999). DHEA and DHEA-S: A review. *Journal of Clinical Pharmacology* 39 (4):327–348.

Labrie, F., A. Belanger, et al. (1997). Marked decline in serum concentrations of adrenal C19 sex steroid precursors and conjugated androgen metabolites during aging. *Journal of Clinical Endocrinology and Metabolism* 82 (8):2396–2402.

Linkowski, P., A. Van Onderbergen, et al. (1993). Twin study of the 24-h cortisol profile: Evidence for genetic control of the human circadian clock. *Am J Physiol* 264 (2 Pt. 1):E173–181.

Liotti, M.F., H.S. Mayberg, et al. (2000). Differential limbic—cortical correlates of sadness and anxiety in healthy. *Biological Psychiatry* 48 (1):30–42.

Liu, D., J.S. Dillon. (2002). Dehydroepiandrosterone activates endothelial cell nitric-oxide synthase by a specific plasma membrane receptor coupled to Galpha(i2,3). *Journal of Biological Chemistry* 277 (24):21379–21388.

Lu, N.Z., J.A. Cidlowski. (2004). The origin and functions of multiple human glucocorticoid receptor isoforms. *Annals of New York Academy of Science* 1024:102–123.

Lupien, S.J., S. King, et al. (2000). Child's stress hormone levels correlate with mother's socioeconomic status and depressive state. *Biological Psychiatry* 48 (10):976–980.

Lupien, S.J., S. King, et al. (2001). Can poverty get under your skin? Basal cortisol levels and cognitive function in children from low and high socioeconomic status. *Development and Psychopathology* 13 (3):653–676.

Lupien, S.J., and M. Lepage (2001). Stress, memory, and the hippocampus: Can't live with it, can't live without it. *Behaviour and Brain Research* 127 (1–2):137–158.

Lupien, S.J., C.W. Wilkinson, et al. (2002). The modulatory effects of corticosteroids on cognition: Studies in young human populations. *Psychoneuroendocrinology* 27 (3):401–416.

Lupien, S.J., C.W. Wilkinson, et al. (2002). Acute modulation of aged human memory by pharmacological manipulation of glucocorticoids. *Journal of Clinical Endocrinology and Metabolism* 87 (8):3798–3807.

Marx, C., S. Petros, et al. (2003). Adrenocortical hormones in survivors and nonsurvivors of severe sepsis: Diverse time course of dehydroepiandrosterone, dehydroepiandrosterone-sulfate, and cortisol. *Critical Care Medicine* 31 (5):1382–8.

Mayberg, H.F., M. Liotti, et al. (1999). Reciprocal limbic-cortical function and negative mood: Converging PET *American Journal of Psychiatry* 156 (5):675–682.

McBurnett, K., B.B. Lahey, et al. (2000). Low salivary cortisol persistent aggression in boys referred for disruptive behavior. *Arch Gen Psychiatry* 57 (1):38–43.

Meinlschmidt, G., and C. Heim. (2005). Decreased cortisol awakening response after early loss experience. *Psychoneuroendocrinology* 30 (6):568–576.

Meyer, J.H., S.B. Kapur, J. Eisfeld, et al. (2001). The effect of paroxetine on 5-HT(2A) receptors in depression. *American Journal of Psychiatry* 158 (1):78–85.

Murphy, B.E. (2003). Urinary free cortisol levels in PTSD offspring. *Psychoneuroendocrinology* 28 (4):594–595; author reply 595–596.

Nemeroff, C.B. (2002). New directions in the development of antidepressants: The interface of neurobiology and psychiatry. *Human Psychopharmacology* 17 (Suppl 1): S13–16.

Newcomer, J.W., G. Selke, et al. (1999). Decreased memory performance in healthy humans induced by stress-level cortisol treatment. *Archives of General* Psychiatry 56 (6):527–533.

Neylan, T.C., A. Brunet, et al. (2005). PTSD symptoms predict waking salivary cortisol levels in police officers. *Psychoneuroendocrinology* 30 (4):373–381.

Pajer, K., W. Gardner, et al. (2001). Decreased cortisol levels in adolescent girls with conduct disorder. *Arch Gen Psychiatry* 58 (3):297–302.

Park, S.B., D.J. Williamson, et al. (1996). 5-HT neuroendocrine function in major depression: Prolactin and cortisol responses to D-fenfluramine. *Psychological* Medicine 26 (6):1191–1196.

Parker, C.R., Jr. (1999). Dehydroepiandrosterone and dehydroepiandrosterone sulfate production in the human adrenal during development and aging. *Steroids* 64 (9):640–647.

Plotsky, P.M., M.J. Owens, et al. (1998). Psychoneuroendocrinology of depression. Hypothalamic-pituitary-adrenal axis. *Psychiatric Clinics of North America* 21 (2):293–307.

Portella, M.J., C.J. Harmer, J. Flint, P. Cowen, G. Goodwin, (2005). Enhanced early morning salivary cortisol in neuroticism. *American Journal of Psychiatry* 162 (4):807–809.

Pruessner, J.C., D.H. Hellhammer, et al. (1999). Burnout, perceived stress, and cortisol responses to awakening. *Psychosomatic Medicine* 61:197–204.

Pruessner, J.C., Wolf, O.T. et al. (1997). Free cortisol levels after awakening: A reliable biological marker for the assessment of adrenocortical activity. *Life Sciences* 61:2539–2549.

Raine, A., P. Brennan, et al. (1997). Interaction between birth complications and early maternal rejection in predisposing individuals to adult violence: Specificity to serious, early-onset violence. *Am J Psychiatry* 154 (9):1265–1271.

Raine, A., J.R. Meloy, et al. (1998). Reduced prefrontal and increased subcortical brain functioning assessed using position emission tomography in predatory and affective murderers. *Behav Sci Law* 16 (3):319–332.

Raine, A., T. Lencz, et al. (2000). Reduced prefrontal gray matter volume and reduced autonomic activity in antisocial personality disorder. *Arch Gen Psychiatry* 57 (2):119–27; discussion 128–129.

Rosmond, R., Y.C. Chagnon, et al. (2000). A polymorphism of the 5'-flanking region of the glucocorticoid receptor gene locus is associated with basal cortisol secretion in men. *Metabolism* 49:1197–1199.

Rosmond, R., Chagnon, M., et al. (2001). A polymorphism in the regulatory region of the corticotropin-releasing hormone gene in relation to cortisol secretion, obesity, and gene-gene interaction. *Metabolism* 50:1059–1062.

Schmidt, P.J., R.C. Daly, M. Bloch, M.J. Smith, et al. (2005). Dehydroepiandrosterone monotherapy in midlife-onset major and minor depression. *Archives of General Psychiatry* 62 (2):154–162.

Seminowicz, D.A., H.S. Mayberg, et al. (2004). Limbic-frontal circuitry in major depression: A path modeling metanalysis. *Neuroimage* 22 (1):409–418.

Smoller, J.W., J.F. Rosenbaum, et al. (2001). Genetic association analysis of behavioral inhibition using candidate loci from mouse models. *American Journal of Medical Genetics* 105:226–235.

Smoller, J.W., J.F. Rosenbaum, et al. (2003). Association of a genetic marker at the corticotropin-releasing hormone locus with behavioral inhibition. *Biological Psychiatry* 54:1376–1381.

Southwick, S.M., S.R. Axelrod, et al. (2003). Twenty-four-hour urine cortisol in combat veterans with PTSD and comorbid borderline personality disorder. *Journal of Nervous and Mental Disease* 191 (4):261–262.

Stone, A.A., J.E. Schwartz, et al. (2001). Individual differences in the diurnal cycle of salivary free cortisol: A replication of flattened cycles for some individuals. *Psychoneuroendocrinology* 26 (3):295–306.

Strickland, P.L., J.F. Deakin, et al. (2002). Bio-social origins of depression in the community. Interactions between social adversity, cortisol and serotonin neurotransmission. *Britsh Journal of Psychiatry* 180:168–173.

Strous, R.D., R. Maayan, et al. (2003). Dehydroepiandrosterone augmentation in the management of negative, depressive, and anxiety symptoms in schizophrenia. *Archives of General Psychiatry* 60 (2):133–141.

Suzuki, M., L.S. Wright, et al. (2004). Mitotic and neurogenic effects of dehydroepiandrosterone (DHEA) on human neural stem cell cultures derived from the fetal cortex. *Proceedings of the National Academy of Sciences USA* 101 (9):3202–3207.

Van Goozen, S.H., W. Matthys, et al. (1998). Salivary cortisol and cardiovascular activity during stress in oppositional-defiant disorder boys and normal controls. *Biol Psychiatry* 43 (7): 531–539.

Van Goozen, S.H., E. Van den Ban, et al. (2000). Increased adrenal androgen functioning in children with oppositional defiant disorder: a comparison with psychiatric and normal controls. *J Am Acad Child Adolesc Psychiatry* 39 (11)L 1446–1451.

Van Niekerk, J.K., F.A. Huppert, et al. (2001). Salivary cortisol and DHEA: Association with measures of cognition and well-being in normal older men, and effects of three months of DHEA supplementation. *Psychoneuroendocrinology* 26 (6):591–612.

Viding, E., R.J. Blair, et al. (2005). Evidence for substantial genetic risk for psychopathy in 7-year-olds. *Journal of Child Psychology and Psychiatry* 46 (6):592–597.

Watson, S., P. Gallagher, et al. (2002). Hypothalamic-pituitary-adrenal axis function in patients with chronic depression. *Psychological Medicine* 32:1021–1028.

Weaver, I.C., Cervoni, N., et al. (2004). Epigenetic programming by maternal behavior. *Nature Neuroscience* 7 (8):847–854.

Wissink, S., O. Meijers, et al. (2000). Regulation of the rat serotonin-1A receptor gene by corticosteroids. *Journal of Biological Chemistry* 275:1321–1326.

Wolkowitz, O.M., V.I. Reus, et al. (1999). Double-blind treatment of major depression with dehydroepiandrosterone. *American Journal of Psychiatry* 156 (4):646–649.

Yehuda, R., S.L. Halligan, et al. (2004). Effects of trauma exposure on the cortisol response to dexamethosone administration in PTSD and major depressive disorder. *Psychoneuroendocrinology* 29 (3): 398–404.

Yehuda, R., J.A. Golier, et al. (2005). Relationship between cortisol and age-related memory impairments in Holocaust survivors with PTSD. *Psychoneuroendocrinology* 30 (7):678–687.

Yehuda, R., and Golier, J.A. et al. (2005). Circadian rhythm of salivary cortisol in Holocaust survivors with and without PTSD. *American Journal of Psychiatry* 162 (5):998–1000.

Yehuda, R., S.L. Halligan, et al. (2002). Cortisol levels in adult offspring of Holocaust survivors: Relation to PTSD symptom severity in the parent and child. *Psychoneuroendocrinology* 27 (1–2):171–180.

Chapter Three

Promoting Children's Adjustment: Parenting Research from the Perspective of Risk and Protection

Thomas G. O'Connor
and
Stephen B. C. Scott

In the past several decades, researchers studying parent-child relationships and children's adjustment have reported a mix of useful, controversial, and monotonous results. These findings derive from a rich array of scientific disciplines and philosophical perspectives. To a considerable, but not always predictable, extent these findings have attracted interest from educators and health professionals—as well as parents themselves. And as the notion of parenting as a public health issue gains prominence, these findings have garnered attention from policy makers, for whom there is a growing expectation that modifying the family environment may be one of the most potent ways of improving children's lives and life chances.

The aim of this chapter is to underscore parenting as a clinical and public health concern. Toward that end, we (1) review basic concepts and methods now commonplace in parenting research, (2) consider some of the relevant research findings gleaned from decades of research, and (3) emphasize the now substantial body of intervention research that has provided some of the most significant findings and challenges.

This chapter is not intended as an exhaustive review. It is instead oriented toward a selective and illustrative review of key conceptual-methodological findings that deserve particular attention. There are many helpful reviews of this research from a range of empirical and conceptual perspectives (O'Connor, 2002; Rothbaum and Weisz, 1994), and we will not duplicate those efforts here. In this regard, we leave off our agenda several debates, such as differences between mother-child and father-child relationships. In addition, we can make only passing reference to experimental animal work that has provided clues for integrating biological explanations into models of caregiving (Francis et al., 2002).

THEORIES ACCOUNTING FOR LINKS BETWEEN PARENT-CHILD RELATIONSHIPS AND CHILD OUTCOMES

Several theories have been developed to clarify the psychological signifi-cance of parent-child relationships and to account for the observed associa-tions between parent-child relationship quality and child well-being. A his-torical perspective on this field shows how the existing theories and methods reflected broader theoretical movements in the field of psychology (Sears et al., 1957). It is predictable, then, that there was a discourse (or at least com-petition) between, for example, the behaviorism of Watson and Skinner, on the one hand, and psychoanalytic and neoanalytic explanations of Freud and Blos on the other. What distinguished these early ideas was not so much the evidence base (there was little of that), but rather a setting up of conceptual models and outcomes and predictors of interest to be incorporated into em-pirical investigation.

Our emphasis on the theoretical underpinnings of current research includes two dominant perspectives, social learning theory and attachment theory. These models are useful to review because they shape much of the naturalis-tic and intervention studies now being conducted and because they are often viewed — somewhat unfairly — as incompatible or disjunct approaches.

Social Learning Theory

Social learning theory is closely associated with the conceptual and empirical work of Bandura (e.g., Bandura, 1977). Patterson (1969, 1996) has been per-haps the most influential thinker applying social learning principles to parent-child relationships and children's development. Briefly stated, the social learning model describes the processes by which the child's exposures to cer-tain parental behaviors or relationship qualities (e.g., to parental hostility) in-crease the likelihood of certain behavioral outcomes (e.g., antisocial behav-ior). "Traditional" behavioral principles of reinforcement and conditioning are important explanatory tools in the model. For instance, it would be pro-posed that a child who exhibits high levels of antisocial behavior has had his or her antisocial behavior reinforced, through any of a number of ways. Pat-terson described the coercive cycle model. In this example, the child's dis-ruptive or coercive, or otherwise petulant, behavior is met with a negative, co-ercive parental behavior. Rather than extinguishing his or her irritable behavior, the child instead amplifies, and the parent matches and accentuates this pattern. This cycle of behavior persists until the parent eventually gives up — as tired, weary, and unskilled parents are sometimes inclined to do. The net effect is to reinforce the child's aggressive, coercive strategy. That approach is then taken to other settings, such as the classroom and playground, where it may be further reinforced. Other observational studies illustrate other examples of the need to consider contingencies or patterns of reinforcement for explaining children's behavior (LaFreniere and Dumas, 1992).

The social learning model would not always or necessarily incorporate an explanation for how these exposures lead to behavioral outcomes in the child, that is, what it is that happens in the child's mind that mediates the observed links between parent behavior and child behavior. There is, however, a very productive line of research that seeks to do just that. So, for example, some authors in this theoretical tradition consider the internalization of experiences into cognitive models, notably expectations and attributions (Bugenthal et al., 1989; Dodge et al., 1995). Particularly for young children, the parent-child relationship and the family environment is the primary source of modeling and for learning strategies about managing emotions, resolving disputes, and engaging with others. Cognitive extensions of the social learning theory framework set out testable predictions for how these experiences are carried forward to influence the child's behavior in other settings. However, although there is now a heavy emphasis on cognitive-behavioral approaches—the synchrony between thoughts and behavior—this is not always needed and by no means always evident in social learning theory models or explanations.

Given its traditional focus on altering disruptive, aggressive behavior in the child, social learning theory studies emphasize parental conflict and consistent discipline—parallel behaviors in parents and children. Positive dimensions of parenting and of the parent-child relationship have attracted attention only recently. What these studies show is the importance of promoting child positive behavior, improving the pleasurable nature of parent-child interaction, and providing a positive and effective relationship context for parental discipline.

Attachment Theory

Attachment theory derives from the integrative theoretical work of Bowlby (1969/1982) and the creative empirical and conceptual studies by Ainsworth et al. (1978) and many others (Cassidy and Shaver, 1999). Attachment theory is rooted in a broad theoretical base, including ethology and cognitive psychology. A level of explanation particular to attachment theory is the nature, significance, and function of a child's tie to his or her parent. Attachment theory was strongly rooted in clinical observations, especially of children who experienced deprived caregiving; it has since been applied widely to normal and abnormal development.

Parent-child *attachment* is not synonymous with parent-child *relationship*. Because of its ethological base, attachment theory emphasizes fundamental issues of safety and protection; translated into psychological terms, attachment theory emphasizes how the relationship provides (or not) the child with protection against harm and with a sense of emotional security—what Bowlby described as a secure base for exploration. Many components of the parent-child relationship that might be routinely assessed in most clinician offices or research laboratories (e.g., teaching) would not be central to an attachment assessment; and core aspects of attachment would not be assessed in the routine assessment approach taken in clinical or research contexts. Attachment theory is therefore both more limited in focus and more fundamental than most models.

There are other particular aspects of attachment theory that deserve attention. One is the notion that children develop attachment relationships with a limited number of caregivers; the emphasis on a limited number of relationships means that attachment relationships are not diffuse and that changing parents (in the case of adoption or remarriage) is a significant and inherently challenging task for the child. Children also develop different patterns of attachment with different caregivers (Steele et al., 1996). Attachment theory further proposes that the quality of care provided by the caregiver, particularly sensitivity and responsiveness, leads to a secure (optimal) or insecure (nonoptimal) relationship. Early caregiving experiences predict, in a probabilistic manner, later development by setting in place adaptive or maladaptive pathways. The term *pathways* makes explicit the notion that early attachments do not *determine* later development (Bowlby, 1988). Secure attachments offer a child resilience to manage stress and form positive, adaptive experiences with others. In contrast, insecure attachments increase the risk for later social, personal, and emotional difficulties, as diverse as problems in self-regulation in infancy to peer rejection in middle childhood. The process by which attachment relationships are internalized and carried forward was referred to by Bowlby as an "internal working model." Stated simply, a history of consistent and sensitive care is predicted to lead to the child developing a model of self and others as lovable and helpful.

An insecure attachment is not synonymous with psychopathology, just as a secure attachment does not immunize the individual from psychopathology. On the other hand, it is evident that a specific form of insecure attachment, disorganized, is substantially linked with psychopathology and other forms of social and emotional maladjustment (Greenberg, 1999). Following this lead, disorganized attachment has been used to identify parents and children in need of clinical intervention.

In the simple example of the antisocial child previously noted, an attachment theory explanation would focus not only on the history of interactions for the child but also on the meaning these experiences have for the child. Thus Bowlby discussed the role of anger in relation to attachment needs and, more to the point, the impact of disrupted or frustrated attachment relationships. Others within this perspective offer a somewhat less direct account of how certain kinds of parenting environments may lead to angry, antisocial behavior. For example, attachment relationships are proposed to set an emotional regulating context; that is, infants and children learn to regulate (control, make sense of) their anger within the context of an attachment relationship in which the child's feelings are accepted and managed. Attachment relationships that, for example, reject the child's experience of anger are considered insecure; these insecure relationships increase the likelihood of the child's anger not being regulated or made sense of. As a result, the child will be less able to modulate his or her anger when it arises and it may have more disruptive impact on the child than those with whom he or she interacts.

Parenting Styles

A further approach to studying parent-child relationship quality has adopted a more descriptive and less mechanistic approach. An advantage of a descriptive approach is that it can traverse the usual disjunctions between theories. That is, we can ask, What does parental behavior look like? separate from asking how it may confer risk or resilience to the child. One dominant descriptive approach can broadly be described as parenting styles. This research derives in large part from the naturalistic studies of Baumrind in the 1960s (Baumrind, 1991); this work has been extended and repeatedly replicated by numerous other investigators (Hetherington et al., 1999; Maccoby and Martin, 1983; Steinberg et al., 1994). Two central dimensions of parent-child relationship quality that emerged from research were warmth and positivity (versus conflict) and control. It has been shown in many samples using observational and questionnaire data that four typologies adequately describe parent-child relationships: authoritative relationships are high in warmth and exhibit positive or assertive parental control; authoritarian relationships exhibit low warmth, high conflict, and coercive control attempts; permissive parenting styles are characterized by high warmth and low control attempts; and neglectful or disengaged parents are low in warmth and low in control attempts.

The dimensions of warmth, conflict, and control are remarkably common across many studies of the parent-child relationship. Each of these constructs can be further differentiated or specified. Thus warmth might be operationalized not as a broad-based construct but as more specific constructs such as sensitivity, responsiveness, or mutuality. Researchers are sometimes guilty of adopting a form of communication that does not do justice to a construct, usually because it is easier to use a broad if somewhat vague term. It is therefore important not to avoid the small print of the methods section when conceptualizing what it is that the investigators actually measured. Similarly, there are many forms of control, and that term has been used both to imply a negative (e.g., coercive control, psychological control) and a positive (clear expectations, autonomy support). In any event, although additional constructs appear in the research literature, the above dimensions set the minimum standard for a psychological investigation of the parent-child relationship.

A related issue for descriptive studies is how best to bring together the forms of parenting that are assessed. That is, the assessment task is to evaluate how a *particular* parent or, more to the point, a parent-child relationship, can be characterized on warmth, conflict, and control. This is an important challenge for clinicians and intervention work as well. That is because most interventions seek to alter parenting behavior in several ways, including improving their consistency in control or discipline and positive engagement of the child, and decreasing negative or harsh treatment of the child. The parenting typology method seeks to do this by describing parents rather than describing (only) certain parenting behaviors.

Several sets of explanations support the hypothesis that the quality of parent-child relationships will be associated with children's psychological development. It will be apparent from the preceding brief review that these explanations have different theoretical roots and emphases. Of the two theories reviewed here, neither has been found to be any more useful or predictive than the other. That is largely because of the absence of research that seeks to compare theories and models directly—an unfortunate limitation of the current research strategies. Also under development is work that seeks to examine the boundaries of parental influence. The above psychological theories are targeted to broad behavioral outcomes; whether these theories prove just as pertinent for a range of other health-related outcomes is not yet clear (see later discussion). Another area of research sure to attract more attention in the future is the biological bases of parenting and the effects of parenting on children. That is, whereas experimental animal research has described the biological underpinnings of how certain parenting environments shape biobehavioral outcomes in the offspring, no strongly parallel data set exists for humans. Translating animal findings to humans is therefore much needed. Fortunately, this is now feasible because of the ready availability of techniques for testing biological explanations and the clear set of hypotheses that the animal studies have produced.

METHODS USED TO STUDY PARENT-CHILD
RELATIONSHIPS AND THEIR EFFECTS

We are clinical researchers with regular contact with parents, clinicians, policy makers, granting agencies, and the media. In the course of these diverse discussions, it is apparent that the appreciation for the methodology that undergirds the research base on parent-child relationships is underappreciated. In other words, the way the research was carried out is largely neglected. Yet there are several reasons for taking methodology seriously. The first is that there is no best standard for assessing parent-child relationship quality. Although no single approach is considered the gold standard, several methods have been shown to be useful. Each method discussed below has its particular profile of strengths and weaknesses in reliability and validity, and these must be considered when interpreting the findings. To a considerable extent, the choice of assessment method has little to do with the theory being tested. Or in other words, most theories can be translated into a questionnaire, interview, or observation methodology.

Studies using different methods are likely to find (somewhat) different results. That is inevitable, however frustrating it may be for a policy maker who needs to know what the expected effect will likely be (ranges of effect are not usually a welcome complication). Thus, for example, a questionnaire assessment will typically relate more strongly with another questionnaire assessment—seemingly regardless of who completes it—than it will with an observational measure. Ignoring what is referred to as "method variance" will lead to wide variation in results and perhaps misleading claims about parent-child relationship quality or an intervention effect.

Given that there is no gold standard, the most rigorous research adopts a multiagent, multimethod approach in which a particular aspect of the relationship is indexed not by a single measure or method but rather by two (or more) methods. However, because this sort of triangulation is expensive and time intensive, only well-funded studies can invest in this approach to assessment.

Three of the most established methods are questionnaire, interview, and observation. Questionnaires are inexpensive to administer and have adequate reliability and validity. They are widely adaptable for parents and teachers and, from about age eight, children themselves. But, questionnaires have obvious limitations. The most obvious is that they are subject to a social desirability bias and other forms of misreporting, including intentional misreporting. For example, it is easy on a questionnaire to overreport positive parenting behaviors and, unless information is also obtained from another parent or child, that misreporting will go unchecked. A second method, interviews, comes in a variety of styles. On one extreme is a virtual questionnaire; at the other is a detailed assessment in which examples of certain behaviors are obtained and the interviewer makes a determination of whether the dimension of interest was evident and, if so, to what degree. The latter, investigator-based approach is well established in psychiatric epidemiology, but its value in studies of parent-child relationships is not well established. A further type of interview, derived largely from the attachment field, examines the parent's responses according to the quality of the overall narrative, in addition to specific coding of certain key questions.

If there were a gold standard in measuring parent-child relationship quality it would likely be behavioral observation. Collecting observational data is more time intensive and intrusive than the other methods—although not necessarily dramatically so. It has different sorts of methodological strengths and weaknesses. Compared with questionnaire data collection, observational research has more face validity and is less susceptible to obvious sorts of bias because it is coded by independent coders (who are kept blind to other key information, such as whether the mother is depressed or not). Perhaps for this reason observational data have essentially gold-standard status in the intervention field. On the other hand, observational methods inevitably collect a limited slice of behavior that may have limited generalizability; established methods range from several minutes to hours. Researchers have learned a good deal about how to collect observational data, and there is now a set of techniques that have proved clinically useful and scientifically valid (Forgatch and DeGarmo, 1999; Patterson and Bank, 1989).

As regards the coding of the interactions, there is also a consensus on which dimensions of behavior deserve particular attention, namely, conflict, warmth or support, and control. These behavioral dimensions surface in all of the strongly evidence-based coding systems; other dimensions also arise, but not with the near universality of the previously mentioned dimensions. Observational research strategies generally favor one of two approaches, time- or behavioral-sampling methods in which specific behaviors are tallied or continuous ratings scales indicating how often (e.g., on a 5-point scale) a particular behavior or pattern was observed. There seems to be strikingly little evidence showing that one approach of coding is better than another—although this question has not received the sort of empirical attention that it deserves.

GENERAL FRAMEWORKS FOR
INTERPRETING RESEARCH FINDINGS

Synthesizing current thinking about and findings on parent-child relationship quality and children's adjustment is a daunting task. A framework we propose emphasizes cause, context, and convertibility.

By *cause* we mean the identification of the mechanisms by which the quality of parent-child relationships directly or indirectly influences child psychological development. The notion that a causal link might be drawn from research findings has a substantial and complex history. And it is both impressive and humbling that rudimentary questions about cause-effect relations linger following nearly a half century of research activity. A lack of definitive progress in resolving this issue does not necessarily imply that little progress has been attained. That is because the history of the cause-effect debate in parenting research has metamorphosed considerably, taking on new challenges, including genetics and more broadly biological factors. In other words, the research on causal hypotheses has had to take on board previously unknown considerations. This dialectic has led to advances in study design and a focus on biopsychosocial mechanisms, but the debate is far from over. On the other hand, the lack of scientific closure on this issue means that researchers and policy makers still must attend to the study methodology and tolerate ambiguity in results across studies.

By *context* we mean the extent to which findings from one design, sample, measure, and culture can be generalized to another. In other words, the key context question is, are there universals or near universals in how parent-child relationships may be linked with children's well-being? This follows from the cause-effect debate. Once it is established that there may be a causal link between A and B, the context question asks, is that so for other or all samples? Contemporary research has operationalized the contextual question in terms of child age, ethnicity, family constellation, temperament, and cohort, among others. As we discuss later, there is now a good deal of interest in showing that factors as diverse as neighborhood dangerousness to child temperament moderate the association between parenting and outcome. Moreover, cross-cultural research is showing how certain aspects of parenting such as corporal punishment may carry different meanings and effects across cultures (Lansford et al., 2005).

By *convertibility* we mean the extent to which findings from naturalistic studies can inform (preventive) interventions. In other words, what is the clinical or policy relevance of the finding and how can it be translated directly to shape clinical practice or social policy? The convertibility question, like the context question, follows from a basic demonstration or implicit assumption of cause. It is noteworthy that major programs based on solid empirical and theoretical grounds have not always produced clinically meaningful benefits (e.g., Barkley et al., 2000). Findings such as these have highlighted problems of translation and have also underscored the value of intervention studies to test basic hypotheses about causal mechanisms. An additional aspect of the convertibility issue is the very substantial amount of work that is needed to translate a basic finding into an applied program. Evidence that convertibility is a distinct form of research is obvious to those who have tried to institute an intervention program. For example, we now know that information on how best to intervene cannot be derived from nonintervention research. Indeed, a specialty area exists that addresses the practical issues of how to recruit and retain families for interventions.

LINKS BETWEEN PARENT-CHILD RELATIONSHIP
QUALITY AND CHILD OUTCOMES:
KEY AND ILLUSTRATIVE FINDINGS

It is neither possible nor desirable to review exhaustively the data showing correspondences between parent-child relationship quality and child outcomes. Of course, there are reasonably comprehensive reviews, based either on empirical meta-analysis (Rothbaum and Weitz, 1994) or on a more conceptual meta-analysis (Maccoby and Martin, 1983). What we aim to highlight here are central illustrative findings that seem robust across samples and methods.

Aggression and Delinquency

Research on the parent-child relationship origins of aggressive behavior and delinquency is one of the most active areas of study. Such is the strength of existing research that it would be remarkable if a newly conceived study did not find a link between harsh, coercive, punitive parenting and child antisocial behavior. Evidence of a robust link is derived from large-scale epidemiological investigations in several countries (admittedly mostly Western), intensive clinical investigations, and numerous naturalistic studies of diverse convenient samples using a mixture of methods (Dodge et al., 1995; Denham et al., 2000; Dunn et al., 1998; Hetherington et al., 1999; Kilgore et al., 2000; Patterson and Bank, 1989). It is noteworthy that these studies define aggression in a number of ways, from bona fide antisocial criminal acts to observed coercive behavior within a somewhat contrived setting. Just as important, antisocial outcomes linked with coercive, punitive parenting arise no matter if police records, parents, teachers, or peers are the source of the child's target behaviors. This diversity of measurement provides assurance that the link between parental hostility, conflict, and coercion and child aggressive behavior is not peculiar to one method or measure. That, in turn, implies that the association—whatever its degree of causality—is real.

Aggression-related outcomes are mostly frequently linked with coercive, punitive, harsh, or otherwise negative parenting and parent-child relationship quality. It is less clear if this dimension or style of parenting or relationship is especially likely to lead to antisocial outcomes in the child. Less common, but still numerous, are studies connecting lack of warmth, permissive or ineffectual control, and lack of monitoring (or awareness of the child's whereabouts) with aggression-related outcomes (Fletcher et al., 2004; Kerr and Stattin, 2000). Analytically, several studies (see earlier discussion) show that the prediction of aggression is improved when one considers additional sources of parenting behaviors or parent-child relationship dimensions. That means that there is more than one parenting route to aggression-related outcomes in the child or adolescent. And, of course, relationships that are coercive and hostile are also likely to lack warmth, firm authoritative control, and developmentally sensitive monitoring. In other words, it is probably unrealistic to find that there is a silver bullet parenting style or relationship type that predicts outcomes.

Similarly, multiple studies show that the connection between parent-child relationships and externalizing problems exists for variation within the normal range as well as for clinical disturbance. This presumed dose-response pattern suggests causality, but more importantly suggests that a net improvement in parent-child relationship quality might have very broad effects on a sample or population.

Depression and Anxiety

Probably the second-most investigated outcome of parent-child relationship is depression or anxiety, or the broadband dimension often referred to as internalizing. Evidence of a link between parent-child relationships and internalizing is about as robust as it is for aggression-related outcomes. Moreover, the findings also derive from an impressive array of epidemiological, clinical, and convenience samples (Dadds et al., 1996; Garber et al., 1998). Neither is there any evidence that the connection is specific to a particular way of measuring either parent-child relationship quality or internalizing in the child. As a result, there is no longer a tenable null hypothesis that parent-child relationship quality is not significantly associated with child internalizing symptoms and disorders. Identifying those aspects of the relationship that may be most important is no easier than it was in the case of aggression-related outcomes. Thus no single relationship or parenting characteristic is suggested, but the roles of parental warmth or sensitivity and conflict or coerciveness are most often investigated.

Cognitive Ability and Achievement

Cognitive theorists dating back to Vygotsky (see Rogoff and Lave, 1984) proposed that the parent-child relationship context is an essential component to the child's developing cognitive abilities. The capacity to achieve at school has also long been connected to expectations and facilitations that began in the early parent-child relationship. Parents who are sensitively tuned to the child's cognitive ability provide an optimal scaffolding environment for the child to learn and to want to learn. Other mechanisms of parental influence rely on social learning hypotheses. Parents may shape aspirations and achievement motivation by acting as role models and setting expectations for success (Bell et al., 1996; Gutman and Eccles, 1999).

These psychological processes would predict intergenerational transmission of socioeconomic status, and that has been repeatedly found; the roles of other factors, including genetics and assortative mating, are likely to be just as important.

It is perhaps no surprise that many research groups have found that children of authoritative parents have higher rates of school achievement than children with authoritarian, permissive, or disengaged parenting styles (Glasgow et al., 1997; Stevenson and Lee, 1990). Several groups have also shown that reading ability is predicted from the parent-child rearing environment, including the degree to which the parent reads to the child. In addition to implicating genetic explanations, this association also may imply that social learning processes may have a real role to play in improving children's reading ability (Scott and Sylva, 1998).

Of course, parents have multiple routes for shaping children's school success. One important mode of influence seems to be by sustaining links with the child's teachers and school environment. This type of monitoring has been shown to be a robust predictor of educational outcomes, from improved grades to preventing school drop out. This type of educational research is important for many reasons, not least of which is to show how the role and impact of parenting extends far beyond the household.

Social Competence and Peer Relationships

Symptomatology (aggression and internalizing) and educational outcomes have received the lion's share of psychological research attention. Research into how parent-child relationships foster competence in children has largely been based on the same set of conceptual models as those reviewed previously. Here the aim is to understand not merely the absence of problems but the presence of competence. However, assessing competence is demonstrably more difficult than assessing psychopathology. For instance, there are no established measures of prosocial behavior that have attracted widespread interest. Accordingly, rather than define a construct as broad as competence, investigators typically assess competence in several narrowly defined realms. Probably the most common is peer relationships. The evidence linking parent-child relationship quality with competence with peers is substantial. For instance, a secure child-parent attachment in infancy and early childhood predicts peer competence, defined in terms of peer-nominated competence and other methods (Cassidy et al., 1996; Moss et al., 1998). That is, peers rate as more likable and prosocial those children who concurrently or previously were judged to have a secure attachment relationship.

Social learning models of parenting-peer correspondences are equally well established (Dishion and McMahon, 1998; Pettit et al., 1988). Whether the emphasis is on social cognitions or learned behavioral strategies, social learning and related theories predict and observe significant carryover from the parent-child to the child-peer relationship. Thus detailed developmental research has shown how emotional understanding, perspective taking, and emotional regulation that are expressed in the early parent-child relationship can be carried forward or generalized to later social relationships, including those with peers (Carson and Parke, 1996; Dunn, 1992).

It will not be a surprise to hear that research has not identified a specific aspect of the parent-child relationship that has particular import value into the peer domain. Thus warmth, reciprocity, conflict, aggression, and empathy can all be transferred from one relationship to another; different and not incompatible explanations for how that happens exist, as we outlined earlier. Another lesson from the parenting-peer research is that parents have a number of ways of influencing their children's peer relationships and peer standing. One may be by modeling, but it may be just as important for parents to monitor with whom their children have contact. In early childhood this takes the form of directly controlling access to preferred and nonpreferred peers; in adolescence, this takes the form of monitoring contact with preferred and nonpreferred peers.

Another specific area under the heading of competence that has been the subject of significant developmental and clinical research is self-concept, self-esteem, or identity—that is, how children think about themselves. Attachment theory is perhaps the most explicit in describing the ways children will internalize their experiences, but the notion that that happens—in some manner—is accepted in most theoretical circles. Children's internalization of their relationship or attachment experiences are predicted to influence the way the child constructs his or her view of himself or herself as lovable, competent, capable. Direct tests of this hypothesis are still modest. Confounding the story is that measures of self-esteem are complex and provide somewhat confusing data, such as the finding that antisocial children have completely positive self-esteem. It would be easy to argue that that is a defensive strategy (if it is), but the results from most measures of self-esteem will be confounded nonetheless.

An important direction for this research is to examine how caregiving experiences connect with more subtle measures of the child's sense of self. Good examples using narrative and projective approaches have been reported (Toth et al., 2000). Another interesting line of research investigates how positive or negative cognitive biases emerge, including those that may shape the young child's sense of self-competence (Cassidy et al., 1996; Laible and Thompson, 1998). The adolescence research literature is confounded by the complex and sometimes unsatisfying way that self-esteem and identity have been assessed. But there are some interesting examples of how identity processes, such as open exploration of identity, are linked with positive connectedness to parents (Grotevant and Cooper, 1985).

General Health and Biological Development

Smoking, illicit drug use, alcohol use, and sexually risky behaviors carry significant and fairly immediate public health significance. For that reason, they have attracted considerable attention, some from the perspective of the parent-child relationship. Although it is still early in the evolution of this form of parenting research, several observations are noteworthy. These include the links between parent smoking and child smoking (Green et al., 1990), the better known parent-child resemblance in alcohol and other drug use (Hicks et al., 2004; Steinglass, 1981), and the further evidence that parents may create an environment in which children may be more susceptible to peer pressure to use substances (Steinberg, 1987). There is also growing evidence that parenting quality is linked with the likelihood of physical injury of or accident to the child (Bijur et al., 1991; O'Connor et al., 2000). The findings have been convincing enough to generate a number of parenting interventions to reduce serious accident and injury in children. A further example, and one that will attract growing interest, is how the parenting environment may predict health behaviors leading to childhood obesity (Faith et al., 2004; Jebb et al., 2004).

ADDITIONAL DEVELOPMENTAL AND CLINICAL QUESTIONS ABOUT THE RESEARCH LITERATURE

We consider briefly developmental concerns embedded in the research. The first has to do with stability. Although it will be obvious that parent-child relationships change dramatically from infancy to late adolescence—normative developmental change—there is just as much evidence that the individual differences are fairly stable. Thus Bowlby described the emergence of a "goal-corrected" partnership in the preschool years, and several authors have described a reorganization in parent-child relationships around adolescence toward greater child autonomy (Allen and Land, 1999; Smetana and Asquith, 1994). These are examples of normative developmental change corresponding to changes in child cognitive, social, and emotional development. These changes notwithstanding, developmental research also shows how remarkably stable individual differences are in the quality of the parent-child relationship, even when different methods are used (Allen et al., 1996; Loeber et al., 2000; Waters et al., 2000).

Long-term longitudinal research also shows that the quality of parent-child relationships in childhood predicts important adult outcomes. For example, in their analysis of the 1958 British Birth Cohort data, Flouri and Buchanan (2002) reported that the quality of adolescent-parent relationships with mother and father predicted self-reports of conflict with a partner at age thirty-three, after controlling for covariates such as socioeconomic status. Furthermore, Conger and colleagues (Conger et al., 2000) reported that observer reports of nurturant-involved parenting of adolescents forecast (different) observer reports of warmth toward romantic partners in young adulthood—eight years later. These demonstrations of nearly intergenerational links provide one of the most important sets of findings in the parenting literature.

CAUSAL CLAIMS AND CHALLENGES IN FAMILY RESEARCH

No discussion of the parenting literature would be complete without some consideration of the challenges to the causal claims implied or made explicit in the research. These criticisms have largely ignored the findings from intervention studies, which are reviewed below, but require careful attention for what they say about research designs and methods.

The most vocal criticisms of the claim that parent-child relationships may be causally linked with child outcomes derive from the behavioral genetics literature. These studies make use of genetically informative designs, including twins, or adoptive and nonadoptive siblings. If it is found, for example, that monozygotic twins, whose genetic makeup is identical, are more similar on a measure of parent-child relationship than are dizygotic (or fraternal) twins, then it might be inferred that relationship quality is not merely about the social environment or history. Moreover, if the association between parent-child relationship quality and child outcome is significantly stronger in biologically related than adoptive parent-child dyads, then some degree of genetic mediation might be inferred. It is impressive how consistently the research findings fit these patterns.

For example, carefully conducted observational studies show that genetic resemblance between siblings is associated with the similarity in parenting environment (Lytton, 1977; O'Connor et al., 1995). In fact, one study (Deater-Deckard and O'Connor, 2000) found a high degree of replication in two very different samples of preschool-age children using both a twin and adoptive sample from two countries. More to the point, that study assessed observations of parent-child shared affect, parental sensitivity, and a mutual, give-and-take interaction style. The findings are noteworthy in showing that dynamic, moment-to-moment interchanges in the parent-child relationship are no less likely to be under some sort of genetic influence than, say, the stalwarts of genetic research such as personality and psychopathology.

82   *Thomas G. O'Connor and Stephen B. C. Scott*

A further illustrative finding was reported by McGue, Sharma, and Benson (1996) in a sample of adopted and biologically related parent-child dyads. Across a number of measures, there was a consistent pattern in which the magnitude of association between parent-child relationship quality and child adjustment index was greater for biologically related parent-child dyads than adoptive dyads. Numerous other demonstrations of the importance of genetic factors have been reported. In one study based on a normal-risk adoption sample (O'Connor et al., 1998), the authors reported that adopted children who had a biological mother with a history of mild antisocial behavior were more likely to evoke negative, coercive parenting from their adoptive parents (who were unaware of the biological parentage), compared with adoptees whose biological mothers were not antisocial. Similar findings were reported by Ge et al. (1996) in their high-risk adopted offspring study. The net result of these studies is that theories that fail to attend to the possibility of genetic mediation will almost certainly exaggerate the importance of the parenting environment. Findings such as these spur research to incorporate the interplay between nature and nurture.

A different sort of challenge to the causal claim in parenting research has been termed the "child effects" finding (Bell and Harper, 1977). In a classic study, researchers (Anderson et al., 1986) crossed parent-child dyads in a 2 -2 experimental design. Children with and without bona fide antisocial behavior were paired with parents of children with and without antisocial behavior. Observations of these interactions showed that parents of non-antisocial children exhibited increased negativity toward the antisocial child—and more so than did parents of the antisocial children exhibit elevated conflict toward the non-antisocial child. The study documented what teachers surely know, which is that their own behavior is shaped by the child's. Other research offers a clinical application, such as the finding that parental behavior to the attention-deficit/hyperactivity disorder (ADHD) child is influenced by whether the child is taking medication (Barkley, 1981). These findings challenge the parent-causes-child-outcome model by demonstrating that the parental effect may be inflated.

A third example of research that modifies more than challenges the causal claims of parenting researchers was anticipated in our earlier discussion. This set of studies seeks to show that children will respond differently to parenting, depending on, for example, the social context or temperament (Kochanska, 1997). One study (Pettit et al., 1999) found that parental monitoring of a child (knowing who she or he is with and what they are doing) was especially protective against delinquency for adolescents living in violent and high-risk neighborhoods; the effect was more modest for those not living in high-risk settings. The real value in these studies is the empirical demonstration that the effects of parenting are unlikely to be sample- or population-wide, an important message when devising large-scale parenting interventions. The notion that there is a causal link between parent-child relationship quality and child outcomes has been challenged. To a considerable extent, these criticisms hinge on the inherent problems of naturalistic or nonexperimental designs. Research studies that do employ experimental control, namely interventions, are therefore especially valuable in tackling causal questions. These studies are considered in the next section.

INTERVENTION STUDIES AND THEIR PRACTICAL IMPLICATIONS

Parent-child relationship programs, initially referred to as "parent training" programs, are the most widely researched psychological intervention for child antisocial behavior (Patterson, 1974; Forehand et al., 1980; Scott, 2002). Their effectiveness has been known for several decades, although there have been a number of unsuccessful interventions and, as we discuss later, there is wide variation in treatment response that needs to be accounted for. Predictably, the form and format of proposed interventions continues to be modified, and there is an ever-growing set of new and revised programs for implementation.

A key feature of the programs with a sound evidence base is a written manual for therapists and handouts for parents, and many make use of videotape materials (Barkley, 1997; Forehand and Long, 1996; Sanders et al., 1999; Webster-Stratton and Herbert, 1994). The aim in these manuals is not merely to prescribe the interventionist's behavior; indeed, most programs provide considerable latitude for the clinician. Instead, the real benefit of a good manual is that is clearly communicates to the clinician (and usually the parent) what is being done, how, and why. Of course, components of any sound clinical intervention are explicit; a manualized treatment has the benefit of communicating these features to fellow clinicians and researchers.

The demand for evidence-based interventions has reached a critical point; correspondingly, there is an acute need for disseminating materials and making them applicable and accessible to prospective clinicians, sometimes without extensive training (i.e., relying on clinical psychologists to provide these interventions is not financially feasible, nor is it even necessary). The role of manualized treatments needs also to be seen in this context, as there is an undeniable need to improve access to evidence-based interventions for needing families.

Alongside the obvious clinical value of parenting interventions, their scientific value cannot be underestimated. That is because experimental interventions using the state-of-the-art randomized control trial method are one of the most compelling ways to show causal effects in the literature on parent-child relationships. If a parenting intervention that only included the parent (that is, the child is not included in the intervention) shows positive effects on child behavior, it may be inferred with some confidence that the change in parental behavior mediated the change in child behavior. Of course, this can also be shown empirically by demonstrating that the intervention effect on child behavior was statistically mediated by observed changes in parenting qualities. That, in fact, has been shown in many studies (e.g., Scott et al., 2001).

Specifics, Mechanics, and Effects of Interventions

The approach adopted in most parenting interventions has moved well beyond the behaviorism that is often associated with training programs. Indeed, most programs specifically address parents' feelings and beliefs; the therapist works to convey to the parent the sense that she or he is understood (Puckering et al., 1994; Webster-Stratton and Herbert, 1994). Similarly, the context for parenting interventions has broadened to include, for example, the school environment. For instance, the Webster-Stratton school-age program (Webster-Stratton and Hammond, 1997) includes coaching parents in how to negotiate with teachers and how to help children complete homework. The emphasis on parent-school links is also explicit and substantial in other programs, some of which now also incorporate reading programs as a way of improving school success and preventing delinquency and school failure (Scott and Sylva, 1998).

Arguably the most model of programs is the FasTrack project (Conduct Problems Prevention Research Group, 1999), a state-of-the-art multimodal intervention study of nearly 900 children who were rated as extremely high risk for antisocial behavior. Consistent with the theories of antisocial behavior and what is known about the context of antisocial behavior, the program adopted a multimodal intervention that includes parent training, mentoring, social skill training, and home visits. The effects of the intervention, which is still ongoing, are now being widely reported. Almost modest in magnitude—effect size typically ranges from 0.1 to 0.2 of a standard deviation (SD)—the net effect on the costly outcomes still makes the program cost effective.

Meta-analyses of the large and growing parenting intervention literature are encouraging. Serkitch and Dumas (1996) calculated a mean effect size of 0.86 SD for child behavior change. Hoag and Burlingame (1997) calculated an effect size of 0.69 SD. Barlow's (1999) review of the literature, with particular attention to the more rigorous studies, indicated that the mean effect size of child behavior change varied according to source of information, as one might anticipate. Not surprisingly, parent-based reports suggested effect sizes in the range of 0.4–1.0 SD, and direct observation suggested an effect size of 0.4–0.6 SD. The latter finding is an important methodological point that needs careful attention.

Clinically significant effect sizes, on average, still leave considerable room for variation in how parents and children respond to the interventions. In fact, it is now conventional wisdom that up to a third of families do not show improvement. That may be for several reasons, and there is now evidence that family risk may undermine treatment success (Dumas and Wahler, 1983). These observations have led to the development of programs with different components and tiers of intervention—although there are particular analytic challenges for studying these clinically sensitive regimens in which families with different needs receive different forms or levels of treatment. Further work of this kind is under development.

A final step is to make good practice part of the culture and to show population-level changes. That is what is implied in a universal intervention model. Sanders et al. (2000) evaluated a 13-episode television series that included elements of an evidence-based intervention. The series, broadcast to millions in New Zealand during peak viewing hours, produced a significant improvement in parent ratings on a studied subsample of volunteers—an impressive achievement. Further demonstrations of population-level studies are under way.

Parenting interventions are no longer dominated by cognitive-behavioral models, such as the programs cited previously. Attachment-based interventions have increased dramatically and have been shown to be clinically effective for a range of clinical problems (Bakermans-Kranenburg et al., 2003; Cicchetti et al., 2000). The focus on attachment means that these programs tend to include younger children, from infancy to preschool, but the differences in emphasis drawn from attachment theory mean that there is no single route to improving parent-child relationship quality and child well-being. That will be no surprise to those familiar with the broader intervention literature, but it is a useful reminder.

Lastly, it may be a surprise that parenting interventions have been shown to work in remarkably adverse settings. For example, Dybdahl (2001) conducted a parenting intervention with displaced families in Tuzla in war-torn Bosnia. Children and parents in families that received a five-month psychosocial intervention that focused on group-based programs to improve parenting and the mother's mental health showed significant improvement compared with families that received intervention of medical care only. Further evidence that parent-based interventions can be clinically valuable in extreme conditions was provided by Cooper et al. (2002) in a shantytown in South Africa. Another, less extreme but just as important for public health, are parenting interventions with foster parents that suggest improvement in child behavior (Pallett et al., 2003). These examples attest to the considerable relevance of conventional interventions and imply that, with perhaps some modification, the value of the interventions may extend well beyond the samples and populations on which they were formulated.

Additional Features and Considerations

The evidence base for parenting interventions is solid, and there are now a handful of established programs. Although most of the research so far has considered families who seek help at a clinic, there is growing interest in using parenting interventions as preventions. That is a necessary step, particularly because few families with clinical need will go to a clinic. It is therefore significant that several reports have shown parenting interventions to be effective when families are recruited from community settings or when families are recruited according to risk exposure rather than existing psychopathology. A good example of the latter sort was reported by Forgatch and DeGarmo (1999), who adopted a preventive strategy for mothers and children who recently experienced a divorce. Additional use of parenting interventions as preventive approaches is needed.

Another direction for parenting intervention research will be the need to consider the additional benefit of whole family interventions. Family-based interventions for conduct disorder and other severe clinical problems have been reported (Henggeler et al., 1997). That contrasts somewhat with the tendency for parenting interventions to include one parent (a second parent, where available, is not excluded but often fails to participate). Further work along these lines will provide valuable information to tackle questions that clinicians have continually asked, such as how important it is to change the whole family if a child's disruptive behavior is to be reduced.

CONCLUSION

Both clinical experience and empirical research have shown that one of the best predictors of children's well-being, perhaps especially for those living in high-risk settings, is a positive, supportive parent-child relationship (Wyman et al., 1999). In fact, studies of mentally ill parents show that it seems that it is not so much (or merely) the psychopathology that predicts poor outcomes for children, but rather the quality of parenting that the mentally ill parent performs. It is natural, then, for parent-child interventions to attract considerable clinical and scientific attention and for parents and policy makers to invest in these programs as a way to improve children's outcomes.

Both the basic and applied research on parent-child relationships has changed in the past decade, instituting lessons learned from improved methodology and theoretical challenges. Among these changes, one of the most important is the slow but steady breakdown of the largely artificial distinction between basic and applied research. That is seen in, for example, the acknowledged need for theory-driven interventions, the inclusion of diverse families and settings in research, and the rigorous evaluation of clinical programs before they are deemed "evidence-based."

ACKNOWLEDGMENT

The authors gratefully acknowledge support from a research methods center grant from the UK Economics and Social Research Council.

REFERENCES

Ainsworth, M.D.S., Blehar, M.C., Waters, E., and Wall, S. (1978). *Patterns of attachment: A psychological study of the strange situation*. Hillsdale, NJ: Erlbaum.

Allen, J.P., Hauser, S.T., O'Connor, T.G., Bell, K.L., and Eickholt, C.M. (1996). The connection of observed family conflict to adolescents' developing autonomy and relatedness with parents. *Development and Psychopathology* 8:425–442.

Allen, J.P., and Land, D. (1999). Attachment in adolescence. In J. Cassidy and P. Shaver (Eds.), *Handbook of attachment* (pp. 319–335). New York: Guilford.

Anderson, K.E., Lytton, H., and Romney, D.M. (1986). Mothers' interactions with normal and conduct disordered boys: Who affects whom? *Developmental Psychology* 22: 604–609.

Bakermans-Kranenburg, M.J., van Ijzendoorn, M.H., and Juffer, F. (2003). Less is more: Meta-analysis of sensitivity and attachment interventions in early childhood. *Psychological Bulletin* 129:195–215.

Bandura, A. (1977). *Social learning theory*. New York: General Learning Press.

Barkley, R. (1997). *Defiant Children: A clinician's manual for assessment and parent training*, Second Edition. New York: Guilford Press.

Barkley, R.A. (1981). The use of psychopharmacology to study reciprocal influences in parent-child interaction. *Journal of Abnormal Child Psychology* 9:303–310.

Barkley, R.A., Shelton, T.L., and Crosswait, C. (2000). Multi-method pyschoeducational intervention for preschool children with disruptive behaviour: Preliminary results at post-treatment. *Journal of Child Psychology and Psychiatry* 41:319–332.

Barlow, J. (1999). *Systematic Review of the Effectiveness of Parent-Training Programmes in Improving Behaviour Problems in Children Aged 3–10 Years (2nd Ed): A review of the literature on parent-training programmes and child behaviour outcome measures*. Health Services Research Unit, University of Oxford.

Baumrind, D. (1991). Effective parenting during the early adolescent transition. In P. Cowan and E.M. Hetherington (Eds.), *Family transitions* (pp. 111–163). Hillsdale, NJ: Erlbaum.

Bell, K.L., Allen, J.P., Hauser, S.T., and O'Connor, T.G. (1996). Family factors and young adult transitions: Educational attainment and occupational prestige. In J. Graber, J. Brooks-Gunn, and A.C. Peterson (Eds.), *Transitions through adolescence* (pp. 345–366). Hillsdale, NJ: Lawrence Erlbaum Associates.

Bell, R.Q., and Harper, L.V. (1977). *Child effects on adults*. Lincoln: University of Nebraska Press.

Bijur, P.E., Kurzon, M., Hamelsky, V., and Power, C. (1991). Parent-adolescent conflict and adolescent injuries. *Journal of Developmental and Behavioral Pediatrics* 12:92–97.

Bowlby, J. (1969/1982). *Attachment and Loss: Vol. 1. Attachment*. New York: Basic Books.

Bowlby, J. (1988). Developmental psychiatry comes of age. *American Journal of Psychiatry* 145:1–10.

Bugental, D.B., Blue, J.B., and Cruzcosa, M. (1989). Perceived control over caregiving outcomes: Implications for child abuse. *Developmental Psychology* 25:532–539.

Carson, J.L., and Parke, R.D. (1996). Reciprocal negative affect in parent-child interactions and children's peer competency. *Child Development* 67:2217–2226.

Cassidy, J. and Shaver, P. (Eds.) (1999). *Handbook of attachment*. New York: Guilford.

Cassidy, J., Kirsh, S.J., Scolton, K.L., and Parke, R.D. (1996). Attachment and representations of peers. *Developmental Psychology* 32:892–904.

Cicchetti, D., Rogosch, F.A., and Toth, S.L. (2000). The efficacy of toddler-parent psychotherapy for fostering cognitive development in offspring of depressed mothers. *Journal of Abnormal Child Psychology* 28:135–148.

Conduct Problems Prevention Research Group. (1999). Initial impact of the fast track prevention trial for conduct problems: 1. The high-risk sample. *Journal of Consulting and Clinical Psychology* 67:631–647.

Conger, R.D., Cui, M., Bryant, C.M., and Elder, G.H., Jr. (2000). Competence in early adult romantic relationships: A developmental perspective on family influences. *Journal of Personality and Social Psychology* 79:224–237.

Cooper, P.J., Landman, M., Tomlinson, M., Molteno, C., Swartz, L., and Murray, L. (2002). Impact of a mother-infant intervention in an indigent peri-urban South African context: Pilot study. *British Journal of Psychiatry* 180:76–81.

Dadds, M.R., Barrett, P.M., Rapee, R.M., and Ryan, S. (1996). Family process and child anxiety and aggression: An observational analysis. *Journal of Abnormal Child Psychology* 24:715–734.

Deater-Deckard, K., and O'Connor, T.G. (2000). Parent-child mutuality in early childhood: Two behavioral genetic studies. *Developmental Psychology* 36:561–570.

Denham, S.A., Workman, E., Cole, P.M., Weissbrod, C., Kendziora, K.T., and Zahn-Waxler, C. (2000). Prediction of externalizing behavior problems from early to middle childhood: The role of parental socialisation and emotion expression. *Development and Psychopathology* 12:23–45.

Dishion, T.J., and McMahon, R.J. (1998). Parental monitoring and the prevention of child and adolescent problem behavior: A conceptual and empirical formulation. *Clinical Child and Family Psychology Review* 1:61–75.

Dodge, K.A., Pettit, G.S., Bates, J.E., and Valente, E. (1995). Social information-processing patterns partially mediate the effect of early physical abuse on later conduct problems. *Journal of Abnormal Psychology* 104:632–643.

Dumas, J.E., and Wahler, R.G. (1983). Predictors of treatment outcome in parent training: Mother insularity and socio-economic disadvantage. *Behavioral Assessment* 5:301–313.

Dunn, J. (1992). *Young children's close relationships: Beyond attachment*. Newbury Park, CA: Sage.

Dunn, J., Deater-Deckard, K., Pickering, K., O'Connor, T.G., Golding, J., and the ALSPAC Study Team. (1998). Children's adjustment and prosocial behavior in step-, single, and nonstep-family settings: Findings from a community study. *Journal of Child Psychology and Psychiatry* 39:1083–1095.

Dybdahl, R. (2001). Children and mothers in war: An outcome study of a psychosocial intervention program. *Child Development* 72:1214–1230.

Faith, M.S., Berkowitz, R.I., Stallings, V.A., Kerns, J., Storey, M., and Stunkard, A.J. (2004). Parental feeding attitudes and styles and child body mass index: Prospective analysis of a gene-environment interaction. *Pediatrics* 114(4):e429–36.

Fletcher, A.C., Steinberg, L., and Williams-Wheeler, M. (2004). Parental influences on adolescent problem behavior: Revisiting Stattin and Kerr. *Child Development* 75:781–796.

Flouri, E., and Buchanan, A. (2002). What predicts good relationships with parents in adolescents and partners in adult life: Findings from the 1958 British Birth Cohort. *Journal of Family Psychology* 16:186–198.

Forehand, R.L., and Long, N. (1996). *Parenting the strong-willed child: The clinically proven five-week program for parents of two- to six-year-olds*. Chicago: Contemporary Books.

Forehand, R., Wells, K.C., and Griest, D.L. (1980). An examination of the social validity of a parent training program. *Journal of Behavior Therapy* 11:488–502.

Forgatch, M., and DeGarmo, D.S. (1999). Parenting through change: An effective prevention program for single mothers. *Journal of Consulting and Clinical Psychology* 67:711–724.

Francis, D., Diorio, J., Liu, D., Meaney, M.J. (1999). Nongenomic transmission across generations of maternal behavior and stress response in the rat. *Science* 286:1155–1158.

Garber, J., Little, S., Hilsman, R., and Weaver, K.R. (1998). Family predictors of suicidal symptoms in young adolescents. *Journal of Adolescence* 21:445–457.

Ge, X., Conger, R.D., Cadoret, R.J., Neiderhiser, J.M., Yates, W., Troughton, E., and Stewart, M.A. (1996). The developmental interface between nature and nurture: A mutual influence model of child antisocial behavior and parent behaviors. *Developmental Psychology* 32:574–589.

Glasgow, K.L., Dornbusch, S.M., Troyer, L., Steinberg, L., and Ritter, P.L. (1997). Parenting styles, adolescents' attributions, and educational outcomes in nine heterogeneous high schools. *Child Development* 68:507–529.

Green, G., Macintyre S., West P., and Ecob R. (1990). Do children of lone parents smoke more because their mothers do? *British Journal of Addiction* 85:1497–1500.

Greenberg, M.T. (1999). Attachment and psychopathology in childhood. In *Handbook of attachment* (ed. J. Cassidy and P. Shaver). New York: Guilford.

Grotevant, H.D., and Cooper, C.R. (1985). Patterns of interaction in family relationships and the development of identity exploration in adolescence. *Child Development* 56:415–428.

Gutman, L.M., and Eccles, J.S. (1999). Financial strain, parenting behaviors, and adolescents' achievement: Testing model equivalence between African American and European American single- and two-parent families. *Child Development* 70:1464–1476.

Henggeler, S.W., Melton, G.B., Brondino, M.J., Scherer, D.G., Hanley, J.H. (1997). Multisystemic therapy with violent and chronic juvenile offenders and their families: The role of treatment fidelity in successful dissemination. *Journal of Consulting and Clinical Psychology* 65:831–833.

Hetherington, E.M., Henderson, S., and Reiss, D. (1999). Family functioning and adolescent adjustment of siblings in nondivorced families and diverse types of stepfamilies. *Monographs of the Society for Research in Child Development* 64, no. 4 (Serial no. 259).

Hicks, B.M., Krueger, R.F., Iacono, W.G., McGue, M., and Patrick, C.J. (2004). Family transmission and heritability of externalizing disorders: A twin-family study. *Archives of General Psychiatry* 61:922–928.

Hoag, M.J., and Burlingame, G.M., (1997). Evaluating the effectiveness of child and adolescent group treatment: A meta-analytic review. *Journal of Clinical Child Psychology* 16:57–68.

Jebb, S.A., Rennie, K.L., and Cole, T.J. (2004). Prevalence of overweight and obesity among young people in Great Britain. *Public Health Nutrition* 7:461–465.

Kerr, M., and Stattin, H. (2000). What parents know, how they know it, and several forms of adolescent adjustment: Further support for a reinterpretation of monitoring. *Developmental Psychology* 36:366–380.

Kilgore, K., Snyder, J., and Lentz, C. (2000). The contribution of parental discipline, parental monitoring, and school risk to early-onset conduct problems in African American boys and girls. *Developmental Psychology* 36:835–845.

Kochanska, G. (1997). Multiple pathways to conscience for children with different temperaments: From toddlerhood to age 5. *Developmental Psychology* 33:228–240.

LaFreniere, P.J. and Dmas, J.E. (1992). A transactional analysis of early childhood anxiety and social withdrawal. *Development and Pyschopathology* 4:385–402.

Laible, D.J., and Thompson, R.A. (1998). Attachment and emotional understanding in preschool children. *Developmental Psychology* 34:1038–1045.

Lansford, J.E., Chang, L., Dodge, K.A., Malone P.S., Oburu P., Palmerus K., Bacchini, D., Pastorelli, C., Bombi, A.S., Zelli, A., et al. (2005). Physical discipline and children's adjustment: cultural normativeness as a moderator. *Child Development* 76:1234–1246.

Loeber, R., Drinkwater, M., Yin, Y., Anderson, S.J., Schmidt, L.C. and Crawford, A. (2000). Stability of family interaction from ages 6 to 18. *Journal of Abnormal Child Psychology* 28(4):353–369.

Lytton, H. (1977). Do parents create, or respond to, differences in twins? *Developmental Psychology* 13:456–459.

Maccoby, E.E., and Martin, J.A. (1983). Socialization in the context of the family: Parent-child interaction. In E.M. Hetherington (Ed.), *Mussen manual of child psychology,* Vol. 4 (pp. 1–102). New York: Wiley.

McGue, M., Sharma, A., and Benson, P. (1996). The effect of common rearing on adolescent adjustment: Evidence from a U.S. adoption cohort. *Developmental Psychology* 32:604–613.

Moss, E., Rousseau, D., Parent, S., St-Laurant, D., and Saintonge, J. (1998). Correlates of attachment at school age: Maternal reported stress, mother-child interaction, and behavior problems. *Child Development* 69:1390–1405.

O'Connor, T.G., Davies, L., Dunn, J., Golding, and the ALSPAC Study Team. (2000). Differential distribution of children's accidents, injuries, and illnesses across family type. *Pediatrics* 106:e68.

O'Connor, T.G. (2002). Annotation: The "effects" of parenting reconsidered: Findings, challenges, and applications. *Journal of Child Psychology and Psychiatry* 43:555–572.

O'Connor, T.G., Deater-Deckard, K., Fulker, D., Rutter, M., and Plomin, R. (1998). Genotype-environment correlations in late childhood and early adolescence: Antisocial behavioral problems and coercive parenting. *Developmental Psychology* 34:970–981.

O'Connor, T.G., Hetherington, E.M., Reiss, D., and Plomin, R. (1995). A twin-sibling study of observed parent-adolescent interactions. *Child Development* 66:812–829.

Pallett, C., Scott, S., Blackeby, K., Yule, W., and Weissman, R. (2002). Fostering changes: A cognitive-behavioural approach to help foster carers manage children. *Adoption and Fostering* 26:39–48.

Patterson, G.R. (1969). Behavioural techniques based upon social learning: An additional base for developing behaviour modification technologies. In C. Franks (Ed.), *Behaviour therapy: Appraisal and status*. New York: McGraw Hill.

Patterson, G.R. (1974). Interventions for boys with conduct problems: Multiple settings, treatments and criteria. *Journal of Consulting and Clinical Psychology* 42:471–481.

Patterson, G.R. (1996). Some characteristics of a developmental theory for early onset delinquency. In M.F. Lenzenweger and J.J. Haugaard (Eds.), *Frontiers of developmental psychopathology* (pp. 81–124). New York: Oxford University Press.

Patterson, G.R., and Bank, L. (1989). Some amplifying mechanisms for pathological processes in families. In M. Gunnar and E. Thelan (Eds.), *Systems and development: The Minnesota symposium on child psychology*, vol. 22 (pp. 167–209). Hillsdale, NJ: Erlbaum.

Pettit, G.S., Bates, J.E., Dodge, K.A., and Meece, D.W. (1999). The impact of afterschool peer contact on early adolescent externalizing problems is moderated by parental monitoring, perceived neighborhood safety, and prior adjustment. *Child Development* 70:768–778.

Pettit, G.S., Dodge, K.A., and Brown, M.M. (1988). Early family experience, social problem solving patterns, and children's social competence. *Child Development* 59:107–120.

Puckering, C., Rogers, J., Mills, M., Cox, A.D., and Mattsson-Graff, M. (1994). Process and evaluation of a group intervention for mothers with parenting difficulties. *Child Abuse Review* 3:299–310.

Rogoff, B., and Lave, S. (Eds.). (1984). *Everyday cognition: Development in Social Context*. Cambridge, MA: Harvard University Press.

Rothbaum, F. and Weisz, J.R. (1994). Parental caregiving and child externalizing behavior in nonclinical samples: A meta-analysis. *Psychological Bulletin* 116:55–74.

Sanders, M.R., Markie-Dadds, C., and Turner, K.M.T. (1999). *What is Triple P?* Brisbane: Families International Publishing.

Sanders, M.R., Montgomery, D.T., and Brechman-Toussaint, M.L. (2000). The mass media and the prevention of child behavior problems: The evaluation of a television series to promote positive outcomes for parents and their children. *Journal of Child Psychology and Psychiatry* 41:939–948.

Scott, S.B. (2002). Parent training programmes. In M. Rutter and E. Taylor (Eds.), *Child and Adolescent Psychiatry*, 4th edition. Oxford: Blackwell Science.

Scott, S., Spender, Q., Doolan, M., Jacobs, B., and Aspland, H. (2001). Multicentre controlled trial of parenting groups for child antisocial behaviour in clinical practice. *British Medical Journal* 323:194–198.

Scott, S., and Sylva, K., (1998). *Supporting Parents on Kids' Education (SPOKES): Improving adjustment and raising attainment in young children at school.* Interim project report to the Department of Health.

Sears, R., Maccoby, E.E., and Levin, H. (1957). *Patterns of child rearing.* Evanston, Ill: Row, Peterson.

Serkitch, W.J., and Dumas, J.E. (1996). The effectiveness of behavioral parent training to modify antisocial behavior in children: A meta-analysis. *Journal of Behavior Therapy* 27:171–186.

Smetana, J.G., and Asquith, P. (1994). Adolescents' and parents' conceptions of parental authority and personal autonomy. *Child Development* 65:1147–1162.

Steele, H., Steele, M., and Fonagy, P. (1996). Associations among attachment classifications of mothers, fathers, and their infants. *Child Development* 67:541–555.

Steinberg, L. (1987). Single parents, stepparents, and the susceptibility of adolescents to antisocial peer pressure. *Child Development* 58:269–275.

Steinberg, L., Fletcher, A., and Darling, N. (1994). Parental monitoring and peer influences on adolescent substance use. *Pediatrics* 93:1060–1064.

Steinglass, P. (1981). The alcoholic family at home. Patterns of interaction in dry, wet, and transitional stages of alcoholism. *Archives of General Psychiatry* 38:578–584.

Stevenson, H.W. and Lee, S.Y. (1990). Contexts of achievement: a study of American, Chinese, and Japanese children. *Monographs of the Society for Research in Child Development* 55(1–2):1–123.

Toth, S.L., Cicchetti, D., Macfie, J., Maughan, A., and Van Meenen, K. (2000). Narrative representations of caregivers and self in maltreated pre-schoolers. *Attachment and Human Development* 2:271–305.

Waters, E., Merrick, S., Treboux, D., Crowell, J., and Albersheim, L. (2000). Attachment security in infancy and early adulthood: A twenty-year longitudinal study. *Child Development* 71:684–689.

Webster-Stratton, C. (1994). Advancing videotape parent training: A comparison study. *Journal of Consulting and Clinical Psychology* 62:583–593.

Webster-Stratton, C. and Hammond, M. (1997). Treating children with early-onset conduct problems: A comparison of child and parent training interventions. *Journal of Consulting and Clinical Psychology* 65:93–109.

Webster-Stratton, C., and Herbert, M. (1994). *Troubled Families—Problem Children. Working with Parents: A Collaborative Process.* Chichester: John Wiley & Sons.

Wyman, P.A., Cowen, E.L., Work, W.C., Hoyt, L., Magnus, K., and Fagen, D. (1999). Caregiving and developmental factors differentiating young at-risk urban children showing resilient vs. stress-affected outcomes: A replication and extension. *Child Development* 70:645–659.

Chapter Four

Child Abuse and Neglect: A Mental Health Perspective

Ernesto Caffo, Luisa Strik Lievers,
and Barbara Forresi

Child maltreatment is a major public health issue and worldwide concern. It is clearly evident that research on child maltreatment had a scientific maturation during the last two decades. Nonetheless, as highlighted by the U.S. National Institutes of Health, it still "lacks a level of sophistication necessary to address adequately the critical scientific and clinical issues. There have been only a handful of longitudinal studies on course and outcome of maltreatment in children" (Neglect of child neglect, *Lancet*, 2003).

On the one side, the time has come to address some fundamental questions relating to definitions, classifications, measurement, and interpretation of abuse statistics and effective prevention and treatment interventions. On the other side, research in the field of psychological abuse and neglect has to be promoted. Psychological abuse and neglect seem to remain a low priority, with very few resources, initiatives, and studies. As evidenced in a study by the *International Journal of Child Abuse and Neglect* (Behl et al., 2003), during the past twenty-two years the percentage of articles examining child physical abuse declined while the proportion of research published on sexual abuse rose. At the same time, the percentage of articles examining child neglect and emotional abuse remained consistently low.

In this chapter we present advances in the field of child abuse and neglect, both from a clinical and a research perspective. Central areas will be covered, including epidemiology of child abuse and neglect, definitions, impact of abuse, prevention, and treatment. Similarly, controversial topics, unanswered questions, and the need for further research will be highlighted.

EPIDEMIOLOGY OF CHILD ABUSE AND NEGLECT

What percentage of children and adolescents are exposed to abuse and neglect? Although there is growing awareness among the public and professionals about this issue, the prevalence of victimization among youth remains a source of ongoing debate and controversy.

Child abuse and neglect is often associated with social stigma, and it frequently occurs inside families, resulting in severe consequences after disclosure. The majority of these cases fail to reach official attention: only a limited number are known to welfare agencies and reported to child protection services, social services, police, or the courts.

Therefore statistics do not accurately describe the prevalence, the incidence, or the time trends in rates. Moreover, there is a high variability in data. Multiple factors may explain this feature. First of all, data on child abuse and neglect come from a variety of sources, including official statistics, case reports, and population-based surveys. In the United States the main sources of epidemiological data are the National Child Abuse and Neglect Data System—which presents data compiled from state child-protective services (CPS) agencies of known maltreatment cases—and the National Incidence Study, which samples CPS, law enforcement, juvenile probation, public health, hospitals, school day care, and mental health and social service agencies.

According to *Child Maltreatment 2003* (U.S. Department of Health and Human Services, 2005) an estimated 906,000 children were determined to be victims of child abuse or neglect. Almost 19% were physically abused, 10% were sexually abused, and 5% were emotionally maltreated. Children ages birth to three years had the highest rates of victimization; girls were slightly more likely to be victims than boys. Pacific Islander, American Indian, Alaska Native, and African American children had the highest rates of victimization when compared to the national population.

The National Incidence studies found a 67% increase in all forms of child abuse from 1986 to 1993, with the number of abused and neglected children nearly doubled. As far as gender and age are concerned, these data report that girls were sexually abused three times more often than boys, that boys had a greater risk of emotional neglect and serious injury than girls, and that children are consistently vulnerable to sexual abuse from age three on. Children of single parents had a greater risk of being abused and neglected than children living with both parents. Children in the largest families were physically neglected at nearly three times the rate of those who came from single-child families, while children from the lowest income families were more likely to be abused and neglected than children from higher income families (U.S. Department of Health and Human Services, 1996).

In spite of the increasing numbers reported by the National Incidence Study, in the United States officially reported cases of child sexual abuse (CSA) declined in the same period. Reasons for the decrease—and the following increase from 2000 on—are being debated (Jones et al., 2001; Chadwick, 2002; Jones and Finkelhor, 2001, 2002).

Among the other factors, difficulties in interpreting these estimates and cross-national comparisons are complicated by variations in the definition of sexual abuse, physical abuse, psychological abuse, and neglect and by cultural factors. Maltreatment has a heterogeneous nature and may vary from single incident to frequent and multiple acts of abuse. Because it is no longer considered a dichotomous variable (yes/no), the threshold for a behavior being judged inappropriate depends on cultures and normative basis. Furthermore, also among those classified as being exposed to abuse or neglect, there is a significant heterogeneity in the nature of the abuse, which may be more or less violent, severe, and intrusive.

In addition to difficulties in the definitions, variations in the estimates of prevalence may be associated with problems of recall and disclosure of abuse, purpose of the investigations, methods of assessment, sample selection factors, and random sampling errors.

These uncertainties highlight the need for care and caution when presenting and interpreting data on the prevalence of child abuse and neglect.

DEFINITION OF CHILD ABUSE

In 1999, the WHO Consultation on Child Abuse Prevention drafted the following definition (WHO, 1999): "Child abuse or maltreatment constitutes all forms of physical and/or emotional ill-treatment, sexual abuse, neglect or negligent treatment or commercial or other exploitation, resulting in actual or potential harm to the child's health, survival, development or dignity in the context of a relationship of responsibility, trust or power."

There are no universal definitions of child physical abuse, sexual abuse, neglect, or psychological maltreatment. A useful starting point is to consider a general definition of each problem, which usually focuses both on the behavior (or actions) of adults and the harm (or the threat of harm) to the child.

After an extensive review of different countries' definitions of child maltreatment and a consultation on child abuse prevention, WHO (1999) proposed the following definitions:

Physical Abuse

Physical abuse of a child is that which results in actual or potential physical harm from an interaction or lack of interaction, which is reasonably within the control of a parent or person in a position of responsibility, power, or trust. There may be single or repeated incidents.

Sexual Abuse

Child sexual abuse is the involvement of a child in sexual activity that he or she does not fully comprehend, is unable to give informed consent to, or for which the child is not developmentally prepared and cannot give consent, or that violates the laws or social taboos of society. Child sexual abuse is evidenced by an activity between a child and an adult or another child who by age or development is in a relationship of responsibility, trust or power, the activity being intended to gratify or satisfy the needs of the other person. This may include but is not limited to the inducement or coercion of a child to engage in any unlawful sexual activity; the exploitative use of a child in prostitution or other unlawful sexual practices; the exploitative use of children in pornographic performances and materials.

Neglect and Negligent Treatment

Neglect and negligent treatment is the inattention or omission on the part of the caregiver to provide for the development of the child in all spheres: health, education, emotional development, nutrition, shelter and safe living conditions, in the context of resources reasonably available to the family or caretakers and causes, or has a high probability of causing, harm to the child's health or physical, mental, spiritual, moral or social development. This includes the failure to properly supervise and protect children from harm as much as it is feasible.

Emotional Abuse

Emotional abuse includes the failure to provide a developmentally appropriate, supportive environment, including the availability of a primary attachment figure, so that the child can develop a stable and full range of emotional and social competencies commensurate with her or his personal potential, and in the context of the society in which the child dwells. There may also be acts toward the child that cause or have a high probability of causing harm to the child's health or physical, mental, spiritual, moral or social development. These acts must be reasonably within the control of the parent or person in a relationship of responsibility, trust or power. Acts include restriction of movement, patterns of belittling, denigrating, scapegoating, threatening, scaring, discriminating, ridiculing, or other non-physical forms of hostile or rejecting treatment.

The discussion concerning the definition of psychological and emotional maltreatment is particularly active and interesting. The American Professional Society on the Abuse of Children (APSAC, 1995) defines psychological maltreatment as "a repeated pattern of caregiver behaviors or extreme incident(s) that convey to children that they are worthless, flawed, unloved, unwanted, endangered, or of value only in meeting another's needs."

According to this definition, APSAC identifies six forms of psychological maltreatment: spurning (verbal and nonverbal hostile rejecting or degrading); terrorizing (behavior that threatens or is likely to harm physically the child or place the child or the child's loved objects in danger); exploiting or corrupting (encouraging the child to develop inappropriate behaviors); denying emotional responsiveness (ignoring the child's needs to interact, failing to express positive affect to the child, showing no emotion in interactions with the child); isolating (denying child opportunities for interacting or communicating with peers or adults); and mental health, medical, and educational neglect (ignoring or failing to ensure provision for the child's needs).

Given the presence of some difficulties in these definitions (e.g., not evident conceptual basis, possibility of classifying several forms simultaneously), an alternative framework has been provided by Glaser (2002), who identifies the following categories of emotional abuse and neglect: emotional unavailability, unresponsiveness, and neglect; negative attributions and misattributions to the child; developmentally inappropriate or inconsistent interactions with the child; failure to recognize or acknowledge the child's individuality and psychological boundary; and failing to promote the child's social adaptation.

In recent years, questions have been asked about the cultural applicability of previous categories of abuse and neglect. Researchers are still debating if there may be a general agreement across different cultures on what constitutes acceptable parenting practices and consequently what is to be considered child abuse and neglect.

RISK FACTORS

The multidetermined nature of problems such as child abuse and neglect has been explicated by decades of research. According to an ecological model (Bronfenbrenner, 1979; Belsky, 1980; Cicchetti and Linch 1993), an episode of maltreatment is more likely to occur when risk factors overtake protective ones. Risk factors for child maltreatment, as for other forms of violence, occur on multiple levels, ranging from biological and individual-level factors, to family and community levels.

First of all, what emerge from this literature are limitations and uncertainties: recall bias and sample-selection bias may lead to unreliable or inaccurate accounts. Second, when adopting a risk-based approach, the following caution should be considered. The development of a profile of a child who is most likely to be abused or neglected would naturally lead to the thought that child, family, community, and cultural characteristics may be used to identify children at risk. Conversely, a number of authors concluded that this identification is likely to be highly imprecise and potentially misleading (Fergusson and Mullen, 1999; WHO, 1999):

> Theories that propose single factors or combinations of risk factors as invariably leading directly to child abuse will stigmatize families which fall within the profile and lead to missed cases of child abuse, which do not fit the profile. In families where child abuse does exist, they may be more likely to hide the abuse as it now carries a public condemnation. In families where it is not present, stigmatization may translate into marginalization of the family, including the children. (WHO, 1999, 23)

Individual-Level Risk Factors

Age

There is evidence that vulnerability to child abuse and neglect is significantly associated with age. Children less than one year old, born prematurely or with low birth weight, with disabilities, and children who are boys, twins, or stepchildren are all at increased risk (Reece, 1994). If the age of risk for physical abuse varies from country to country, sexual abuse rates tend to rise after puberty (U.S. Department of Health and Human Services, 1998), with a peak between ages twelve and eighteen (35.9% of cases).

Gender

Research also indicates that, considering the general population, girls are at higher risk for sexual abuse and neglect, while male children appear to be at greatest risk of physical abuse (Krug et al., 2002). It is calculated that girls have a 2.5 to 3 times higher risk of sexual abuse than boys (Putnam, 2003). It has to be taken into account that boys' rates could be underestimated and that mental health professionals rarely investigate sexual abuse of males (Lab et al., 2000). Nevertheless, in the last decade there is growing recognition of sexual abuse of boys (Beitchman et al., 1991).

Physical and Mental Health

Another risk factor relates to the presence of poor physical or mental health. It is proposed that families with children with disabilities may have higher emotional, physical, and social demands and, in some cases, challenges that make the child more likely to be victimized. Interestingly, it seems that boys are overrepresented among sexually abused children with disabilities rather than in the nondisabled samples (Sobsey et al., 1997). Similarly, children's personality features, difficult temperament, and behavior problems (e.g., socialized aggression, attention deficits, and internalizing and externalizing problems) appear to be associated with increased risk for child physical abuse and neglect (Schumacher et al., 2001; Black et al., 2001).

If child physical abuse has the richest risk-factor research literature of any form of family violence, there is a very limited body of research on risk factors for psychological abuse, which may be due to the lack of consensus on the definition. However, as evidenced by recent studies, some personality factors (e.g., aggression and hostility) appear to be related to psychological abuses (Black et al., 2001).

Family and Environmental Risk Factors

Social and Family Factors

A growing number of studies examined social and family characteristics of children exposed to abuse and neglect. Although there is consensus that child abuse and neglect occur across all socioeconomic and cultural groups, some family and social factors appear to have important implications.

Physical and Sexual Abuse. Children at greatest risk of physical and sexual abuse appear to come from families characterized by multiple sources of difficulties and dysfunctions, including marital conflict, parental separation, step-parenthood, parental psychopathology, and impaired parent-child relationship (Cummings, 1997; Krug et al., 2002; Fergusson and Mullen, 1999). The literature evidences a high comorbidity of domestic violence and child maltreatment, which ranges from 30% to 60% (Edelson, 1999). Similarly, a number of studies highlight that children who are exposed to sexual abuse have also been physically and emotionally abused (Fergusson and Mullen, 1999), possibly because the same family difficulties may be associated with different types of abuse.

Furthermore, a study on child sexual abuse highlighted that children exposed to intrafamilial abuse and extrafamilial abuse came from similar family backgrounds (Fergusson et al., 1996a); family dysfunctions indeed place children at risk of both intrafamilial and extrafamilial sexual abuse.

Family and social variables, including poverty, unemployment, low education, and lack of social support, can contribute to increased risk for physical abuse, neglect, and emotional abuse (WHO, 2002; Zelenko et al., 2001) but seem to have much less impact on child sexual abuse (Finkelhor, 1993).

Child Neglect.   The risk for child neglect is associated with many maternal variables, such as psychological factors, dimensions of social support, self-esteem, impulsivity, and personal history of child neglect (Schumacher et al., 2001). Certain community factors, such as disadvantaged communities and a low socioeconomic status, may also be associated with increased risk for child neglect; however, it is not yet clear whether in disadvantaged communities child neglect occurs more often or it is more reported and substantiated (Schumacher et al., 2001).

Psychological Abuse.   Environmental stressors (e.g., very low income) and proximal variables (verbal and physical aggression between parents) also appear to be related to psychological abuse (Black et al., 2001).

Abusive Parents.   As far as abusers are concerned, many studies suggest that abusive parents tend to be young and have more unrealistic expectations, rigid attitudes, and impulsivity. Similarly, other studies have found that abusive parents are more prone to feelings of inadequacy, loneliness, depression, and unhappiness. Substance abuse and negative childhood experiences, including history of abuse and neglect, have been found to have a role in the onset of abusing and neglecting behaviors. More proximal variables that increase the probability of parents, especially mothers, employing severe abuse include those related to stress (e.g., stressful life events) and coping (most likely a protective factor, including problem solving and social support) (Nagler, 2002; Zelenko et al., 2001).

Little is known about the intergenerational transmission of abuse. Many observational studies in the field of physical as well as sexual abuse, longitudinal or retrospective, have attempted to elucidate this link but have inconsistent results (Ertem et al., 2000; Bagley et al., 1994; Watkins and Bentovim, 2000). It appears that past abuses may represent a contributory factor, not a necessary factor—among a number of other abusive experiences.

Whether the abuser is more likely to be male or female appears to be related to the type of abuse. In the case of CSA, for example, males are the predominant perpetrators when the victim is female, although one in five perpetrators are female when the victim is male (Fergusson and Mullen, 1999).

Cultural-Level Risk Factors

Ethnicity and Culture

Only few studies have highlighted the relationship between culture and risk of abuse. Some examined the role of ethnicity and culture on sexual abuse (Kenny and McEachern, 2000). In an interesting article about methodological aspects in the study of culture, Korbin (2002) evidenced the risk of considering the culture as an isolated variable that may have an impact on its own. It is difficult, and extremely dangerous, to state that in a specific cultural group there is a higher risk of abusive behaviors toward children. Culture has to be considered as an ecological framework and in interaction with other variables (e.g., migration, socioeconomic status, etc.) at different ecological levels. Therefore, it can offer both risk and protective factors, whose impact varies not only between different cultures but also within a specific culture.

RECOGNITION AND ASSESSMENT OF CHILD ABUSE AND NEGLECT

How can we distinguish between children who are sexually abused or neglected from those who are not? Although the literature, as discussed previously, provides several bases for defining abuse and neglect, we still do not have a generally accepted set of normative, moral, and clinical standards that determine which acts are to be classified as abusive and which are not.

Some clinicians, for example, consider that exposure to sexual or physical abuse is associated with a characteristic and specific pattern of symptoms. According to recent evidence, however, there is no single sign, physical or behavioral symptom, or any interactional patterns that can be considered specific to exposure to abuse or neglect.

The behavioral profiles of children and adolescents exposed to abuse or neglect, in fact, have considerable similarity to the behavioral profiles associated with a wide range of early adversities and difficulties.

When dealing with self-reporting by caregivers, clinicians also have to consider the high potential for nondisclosure or conversely for false positive cases (for example, in cases of parental divorce, separation, or conflict). In the case of self-report made by victimized children, moreover, there is a high risk of minimization of the actual experience of maltreatment or of nonreporting early life experiences.

From a clinical point of view, some researchers (Fergusson and Mullen, 1999) considering CSA cases highlight the need to move away from definitions that aggregate a diverse set of experiences into a general category of abuse and toward approaches that describe the nature, extent, and intrusiveness of the experience and how it affects the development of children and adolescents.

THE DEVELOPMENT OF CLASSIFICATIONS

A correct recognition of abuse and neglect, as well as distinguishing among severe, moderate, and inferred cases of abuse, is therefore of primary importance.

The development of adequate classifications could represent the first step to providing supportive interventions and, in the most serious cases, coercive interventions. Moreover, many parents labeled as abusive are facing a temporary situation of stress and may be more likely to benefit from supporting interventions instead of repressive interventions.

Some work in this direction has already begun. One study (Sedlak and Broadhurst, 1996) defines serious injury as "a threatening condition or long-term impairment of physical, mental or emotional capacities, or requiring professional treatment aimed at preventing such long-term impairment." Moderate injury is defined as an injury that "persisted in observable form (including pain or impairment) for at least 48 h[ours] (e.g., bruises, depression or emotional distress not serious enough to require professional treatment)." Inferred harm is defined as the "nature of the maltreatment itself [giving] reasonable cause to assume the injury or impairment probably occurred."

The Maltreatment Classification System (Barnett et al., 1993) is a comprehensive framework for quantifying maltreatment among multiple dimensions potentially related to psychological outcome. They include subtype, severity and timing of maltreatment (age of onset, frequency, chronicity, developmental period), relationship with perpetrator, occurrence of separations, and placements. Some studies aiming to better understand the importance of severity dimensions of maltreatment in determining outcomes used the Maltreatment Classification System. In an interesting study Litrownik et al. (2005) suggest that maximum severity subtype is the most appropriate way to classify maltreatment severity: sexual abuse severity seems to be primarily related to the intrusiveness of abusing behavior (e.g., exposure, penetration); physical abuse is related to physical injury to the child (e.g., cuts, bruises); severity of neglect is associated with the risk of harm in situations where the child is not supervised or not provided with essential needs.

According to our knowledge, very few studies deal with the question of the severity of emotional maltreatment. Hamarman and Bernet (2000) suggested the following three levels of severity, borrowed from legal precedents:

> An action that is both committed with intent to inflict harm and has a high probability of causing harm is considered to be severe emotional abuse. Conversely, an action that contains neither intent nor high probability of harm is considered mild. Actions falling in the middle, with either intent or harm but not both, may be classified as moderate. (929)

This attempt to classify and quantify maltreatment being not yet exhaustive, future efforts should address the need for more refined classifications, distinguishing among different levels of abuse and neglect.

SEQUELAE

It is now increasingly accepted that abused and neglected children are at risk for a wide range of mental health disorders and adjustment difficulties. Apart from physical consequences that go beyond the aim of this chapter, the experience of having been abused or neglected may be significantly associated with a wide range of psychological difficulties, which may persist in adolescence and adulthood. Conversely, a substantial minority of children and adolescents known to have been exposed to abuse or neglect do not develop any significant adjustment difficulties.

To what extent does exposure to child abuse and neglect lead to the onset of mental health difficulties in childhood and adolescence? What factors influence the resilience of abused and neglected children?

Mental Disorders and General Health Problems

Although some study bias—such as sample selection processes and failure to control for confounding factors—may lead to an overestimation of the causal effect of child abuse and neglect on childhood adjustment, it may be argued that exposure to abuse and neglect does in fact lead to a wide range of mental health difficulties. Some children do not develop any clear symptomatology; others have just a few symptoms that do not reach clinical level of concern, whereas others meet full criteria for mental disorders. According to some reviews, victims of abuse and neglect show higher rates of substance abuse, depression, post-traumatic stress disorder (PTSD) and anxiety disorders, suicide, conduct disorders, oppositional disorders, attention deficit/hyperactivity disorder, and eating disorders (Paolucci et al., 2001; Kendall-Tackett et al., 1993; Berliner and Elliot, 2002; Cohen, et al., 2003; Rogers, 2003; Evans et al., 2005; Levitan et al., 1998; Gisese et al., 1998; Zlotnick et al., 2001; Miller et al., 1993; Kaplan et al., 1999).

Researchers have also documented a higher incidence of general health problems among adult survivors of victimization: more medical consultations (Felitti, 1991), more surgery (Kendall-Tackett et al., 2000), and higher risk of having one or more chronic pain syndromes (Kendall-Tackett, 2000).

Neurobiological Consequences

Neuroanatomical Changes

From the standpoint of neurobiology, exposure to abuse during specific sensitive periods may produce enhanced stress responsiveness. Early stress, in fact, can influence neurogenesis, synaptic overproduction and pruning, and myelination. Studies of the biological correlates of abuse and neglect are still relatively rare, especially studies that include children or adolescents as subjects. Nonetheless, several structural and functional neurobiological consequences of early traumatic events have been identified: they include reduced corpus callosum size; attenuated development of the left neocortex, hippocampus, and amygdala; enhanced electrical irritability in limbic structures; and reduced functional activity of the cerebellar vermis (Teicher et al., 2003). Some studies show the presence of neuroanatomical alterations: smaller intracranial and cerebral volumes have been found in abused children compared with matched controls (De Bellis et al., 1999), and a greater impact has been documented in boys rather than girls. Brain volumes were strongly correlated with age of onset (positively) and duration of abuse (negatively). Adults with PTSD associated with severe childhood physical or sexual abuse show a decreased hippocampal size, which may explain memory impairment (Bremner et al., 2003). In a population of psychiatric inpatient children with a history of physical or sexual abuse, frontotemporal and anterior brain electrophysiological abnormalities were found (Ito et al., 1993).

Endocrine, Autonomic, and Behavioral Stress Responsiveness

According to Heim and Nemeroff (2001), who summarized findings from animal and human studies, early stress may induce hyperactivity and sensitization of central nervous system corticotropin releasing factor, resulting in enhanced endocrine, autonomic, and behavioral stress responsiveness. De Bellis and Putnam (1994) found an increased morning-plasma-cortisol level in a sample of sexually abused girls, while King et al. (2001) showed a significant reduction. Hormonal changes, including changes in the hypothalamic-pituitary-adrenal axis, have also been related to physical abuse (Hart et al., 1996). In particular, Hart and colleagues reported elevated afternoon-cortisol levels in maltreated children, as well as an unexpected pattern of increased afternoon-cortisol levels in depressed maltreated children, which was not found in depressed nonmaltreated children. Differences in growth hormone levels of physically maltreated and comparison children have also been found, suggesting delayed growth as a possible correlate of maltreatment (Jensen et al., 1991).

Alterations in the structure and in the functioning of these areas may represent the biological substratum for the amnesiac, dissociative, anxiogenic, and disinhibitory aspects of PTSD; for aggressive behaviors; and for difficulties in information processing (attention, language, etc.). Neurobiological changes, as a consequence of early abuse, play a significant role in the emergence of a wide array of psychiatric disorders (Teicher et al., 2003; Heim and Nemeroff, 2001). As reviewed by Kendall-Tackett (2000), the chronic state of hyperarousal due to past traumatic events can sensitize the victims to current life stressors and play a role in the development of sequelae of PTSD, depression, and irritable bowel syndrome.

Developmental Consequences

Most research focuses on psychiatric outcomes of child abuse and neglect, but psychological consequences are best described as a process that unfolds over time. According to a developmental psychopathology model, each stage of development confronts children with new challenges. An individual who has adaptively met the developmental tasks of a particular stage will be better equipped to meet successive new challenges in development. In contrast, incompetence in development leads to difficulties or maladaptive efforts to resolve the challenges of a certain period. The progression is probabilistic, not inevitable: changes in the environment may lead to improvements in the ability to deal with developmental challenges, resulting in a redirection in the developmental course (Cicchetti, 2002; Cummings et al., 2000; Cicchetti and Cohen, 1995). Using this model, Cicchetti and Toth (1997) have described how child abuse and neglect may disrupt the normal course of child development, such as deformation of attachments, affects regulation, the self system, and peer relationships.

Academic Performance

During the last decade, studies have consistently documented that childhood maltreatment may impair the development of cognitive abilities and subsequent academic performance. Severe cognitive and language problems are frequently associated with early abuse and neglect (McFadyen and Kitson, 1996; Hildyard and Wolfe, 2002). Abused children and adolescents may also show a negative cognitive style, tending to attribute the occurrence of negative events to internal, stable, and global causes. This may leave the child with a higher sense of danger and adversity in the environment, leading to chronic low self-esteem and feelings of helplessness, powerlessness, and depression (Gibb, 2002).

According to Van der Kolk (1994), early trauma may interfere with semantic memory and may render an adult particularly vulnerable to post-trauma flashbacks, physiological arousal, and kinesthetic memories of the abuse.

Social Functioning

Deficits in social functioning of abused and neglected children have been found in a number of studies. In cases of abused infants, these deficits may be seen as insecure patterns of attachment (Cicchetti and Barnett, 1992) which can influence later peer and intimate relationships, revictimization, or victimization of others. Emotional neglect appears to be particularly detrimental in the beginning stages of life: over the course of several months, emotionally neglected children may have very severe attachment problems (Hildyard and Wolfe, 2002). Because caregivers provide a model for the child and teach him or her how to manage a stressful situation, maltreated children may have severe difficulties in adapting to any form of stress, as they are deprived of positive adult relationships, lack models of problem solving, and have no trust in the predictability of the future.

Physically abused children have been found to be less popular and more disliked than their nonabused peers; even with friends they show less intimacy and more conflicts than nonabused children (Parker and Herrera, 1996). Similarly, abused adolescents also report impaired patterns of attachment, engage in more aggressive peer relationships, and display more abusive behavior in dating relationships (Wolfe et al., 1998).

Although neglected children appear to have less coping abilities and to be less likely to exhibit externalizing problems than physically abused children, they also may show deficits in social functioning such as greater peer conflicts and fewer reciprocated friendships (Bolger et al., 1998). Interpersonal problems of maltreated children can be understood as relating to emotional-skills deficits (understanding appropriate emotional responses to interpersonal situations) and to limited social problem-solving skills (Rogosch et al., 1995).

Family violence creates social isolation, fragmentation of social networks, and disruption in familial support; many consequences are still evident in adult life. Adult survivors seem to be more frequently dissatisfied with their present relationships, which are often exploitative or victimizing (Fleming et al., 1999). Revictimization is relatively common among adult survivors of childhood abuse, even in community samples (Fergusson et al., 1997). Early sexual abuse represents, for example, a risk factor for a range of interpersonal dysfunctions among adult female survivors, including problems with intimate partner relations, disturbed sexual functioning, and difficulties when in a parental role (DiLillo, 2001).

Behavioral Aspects

An increasing number of studies have also reported that victims of violence are more likely to show high levels of impulsivity and irritability, aggressive behaviors with adults and peers, and delinquent behaviors (Kaplan et al., 1999). Children who experienced physical abuse appear to be 1.9 times as likely to be arrested for violence, and victims of neglect were 1.6 times as likely to be arrested for violence as control participants (Gushurst, 2003). Of maltreated adolescents of a longitudinal study, 74% had at least one adjustment problem, such as clinically deviant levels of aggression, trouble with police, running away from home, pregnancy or impregnating someone, and gang membership, compared with 43% of adolescents who had not been maltreated (Gushurst, 2003).

Risk-taking behaviors and sexualized behaviors appear to be also associated with child abuse. Physically abused children and adolescents are more likely than their nonabused peers to take part in behaviors endangering their health, including cigarette smoking, substance use, and sexual risk taking (Riggs et al., 1990). Sexual risk taking may explain why physical abuse and neglect have also been associated with teenage parenthood for both males and females (Herrenkohl et al., 1998). However, sexualized behaviors are more evident in the case of young children exposed to sexual abuse, proximally to the moment of the abuse (Putnam, 2003). Similarly, rates of risky sexual behaviors are higher in survivors of childhood sexual abuse (Fergusson et al., 1997) and so are rates of earlier pregnancies (Fiscella et al., 1998).

RESILIENCE

An extensive literature has documented over the past thirty years the maladaptive outcomes associated with child abuse and neglect, and a smaller set of studies addressed resilience and protective factors, reporting that some individuals exposed to different adverse events manifest little or no symptomatology.

Little is known about asymptomatic children and even less is known about what happens when abused and neglected children enter adolescence and adulthood. The majority of the studies in this field concerns child sexual abuse. It is estimated, for example, that between 20% and 44% of adults who were sexually abused during their childhood show no apparent sign of negative outcome (Himelein and McElrath, 1996; Spaccarelli, 1994).

The term *resilience* refers to both an individual maintaining his or her adaptive behavior despite the presence of risk factors and maintaining or reestablishing his or her level of functioning in the presence of danger or after a trauma. However, there is a general lack of consensus regarding the definition, conceptualization, operationalization, and measurement of the construct of resilience. This leads to confusion and to inability to compare results across studies.

A number of factors make the concept of resilience particularly difficult to define: (1) avoiding negative outcomes may be due to constitutional as well as environmental factors; (2) successful adaptation of an individual exposed to a high risk situation may affect only one domain of functioning; and (3) it may be time limited. On the one side, investigators may not examine the injured domain or may fail to measure it adequately. On the other side, some children may develop symptoms that are not evident at the time of the assessment. In the specific case of CSA, for example, it is estimated that up to 40% of sexually abused children, evaluated with standard instruments, have few or no symptoms but also that 10% to 20% of them will deteriorate over the next twelve to eighteen months (Finkelhor and Berliner, 1995).

Despite these difficulties, many authors tried to operationalize the concept of resilience when analyzing adjustment consequences of early abuse and neglect. In some cases, it was referred to a single factor, in others it was associated with different areas of functioning. McGloin and Widom (2001), for example, operationalized the construct of resilience across several domains of functioning: employment, homelessness, education, social activity, psychiatric disorders, substance abuse, official arrest records, and self-report of violence. According to this definition, they found that 22% of 676 abused and neglected children, when followed up into young adulthood, appeared to be resilient across several domains of functioning and at different time periods (McGloin and Widom, 2001).

The high variability in the operalization of the construct led to inevitable cautions. With regard to this issue, Cicchetti and colleagues (1993) underlined the importance of assessing various domains of interpersonal functioning as well as including a temporal dimension in order to capture the dynamic nature of child and adolescent development.

WHAT INFLUENCES OUTCOME?

There is evidence that the same type of abuse may have different outcomes in different subjects. At the same time different types of abuse may have similar consequences. As stated by the U.S. Surgeon General's Report on Children and Mental Health (1999), "psychopathology in childhood arises from the complex, multilayered interactions of specific characteristics of the child (including biological, psychological and genetic factors), his or her environment (including parent, sibling, family relations, peer and neighborhood factors, school and community factors, and the larger social-cultural context) and the specific manner in which these factors interact with and shape each other over the course of development."

Number of Risk Factors

The number of variables involved—as well as methodological limitations— mostly influence research outcomes that are often contradictory. Child abuse, in fact, is associated with several risk factors that may account for the apparent relation between abusive behavior and psychological problems: poverty, troubled family environment, as well as genetic liability. Similarly, the effects of these factors may interact with the consequences of abuse. For example, a study by Wind and Silvern (1994) showed that the experience of sexual abuse itself was related to later PTSD symptoms, while depression and low self-esteem were more closely related to a lack of parental warmth.

Moreover, it has to be considered that different forms of child abuse and neglect often coexist. For example, while psychological maltreatment may exist independently, it was found in 90% of children who had been physically abused and neglected (Claussen and Crittenden, 1991) and seems to be more strongly predictive of subsequent impairment than the severity of physical abuse itself (Hart et al., 1996). Similarly, 40% of CSA victims appear to have been exposed also to physical and emotional abuse (Bowen et al., 2000).

Therefore it is not possible to draw a simple cause-effect model, establishing secure links between a specific act of abuse and poor mental health or adjustment problems. However, we can identify some general patterns of variables associated with psychological consequences; among them the nature of the abusive act, individual characteristics of the victim, the nature of the relationship between the child and the abuser, and the response of others to the abuse.

The Nature of the Abusive Act

Subtype of event, severity, and level of exposure seem to predict risk for later psychiatric symptoms (Brown et al., 1999; Fergusson et al., 1996a; Fergusson et al., 1996b). For example, sexually abused children generally appear to display more reexperiencing, avoidance, and hyperarousal phenomena (PTSD symptoms) compared with physically abused and nonabused populations (Deblinger et al., 1989). Hyperarousal may consist of sleep difficulties, hypervigilance, startle response, and intrusive thoughts (Briere and Elliot, 1994). Unlike physical or sexual abuse, which is usually incident specific, neglect often involves chronic situations that are not easily identified as specific incidents. Compared to physically abused children and adolescents, neglected children appear to have more severe cognitive and academic deficits and experience social withdrawal, limited peer interactions, and internalizing problems (Hildyard and Wolfe, 2002). However, psychological and psychopathological consequences in many cases may be related to the coexistence of different forms of abuse and neglect.

Although counterintuitive, some evidence suggests that neglect occurring in the absence of other forms of abuse is associated with worse outcomes than neglect accompanied by physical abuse (Hildyard and Wolfe, 2002).

In the specific case of CSA, risk of psychopathology is increased in case of intrafamilial abuse—which is more likely to last longer and be repeated—and when the child has a close relationship with the abuser (Kendall-Tackett et al., 1993; Trickett et al., 2001). Similarly, an important role is played by type of contact (abuse with contact has poorer psychopathological outcome than abuse without contact; Kendler et al., 2000; Fergusson et al., 1996) and age of the abuser (if the adult is substantially older than the child, there is a worse outcome; Finkelhor et al., 1990).

In general, it seems that acute events that produce relatively little change in the social milieu tend to carry lower risk to either ongoing traumatic events or abuses that lead to long-term disruptions in children's social environment (Terr, 1991).

Recent research has suggested that chronicity, rather than type or severity of maltreatment, best predicts negative outcomes (Bolger and Patterson, 2001).

Characteristics of Children and Families

As far as characteristics of children are involved, sexually abused girls are more likely to manifest internalizing behaviors (depression, anxiety, post-traumatic stress, suicidal ideation), while boys tend to display more oppositional behaviors, aggression, impulsivity, substance abuse, and higher levels of eroticism (Feiring et al., 1999). The assumption that male victims are less adversely affected than females has been discussed by Garnefski and Diekstra (1997), who found in boys considerably more emotional and behavioral problems, including tendency to suicide, than in their female counterparts.

Although the assumption that abuse that occurs at an earlier age is more harmful than abuse that occurs later, no linear relationship has been found (Finkelhor and Kendall-Tackett, 1997). Each stage of development has its own vulnerabilities and its own protections.

Family factors such as parental conflict, parental psychopathology, impaired parent-child relationship, and family disruption that operate prior to or concurrently with CSA may also adversely affect outcome (Fergusson et al., 1996b).

Protective Factors and Resilience

Why, despite harsh life circumstances, do some people survive and later thrive after experiencing trauma? What are the processes associated with a successful departure from abuse and neglect?

Many studies evidenced a range of factors that are hypothesized to protect against the effects of exposure to adverse events. The development of adjustment difficulties is less likely in children and adolescents exposed to abuse that is less severe and of limited duration (Bolger and Patterson, 2001; Fergusson and Mullen, 1999).

A child's personality factors, personal attitudes, and coping skills play an important role in moderating the effect of abuse and neglect (Luthar, 1993; Rutter, 1985). Adaptive cognitive strategies are represented by searching for support, disclosing the abuse, and giving a meaning to the abuse. Conversely, avoidance is not found to be an adaptive coping strategy (Dufour et al., 2000).

Family characteristics, parental attachment, and quality of interpersonal, peer relationships may be influential in determining responses to adverse events. Children reared in supportive and nurturant families are more likely to positively adapt to abuse and neglect (Luthar, 1993; Rutter, 1985).

In the specific case of CSA, several studies indicate that important protecting factors against the development of adjustment problems appear to be the nature and the quality of peer and family relationships (Lynskey and Fergusson, 1997).

Even in the area of resilience, more studies on physical abuse, neglect, and psychological abuse are needed. Moreover, future work needs to address the mechanism that differentiates resilient abused and neglected individuals from their nonresilient abused and neglected peers.

PREVENTION

Although the Convention on the Rights of the Child states that there is a universal need for primary prevention of child abuse and neglect, most interventions focus on tertiary prevention by working with perpetrators and victims after abuse has already occurred. In spite of the importance of tertiary prevention programs in reducing future risk for revictimization, more attention should be paid to primary prevention programs. A World Health Organization report on global violence (Krug et al., 2002), for example, suggests that an ecological model encompassing the four levels of biological and personal factors, close relationships, community context, and broad social factors can be used as a framework for violence and abuse prevention.

Prevention of Physical Abuse

An example of secondary prevention is represented by school-based programs for the prevention of sexual abuse, focused on teaching school children how to resist abuse after it starts and to report it immediately to trusted adults (Daro,

1991). According to two recent meta-analyses, school-based programs are effective in increasing children's self-defense knowledge and skills. The most effective programs were relatively long, involved children in role-playing and taught children skills as well as information (Ripens et al., 1997; Davis and Gidycz, 2000). Conversely, some authors (Taal and Edelaar, 1997) note some possible negative effects such as increased anxiety and feelings of being less in control.

Primary prevention strategies aim to prevent abusive acts from happening. While sexual abuse prevention strategies are often school-based programs, which focus on educating children and youth in avoidance of unsafe situations, primary prevention strategies for physical abuse usually focus on potential abusers (Wurtele and Owens, 1997). As we know that the most serious forms of physical abuse occur in the first three years of life, a great opportunity for prevention is educating parents in high-risk families about childhood development. The first step of prevention is therefore to identify the at-risk families. According to an interesting review by Kaplan et al. (1999), efforts at primary prevention of physical child abuse and neglect have focused on targeting at-risk parents, such as teenagers, single parents, substance-abusing parents, or parents with cognitive limitations. Most prevention programs use home visits to provide some basic social support and education concerning normal child development and parenting strategies.

Early efforts to support the family and strengthen parenting abilities may be particularly successful and cost effective (Dubowitz, 2002). Reviewing home-visitation prevention programs, Olds and Kitzman (1993) concluded that intensive and comprehensive programs are helpful in changing the behavior of parents at risk for perpetrating maltreatment, improving the home environment, and decreasing child behavioral difficulties. There is now some evidence that the benefits of home-visitation programs are durable. A long-term follow-up of a relatively intense nurse visitation program reported that comparison mothers were almost twice as likely to be reported for child abuse or neglect over a fifteen-year period compared with high-risk mothers participating in the program (Olds et al., 1997).

In the United States two home-based models are particularly applied: the healthy families model and the Olds model. They are both focused on socially high-risk families, rely on frequent home visiting (from the prenatal period over a period of time), provide care in the context of a helping relationship, use a curriculum to guide the home visitor, model effective parenting, and connect families to community services.

Some studies demonstrated that families can be helped but also that home visiting does not represent the solution for every problem in families and that well-designed randomized controlled trials are very difficult to conduct (Leventhal, 2001). Therefore, the true effectiveness of many home-visiting programs remains unclear.

However, researchers highlighted several factors that likely contribute to program success:

1. Programs should have clear objectives tied to theoretical models, such as models of behavioural change . . . ;
2. Programs should be perceived as relevant and needed by the population served . . . ;
3. Interventions need to have structured curricula to assure reliability of content, methods, and timing of activities. However, curricula need to allow for some flexibility in order to address differences in populations served. . . .
4. Services must be provided by skilled home visitors with adequate credentials, training, and support. Cultural competence should be considered in hiring and training of home visitors. Debate continues regarding the importance of nurses versus paraprofessionals as service providers.
5. Intensive services should be provided, beginning as early as possible. . . . Services should be provided at least weekly if needed and should be provided long term (several years). . . .
6. Services should include a health improvement component in addition to provision of social services. . . . Such a component may reduce injuries and ingestions and decrease emergency room visits, in addition to improving overall child health. (Rubin et al., 2001, 397)

Need for Further Research

A more limited number of studies examined prevention efforts in the field of child physical abuse directly involving children and adolescents. These studies indicate that even preschool children can learn and retain concepts such as the definition of physical abuse and how to disclose it (Peraino, 1990).

Recent studies reported that both a school-based prevention program (Oldfield et al., 1996) and an intensive media program (Hoefnagels and Baartman, 1997) resulted in significantly more abuse disclosures. However, some unanswered questions are still debated. On one side, it is clearly difficult to evaluate the effectiveness and impact of media campaigns and mass educational programs. On the other side, there is little evidence that classroom instruction reduces the incidence of abuse; in fact, a really effective prevention program should prevent potential molesters from approaching children. According to Hunter and Figueredo (2000), comprehensive treatment for adolescent sexual offenders and for boys who have been sexually abused (and their families) may be an important way to prevent sexual abuse.

We also have to deal with several barriers, including the low and declining number of treatment programs for sexual offenders, the harsh social stigma attached to sexual offenders, and the limited research efforts in the field of the etiology and treatment effectiveness (Daro, 1994).

Prevention of Child Emotional Maltreatment

Another area in need of increased research is the prevention of child emotional maltreatment by parents. Several studies reported that parent-child interactions in the case of mothers with affective or substance-abuse disorders may be characterized by verbal aggression and decreased emotional nurturance (Hawley et al., 1995). Nevertheless, interventions focused on mothers with affective disorders have been found to be effective in reducing dysfunctional parent-child emotional interactions (Beardslee et al., 1997) and enhancing rates of secure mother-child attachment (Lyons-Ruth et al., 1990).

TREATMENT

An increasing recognition of the prevalence of child abuse and neglect and their effects on children's and adolescents' mental health has led to a rapid growth of treatments. Despite increased attention, few rigorously conducted clinical trials compared the effects of potentially beneficial treatments and control treatments in children and adolescents exposed to abuse and neglect, the majority address CSA.

Reviews of these studies have been conducted in the past (Finkelhor and Berliner, 1995; Berliner, 1997; Stevenson, 1999; King et al., 2000). More recent reviews have been conducted by Pine and Cohen (2002), Cohen et al. (2003), and Ramchandani and Jones (2003). According to these reviews, cognitive behavior therapy (CBT) for sexually abused children received the most empirical support.

Six studies used CBT to target symptoms of PTSD or anxiety among sexually abused children (King et al., 2000; Cohen and Mannarino, 1996, 1998; Deblinger et al., 1996, 1999; Celano et al., 1996; Berliner and Saunders, 1996). As highlighted by Pine and Cohen (2002), each of them applied sound methodological designs in examining treatment effects, used random assignment, and accepted clinical measures to document effects of treatment.

All the studies targeted children and adolescents (ages three to seventeen years) with a wide range of symptoms: PTSD, mood and anxiety disorders, and behavior disorders. As far as psychiatric symptoms are concerned, the six studies provided relatively strong evidence of the CBT efficacy in reducing children's symptomatology. They evidenced the benefits of CBT over other forms of treatment, including nondirective play therapy, supportive counseling, usual community treatment, or no intervention. It is not yet clear whether the benefits of CBT are the result of exposure, cognitive techniques, coping skills or relaxation training, behavioral interventions, or some combination.

As highlighted by Cohen and Mannarino (1996, 2000), single versus multiple abuse episodes per se did not predict treatment outcome. Indeed, similar interventions might be effective for abused children regardless of the number of traumatic episodes experienced.

Some of these studies have included nonabusing parents in the treatment and shown that CBT not only improves children's symptomatology, but also decreases parental distress or improves parental perceptions. Providing CBT to parents concerning children's symptoms significantly reduces depression and externalizing symptoms (Deblinger et al., 1996, 1999; King et al., 2000). In the study of Celano et al. (1996) the CBT group reported significantly more improvement in parental support for the child and accurate parental cognitions about the abuse.

Kolko (1996) provided empirical support for the efficacy of family therapy as well as CBT for physically abused children. In a randomized controlled trial, he compared three types of intervention: abuse-focused CBT (provided individually to child and parent), family therapy, and routine community services (RCS). Both CBT and family therapy were shown to be superior to RCS in reducing child-to-parent violence, child externalizing behaviors, parental distress and abuse risk, and family conflict.

Another randomized controlled trial is a twelve-year follow-up study comparing abused children assigned to a therapeutic preschool or routine care: treated children had lower levels of violent delinquency and were significantly less likely to have clinical levels of aggression and internalizing behavior problems as reported by caretakers (Moore et al., 1998).

The addition of group therapy to family network therapy did not produce any additional improvement for sexually abused children (Hyde et al., 1995). The same results were found in a study of sexually abused children that compared individual and group therapy (Perez, 1998).

Finally, there are no empirically rigorous studies regarding pharmacological treatments of children and adolescents exposed to abuse. Nonetheless, several noncontrolled studies have been conducted on samples of abused children with PTSD symptoms (Looff et al., 1995; Harmon and Riggs, 1996). A number of points arise out of these reports:

- There is evidence that children exposed to sexual and physical abuse can benefit from a CBT treatment.
- Symptomatic children are more likely to show benefits from therapy.
- Although the evidence is less strong, studies suggest that older children and adolescents might benefit from the same format of CBT.

- The involvement of the nonabusing parent or carer in the therapy is associated with better outcomes for the child.
- A wide range of other treatments is currently used (play therapy, anger management training, social skills training, etc.); however, they have to demonstrate not only their effectiveness but also that they do no harm.

There are many open questions related to treatment that mental health professionals have to deal with in the next years.

Addressing Multicultural Issues

An important issue concerns the relevance of addressing multicultural issues in treatment. Increasing attention is being paid by researchers to child mental health treatment (Lynch and Hanson, 1998) and child abuse victims (Fontes, 1995). There is evidence that ethnicity may influence symptomatology following traumatic events as well as treatment-seeking behaviors. These findings underscore that more research is needed, not only with regard to effective treatments for child abuse victims, but also concerning ethnic minority victims. We need better screening instruments and more acceptable interventions for ethnic minority children, who may be both more symptomatic and less likely to seek or receive treatment following the abuse (Cohen et al., 2001).

Severity of Abuse

Another interesting issue is related to the association between severity of child abuse and treatment efforts. On the premise that more severe maltreatment results in worse outcome for children, more resources tend to be devoted to extreme cases and lower severity cases may be overlooked. Failing to intervene in the lower severity cases may have long-standing detrimental consequences; prior research (Manly et al., 1994) suggests that low severity maltreatment, especially when chronic, results in negative child outcomes that are similar to those of more severe cases.

Indications for Treatment

More attention should also be paid to questions concerning indications for treatment, timing, and targets. The presence of asymptomatic children, in fact, may reflect sleeper effects, in which some children exposed to abuse will eventually develop symptoms that are not evident at the time of the assessment.

Focus on Protective Factors

According to an ecological model that evidences the coexistence among risk and protective factors, the development of new psychotherapeutic interventions may benefit from a recent focus on protective factors leading to adaptive outcomes in high-risk children. Some characteristics of maltreated children showing resilient social and behavioral functioning have already been identified, including self-esteem, the ability to modulate impulses and feelings, and the ability to adapt to environmental challenges (Cicchetti and Linch, 1993).

Access to Treatment

Another issue is the access to treatment and care of high-risk children and families: according to the U.S. Department of Health and Human Services (1999) only 20% of children and adolescents with a mental disorder receive needed care. As a result, mental health and adjustment problems commonly associated with abuse and neglect are likely to go untreated until access to appropriate mental health services for victims is increased.

CONCLUSION

Children from abusive and neglectful families grow up in environments that fail to provide consistent and appropriate opportunities for development.

The first point of interest in this topic is the discussion of the possibility of establishing universal and definitive definitions of the abuse and its subtypes.

Second, the comprehension of the sequelae of the abusive event benefits from an ecological approach, which considers maltreatment as the result of complex interactions among risk factors within the abuser (e.g., psychiatric disorder), the child (e.g., age, gender), his or her family (e.g., single-parent families), and their environment (e.g., social isolation, low socioeconomic status). The final outcome, during childhood and in adulthood, is not likely to improve until each of these factors is addressed.

An important issue of abuse research with children is represented by the limited generalizability of findings, which are often event, population, and culture specific. Effects on children are known to be potentially severe and long lasting: more investigations with better methodological designs, addressing psychological sequelae and management of abuse impact, are needed. Knowledge derived from research in the field of developmental psychopathology bears considerable relevance to the prevention and treatment of high-risk and maladaptive conditions such as child abuse and neglect.

Much more support is needed for the training of child and adolescent psychiatrists and other child mental health professionals in the area of child maltreatment prevention, intervention, and research.

Another challenge is the implementation of well-designed studies to understand current services utilization by abused and neglected children and adolescents and the effectiveness of intervention strategies according to type of abuse.

Much current research remains pathology driven, with a few studies focusing on youth resilience and protective factors. Therefore promotion of protective factors as well as early recognition and intervention in case of risk factors should be the first and most important goal for mental health professionals.

REFERENCES

APSAC. "Psychosocial evaluation of suspected psychological maltreatment in children and adolescents." *Practice Guidelines*. American Professional Society on the Abuse of Children (1995).

Bagley, C., Wood, M., and Young, L. "Victim to abuser: Mental health and behavioural sequels to child sexual abuse in a community survey of young adult males." *Child Abuse and Neglect* 18, no. 8 (1994):683–697.

Barnett, D., Manly, J.T., and Cicchetti, D. "Defining child maltreatment: the interface between policy and research." Pp. 7–73 in *Child Abuse, Child Development and Social Policy*, edited by D. Cicchetti and S. Toth. Norwood, NJ: Ablex, 1993.

Beardslee, W.R., Salt, P., Versage, E.M., Gladstone, T.R.G., Wright, E.M., and Rothberg, P.C. "Sustained change in parents receiving preventive interventions for families with depression." *American Journal of Psychiatry* 154 (1997):510–515.

Behl, L.E., Conyngham, H.A., and May, P.F. "Trends in child maltreatment literature." *Child Abuse and Neglect* 27 (2003):215–229.

Beitchman, J.H., Zucker, K.J., Hood, J.E., et al. "A review of the short term effects of child sexual abuse." *Child Abuse Neglect* 15 (1991):537–556.

Belsky J, "Child maltreatment: An ecological integration." *American Psychologist* 35, no. 4 (1980):320–325.

Berliner, L. "Intervention with children who experience trauma." Pp. 491–514 in *Developmental Perspectives on Trauma: Theory, Research and Intervention*, edited by D. Cicchetti and S. Toth. Rochester, NY: University of Rochester Press, 1997.

Berliner, L., and Elliott, D. "Sexual abuse of children in the field of child maltreatment." Pp. 55–78 in *The APSAC Handbook on Child Maltreatment* (2nd ed.), edited by J. Myers, L. Berliner, J. Myers. London: Sage, 2002.

Berliner, L., and Saunders, B. "Treating fear and anxiety in sexually abused children: results of a two-year follow up study to child maltreatment." *Child Maltreatment* 1 (1996):294–309.

Black, D.A., Heyman, R.E., and Slap, A.M. "Risk factors for child physical abuse." *Aggression and Violent Behavior* 6 (2001):121–188.

Bolger, K.E., Patterson, C.J., and Kupersmidt, J.B. "Peer relationships and self-esteem among children who have been maltreated." *Child Development* 69 (1998): 1171–1197.

Bolger, K.E., and Patterson, C.J. "Pathways from child maltreatment to internalizing problems: Perceptions of control as mediators and moderators." *Developmental Psychopathology* 13, no. 4 (2001):913–940.

Bowen, K. "Child abuse and domestic violence in families of children seen for suspected sexual abuse." *Clinical Pediatrics* 29, no. 1 (2000):33–40.

Bremner, J.D., Vythilingam, M., Vermetten, M., Southwick, S.M., McGlashan, T., Nazeer, A., Khan, S., Vaccarino, L.V., Soufer, R., and Garg, P.K. "MRI and PET study of deficits in hippocampal structure and function in women with childhood sexual abuse and posttraumatic stress disorder." *American Journal of Psychiatry* 160 (2003):924–932.

Briere, J.N., and Elliot, D.M. "Immediate and long-term impacts of child sexual abuse." *The Future of Children* 4 (1994):54–69.

Bronfenbrenner, U. *The ecology of human development.* Cambridge, MA: Harvard University Press, 1979.

Brown, J., Cohen, P., Johnson, J.G., and Smailes, E.M. "Childhood abuse and neglect: specificity of effects on adolescent and young adult depression and suicidality." *Journal of the American Academy of Child Adolescent Psychiatry* 38 (1999):1490–1496.

Celano, M., Hazzard, A., Webb, C., and McCall, C. "Treatment of traumatogenic beliefs among sexually abused girls and their mothers: An evaluation study." *Journal Abnormal Child Psychology* 24 (1996):1–17.

Chadwick, D. "Letter to the editor: Response to why is sexual abuse declining? A survey of state child protection administrators." *Child Abuse Neglect* (2002):887–88.

Cicchetti, D., "Developmental psychopathology: Reactions, reflections, and projections." *Developmental Review* 13 (1993):471–502.

Cicchetti, D., "The impact of social experience on neurobiological systems: Illustration from a constructivist view of child maltreatment." *Cognitive Development* 17 (2002):1407–1428.

Cicchetti, D., and Barnett, D. "Attachment organization in maltreated preschoolers" *Developmental Psychopathology* 3 (1992):397–411.

Cicchetti, D., and Cohen, D.J. "Perspectives on developmental psychopathology." Pp. 3–20 in *Developmental Psychopathology, Vol. 1, Theory and Methods*, edited by Cicchetti, D. and Cohen, D.J. New York: Wiley, 1995.

Cicchetti, D., and Linch, M. "Toward an ecological/transactional model of community violence and child maltreatment: Consequences for children's development" *Psychiatry* 56 (1993):96–118.

Cicchetti, D., and Toth, S. (Eds.), *Developmental Perspectives on trauma: Theory, Research, and Intervention,* Rochester Symposium on Developmental Psychopathology, vol. 8 (1997). Rochester, NY: University of Rochester Press.

Claussen, A., and Crittenden, P. "Physical and psychological maltreatment: Relations among types of maltreatment." *Child Abuse and Neglect* 15 (1991):5–18.

Cohen, J., Mannarino, A. "A treatment outcome study for sexually abused preschool children: Initial findings." *Journal of the American Academy of Child and Adolescent Psychiatry* 35 (1996):42–50.

Cohen, J.A., and Mannarino, A.P. "Factors that mediate treatment outcome of sexually abused preschool children: Six- and 12-month follow-up." *Journal of the American Academy of Child and Adolescent Psychiatry* 37 (1998):44–51.

Cohen, J.A., and Mannarino, A.P. "Predictors of treatment outcome in sexually abused children." *Child Abuse and Neglect* 24 (2000):983–994.

Cohen, J.A., Berliner, L., and Mannarino, A.P. "Psychosocial and pharmacological intervention for child crime victims." *Journal of Traumatic Stress* 16 no. 2 (2003):175–186.

Cohen, J.A., Deblinger, E., Mannarino, A.P., and de Arellano, M.A. "The importance of culture in treating abused and neglected children: An empirical review." *Child Maltreatment* 6 (2001):148–157.

Cohen, J.A., Mannarino, A.P., Zhitova, A.C., and Capone, M.E. "Treating child abuse related posttraumatic stress and comorbid substance abuse in adolescents." *Child Abuse and Neglect* 27 (2003):1345–1365.

Cummings, E.M., Davies, P.T., and Campbell, S.B. *Developmental Psychopathology and Family Process. Theory, Research and Clinical Implications.* New York: Guilford Press, 2000.

Cummings, E.M. "Marital conflict, abuse and adversity in the family and child adjustment: A developmental psychopathology perspective." Pp. 3–26 in *Child Abuse: New Directions in Prevention and Treatment across the Life Span*, edited by Wolfe, D.A., McMahon, R.J., and Josef, R. Thousand Oaks, CA: Sage Publications, 1997.

Daro, D. *The Child Abuse Prevention Movement: Aggregate Gains and Shortcomings.* Chicago: National Committee to Prevent Child Abuse, 1991.

Daro, D. "Prevention of sexual abuse." *The Future of Children* 4 (1994):196–223.

Davis, M.K., and Gidycz, C.A. "Child sexual abuse prevention programs: A meta analysis." *Journal of Clinical Child Psychology* 29 (2000):257–265.

De Bellis, M., Keshavan, M., and Clark, D. et al. "Developmental traumatology, part II: Brain development." *Biological Psychiatry* 45 (1999):1271–1284.

De Bellis, M.D., and Putnam, F.W. "The psychobiology of childhood maltreatment." *Child and Adolescent Psychiatric Clinics North America* 3 (1994):1–16.

Deblinger, E., Lippman, J., and Steer, R. "Sexually abused children suffering posttraumatic stress symptoms: Initial treatment outcome findings." *Child Maltreatment* 1 (1996):310–321.

Deblinger, E., McLeer, S.V., Atkins, M.S., Ralphe, D., and Foa, E. "Posttraumatic stress in sexual abused, physically abused, and nonabused children." *Child Abuse and Neglect* 13 (1989):403–408.

Deblinger, E., Steer, R.A. and Lippman, J. "Two-year follow-up study of cognitive behavioral therapy for sexually abused children suffering post traumatic stress symptoms." *Child Abuse and Neglect* 23 (1999):1371–1378.

DiLillo, D. "Interpersonal functioning among women reporting a history of childhood sexual abuse: Empirical findings and methodological issues." *Clinical Psychology Review* 21 no. 4 (2001):553–576.

Dubowitz, H. "Preventing child neglect and physical abuse: A role for paediatricians." *Pediatrics in Review* 23 (2002):191–196.

Dufour, M.H., Nadeau, L., and Bertrand, K. "Les facteurs de résilience chez les victimes d'abus sexuel: état de la question." *Child Abuse and Neglect* 24, no. 6 (2000):781–797.

Edelson, J. "The overlap between child maltreatment and woman battering." *Violence Against Women* 5 (1999):134–154.

Ertem, I.O., Leventhal, J.M., and Dobbs, S. "Intergenerational continuity of child physical abuse: How good is the evidence?" *Lancet* 2 (2000):814–9.

Evans, E., Hawton, K., and Rodham, K. "Suicidal phenomena and abuse in adolescents: A review of epidemiological studies." *Child Abuse and Neglect* 29 (2005):45–58.

Feiring, C., Taska, L., and Lewis, M. "Age and gender differences in children's and adolescents' adaptation to sexual abuse." *Child Abuse and Neglect* 23 (1999):115–128.

Felitti, V.J. "Long-term medical consequences of incest, rape, and molestation." *Southern Medical Journal* 84 (1991):328–331.

Fergusson, D., Horwood, L., and Lynskey, M.T. "Childhood sexual abuse and psychiatric disorder in young adulthood, II: Psychiatric outcomes of childhood sexual abuse." *Journal of the American Academy of Child and Adolescent Psychiatry* 35 (1996):1365–1374.

Fergusson, D.M., Horwood, L.J., and Lynskey, M.T. "Childhood sexual abuse, adolescent sexual behaviors and sexual revictimization." *Child Abuse and Neglect* 21 (1997):789–803.

Fergusson, D.M., Lynskey, M.T., and Horwood, L.J. "Childhood sexual abuse and psychiatric disorder in young adulthood: I. Prevalence of sexual abuse and factors associated with sexual abuse." *Journal of the American Academy of Child and Adolescent Psychiatry* 35 (1996a):1355–1363.

Fergusson, D.M., Lynskey, T.L., and Horwood, L.J. "Childhood sexual abuse and psychiatric disorder in young adulthood, II: Psychiatric outcomes of childhood sexual abuse." *Journal of the American Academy of Child and Adolescent Psychiatry* 35 (1996b):1365–1374.

Fergusson, D.M., and Mullen, P.E. *Childhood Sexual Abuse: An Evidence-Based Perspective*. Thousand Oaks, CA: Sage Publications, 1999.

Finkelhor, D. "Epidemiological factors in the clinical identification of child sexual abuse." *Child Abuse and Neglect* 17 (1993):67–70.

Finkelhor, D., Hotaling, G., Lewis, I.A., and Smith, C. "Sexual abuse in a national survey of adult men and women: Prevalence, characteristics, and risk factors." *Child Abuse and Neglect* 14 (1990):19–28.

Finkelhor, D., and Kendall-Tackett, K.A. "A developmental perspective on the childhood impact of crime, abuse and violent victimization." Pp. 1–32 in *Rochester symposium on Developmental Psychopathology: Developmental Perspectives on Trauma*, Vol. 8, edited by Cicchetti, D., and Toth, S. Rochester, NY: University of Rochester Press, 1997.

Finkelhor, D., and Berliner, L. "Research on the treatment of sexually abused children: A review and recommendations." *Journal of the American Academy of Child and Adolescent Psychiatry* 34 (1995):1408–1423.

Fiscella, K., Kitzman, H., Cole, R., Sidora, K., and Olds, D. "Does child abuse predict adolescent pregnancy?" *Pediatrics* 101 (1998):620–624.

Fleming, J., Mullen, P.E., Sibthorpe, B., and Bammer, G. "The long-term impact of childhood sexual abuse in Australian women." *Child Abuse and Neglect* 23 (1999):145–159.

Fontes, L. *Sexual Abuse in Nine North American Cultures*. Thousand Oaks, CA: Sage, 1995.

Garnefski, N., and Diekstra, R. "Child sexual abuse and emotional and behavioural problems in adolescence: Gender differences." *Journal of the American Academy of Child and Adolescent Psychiatry* 36 (1997):323–329.

Gibb, B.E. "Childhood maltreatment and negative cognitive styles. A quantitative and qualitative review." *Clinical Psychology Review* 22 (2002):223–246.

Gisese, A., Thomas, M., Dubovsky, S., and Hilty, S. "The impact of a history of childhood abuse on hospital outcome of affective episodes." *Psychiatric Services* 49 (1998):77–81.

Glaser, D. "Emotional abuse and neglect (psychological maltreatment): A conceptual framework." *Child Abuse and Neglect* 26 (2002):697–714.

Gushurst, C.A. "Child abuse: Behavioral aspects and other associated problems." *Pediatric Clinics of North America* 50 (2003):919–938.

Hamarman, S., and Bernett, W. "Evaluating and reporting emotional abuse in children, parent-based, action based focus aids in clinical decision making." *Journal of the American Academy of Child and Adolescent Psychiatry* 39, no. 7 (2000):928–930.

Harmon, J.R., and Riggs, P.D. "Clinical perspectives: Clonidine for posttraumatic stress disorder in preschool children." *Journal of the American Academy of Child and Adolescent Psychiatry* 35 (1996):1247–1249.

Hart, S., Brassard, M., and Karlson, H. "Psychological maltreatment." Pp. 72–89 in *The APSAC Handbook on Child Abuse and Neglect,* edited by Berliner, L., Briere, J., Bulkley, J., Jenny, C., and Reid, T. London: Sage, 1996.

Hawley, T.L., Halle, T.G., Drasin, R.E., and Thomas, N.G. "Children of addicted mothers: Effects of the crack epidemic on the care giving environment and the development of preschoolers." *American Journal of Orthopsychiatry* 65 (1995):364–379.

Heim, C., and Nemeroff, C.B. "The role of childhood trauma in the neurobiology of mood and anxiety disorders: Preclinical and clinical studies." *Biological Psychiatry* 49 (2001):1023–1039.

Herrenkohl, E.C., Herrenkohl, R.C., Egolf, B.P., and Russo, M.J. "The relationship between early maltreatment and teenage parenthood." *Journal of Adolescence* 21 (1998):291–303.

Hildyard, K.L. and Wolfe, D.A. "Child Neglect: Developmental issues and outcome." *Child Abuse and Neglect* 26 (2002):679–695.

Himelein, M.J., and McElrath, J.A. "Resilient child sexual abuse survivors: Cognitive coping and illusion." *Child Abuse and Neglect* 20 (1996):747–758.

Hoefnagels, C., and Baartman, H. "On the threshold of disclosure: The effects of a mass media field experiment." *Child Abuse and Neglect* 21 (1997):557–573.

Hunter, J.A. and Figueredo, A.J. "The influence of personality and history of sexual victimisation in the prediction of juvenile perpetrated child molestation." *Behavior Modification* 24 (2000):241–263.

Hyde, C., Bentovim, A., and Monck, E. "Some clinical and methodological implications of a treatment outcome study of sexually abused children." *Child Abuse and Neglect* 19 (1995):1387–1399.

Ito, Y., Teicher, M., Glod, C., Harper, D., Magnus, E., and Gelbard, H. "Increased prevalence of electrophysiological abnormalities in children with psychological, physical and sexual abuse." *Journal of Neuropsychiatry* 5 (1993):401–408.

Jensen, J.B., Pease, J.J., Bensel, R., and Garfinkel, B.D. "Growth hormone response in sexually or physically abused boys." *Journal of the American Academy of Child and Adolescent Psychiatry* (1991):784–790.

Jones, L.M., and Finkelhor, D. "The decline in sexual abuse cases: Exploring the causes." *Bulletin* Washington, DC: U.S. Department of Justice, Office of Justice Program, Office of Juvenile Justice and delinquency Prevention, 2001.

Jones, L.M., Finkelhor, D., and Kopiec, K. "Why is sexual abuse declining? A survey of state child protection administrators." *Child Abuse and Neglect* (2001):1139–58.

Jones, L.M., and Finkelhor, D. "Letter to the editor: Response to David Chadwick." *Child Abuse and Neglect* (2002):889–9.

Kaplan, S.J., Pelcovitz, D., and Labruna, V. "Child and adolescent abuse and neglect research: A review of the past 10 years. Part I: Physical and emotional abuse and neglect." *Journal of the American Academy of Child and Adolescent Psychiatry* 38 no. 10 (1999):1214–1222.

Kendall-Tackett, K.A. "Physiological correlates of childhood abuse: Chronic hyperarousal in PTSD, depression and irritable bowel syndrome." *Child Abuse and Neglect* 24 (2000):799–810.

Kendall-Tackett, K.A., Marshall, R., and Ness, K.E. "Victimization, healthcare use, and health maintenance" *Family Violence and Sexual Assault Bulletin* 16 (2000):18–21.

Kendall-Tackett, K.A., Williams, L.M., and Finkelhor, D. "Impact of sexual abuse on children: A review and synthesis of recent empirical studies." *Psychological Bulletin* 113 (1993):164–180.

Kendler, K., Bulik, C., Silberg, J., Hettema, J., Myers, J., and Prescott, C. "Childhood sexual abuse and adult psychiatric and substance abuse disorders in women." *Archives of General Psychiatry* 57 (2000):953–959.

Kenny, M.C., and McEachern, A.G. "Racial, ethnic, and cultural factors of childhood sexual abuse: A selected review of the literature." *Clinical Psychological Review* 20 no. 7 (2000):905–922.

King, J., Mandansky, D., King, S., Fletcher, K., and Brewer, J. "Early sexual abuse and low cortisol." *Psychiatry Clin Neurosci* 55 (2001):71–74.

King, N.J., Tonge, B.J., Mullen, P., Myerson, N., Heyne, D. and Rollings, S. "Treating sexually abused children with posttraumatic stress symptoms: A randomized clinical trial." *Journal of the American Academy of Child and Adolescent Psychiatry* 39 (2000):1347–1355.

Kolko, D. "Individual cognitive-behavioral treatment and family therapy for physically abused children and their offending parents: A comparison of clinical outcomes." *Child Maltreatment* 1 (1996):322–342.

Korbin, J.E. "Culture and child maltreatment: Cultural competence and beyond." *Child abuse and Neglect* 26 (2002):637–644.

Krug, E.G., Mercy, J.A., and Dahlberg, L.L. "The world report on violence and health." *Lancet* 360 (2002):1083–1088.

Lab, D., Feigenbaum, J., and De Silva, P. "Mental health professionals' attitudes and practices towards male childhood sexual abuse." *Child Abuse and Neglect* 24 (2000): 391–409.

Leventhal, J.M. "The prevention of child abuse and neglect: Successfully out of the blocks." *Child Abuse and Neglect* 25 (2001):431–439.

Levitan, R., Parikh, S., Lesage, A., Hegadoren, K.M., Adams, M., Kennedy, S.H., and Goering, P.N. "Major depression in individuals with a history of childhood physical or sexual abuse: Relationship to neurovegetative." *American Journal of Psychiatry* 155 (1998):1746–1752.

Litrownik, A.J., Lau, A., English, D.J., Briggs, E., Newton, R.R., Romney, S., and Dubowitz, H. "Measuring the severity of child maltreatment." *Child Abuse and Neglect* 29, no. 5 (2005):553–73.

Looff, D., Grimley, P., Kuller, F., Martin, A., and Schonfield, L. "Carbamazepine for PTSD." *Journal of the American Academy of Child and Adolescent Psychiatry* 34 (1995):703–704.

Luthar, S.S. "Methodological and conceptual issues in research on childhood resilience." *Journal of Child Psychology and Psychiatry* 34 (1993):441–454.

Lynch, E.W., and Hanson, M.J. *Developing Cross-Cultural Competence: A Guide for Working with Children and Their Families.* Baltimore: Brookes Publication, 1998.

Lynskey, M.T., and Fergusson, D.M. "Factors protecting against the development of adjustment difficulties in young adults exposed to childhood sexual abuse." *Child Abuse and Neglect* 12 (1997):1177–1190

Lyons-Ruth, K., Connell, D.B., Grunebaum, H.U., and Botein, S. "Infants at social risk: Maternal depression and family support services as mediators of infant development and security of attachment." *Child Development* 61 (1990):85–98.

Manly, J.T., Cicchetti, D., and Barnett, D. "The impact of subtype, frequency, chronicity and severity of child maltreatment on social competence and behaviour problems." *Development and Psychopathology* 6 (1994):121–143.

McFadyen, R.G., and Kitson, W.J.H. "Language comprehension and expression among adolescents who have experienced childhood physical abuse." *Journal of Child Psychology and Psychiatry* 37 (1996):551–562.

McGloin, J.M., and Widom, C.S. "Resilience among abused and neglected children grown up." *Development and Psychopathology* 13 (2001):1021–1038.

Miller, D.A., McClusky-Fawcett, K., and Irving, L.M. "The relationship between childhood sexual abuse and subsequent onset of bulimia nervosa." *Child Abuse and Neglect* 17 (1993):305–314.

Moore, E., Armsden, G., and Gogerty, P.L. "A twelve-year followup study of maltreated and at-risk children who received early therapeutic childcare." *Child Maltreatment* 3 (1998):3–16.

Nagler, J. "Child abuse and neglect." Current *Opinions in Pediatrics* 14 (2002):251–254.

"The neglect of child neglect." Editorial, *The Lancet* 361, February 8 (2003).

Oldfield, D., Hays, B.J., and Megel, M.E. "Evaluation of the effectiveness of project TRUST: An elementary school-based victimization prevention program." *Child Abuse and Neglect* 20 (1996):821–832.

Olds, D., Eckenrode, J., and Henderson, C. "Long-term effects of home visitation on maternal life course and child abuse and neglect: Fifteen-year follow up of a randomized trial." *Journal of the American Medical Association* 278 (1997):637–643.

Olds, D., and Kitzman, H. "Review of research on home visiting for pregnant women and parents of young children." *The Future of Children* 3, no. 3 (1993):53–92.

Paolucci, E., Genuis, M., and Violato, C. "A meta-analysis of the published research on the effects of child sexual abuse." *Journal of Psychology* 135 (2001):17–36.

Parker, J.G., and Herrera, C. "Interpersonal processes in friendship: A comparison of abused and nonabused children's experiences." *Developmental Psychology* 32 (1996): 1025–1038.

Peraino, J.M. "Evaluation of a preschool antivictimization prevention program." *Journal Interpersonal Violence* 5 (1990):520–528.

Perez, C.L. "A comparison of group play therapy and individual therapy for sexually abused children." *Dissertation Abstracts International* 48 (1998):3079.

Pine, D.S., and Cohen, J.A. "Trauma in children and adolescents: Risk and treatment of psychiatric sequelae." *Biological Psychiatry* 51 (2002):519–531.

Putnam, W.P. "Ten-year research update review: Child sexual abuse." *Journal of the American Academy of Child and Adolescent Psychiatry* 42, no. 3 (2003):269–278.

Ramchandani, P., and Jones, D.P.H. "Treating psychological symptoms in sexually abused children." *British Journal of Psychiatry* 183 (2003):484–490.

Reece, R.M. *Child Abuse Medical Diagnosis and Management.* Philadelphia: Lea and Febiger, 1994.

Riggs, S., Alario, A. and McHorney, C. "Health risk behaviors and attempted suicide in adolescents who report maltreatment." *Journal of Pediatrics* 116 (1990):815–821.

Ripens, J., Aleman, A., and Goudena, P.P. "Prevention of child sexual abuse victimisation: A meta analysis of school programs." *Child Abuse and Neglect* 21 (1997): 975–987.

Rogers, J.R. "Sexual abuse and suicide: Why we may not know what we think we know." *Archives of Suicide Research* 7 (2003):83–91.

Rogosch, F.A., Cicchetti, D., and Aber, J.L. "The role of child maltreatment in early deviations in cognitive and affective processing abilities and later peer relationship problems." *Development and Psychopathology* 7 (1995):591–609.

Rubin, D., Lane, W., and Ludwig, S. "Child abuse prevention." *Current Opinion in Pediatrics* 13 (2001):388–401.

Rutter, M. "Resilience in the face of adversity. Protective factors and resistance to psychiatric disorder." *British Journal of Psychiatry* 147 (1985):598–611.

Schumacher, J.A., Slep, A.M.S., and Heyman, R.E. "Risk factors for child neglect." *Aggression and Violent Behavior* 6 (2001) 231–254.

Sedlak, A.J., and Broadhurst, D.D. *Third National Incidence Study on Child Abuse and Neglect.* Department of Health and Human Services, Washington, DC, 1996, pp. 13–14.

Sobsey, D., Randall, W., and Parrila, R. "Gender differences in abused children with and without disabilities." *Child Abuse and Neglect* 21 (1997):707–720.

Spaccarelli, S. "Stress, appraisal, and coping in child sexual abuse: A theoretical and empirical review." *Psychological Bulletin* 116 (1994):340–362.

Stevenson, J. "The treatment of long term sequelae of child abuse." *Journal of Child Psychology and Psychiatry* 40 (1999):89–111.

Taal, M., and Edelaar, M. "Positive and negative effects of a child sexual abuse prevention program." *Child Abuse and Neglect* 21 (1997):399–410.

Teicher, M.H., Andersen, S.L., Polcari, A., Anderson, C.M., Navalta, C.P., and Kim, D.M. "The neurobiological consequences of early stress and childhood maltreatment." *Neuroscience and Behavioural Reviews* 27 (2003):33–44.

Terr, L.C. "Childhood traumas: An outline and overview." *American Journal of Psychiatry* 148:(1991) 10–20.

Trickett, P., Noll, J., Reiffman, A., and Putnam, F. "Variants of intrafamilial sexual abuse experiences: Implications for short- and long-term development." *Development and Psychopathology* 13 (2001):1001–1019.

U.S. Department of Health and Human Services, Administration on Children, Youth and Families. *Child Maltreatment 2003.* Washington, DC: U.S. Government Printing Office. National Child Abuse and Neglect Data System, U.S. Department of Health and Human Services, 2005.

128   *Ernesto Caffo, Luisa Strik Lievers, and Barbara Forresi*

U.S. Department of Health and Human Services—Children's Bureau. *Child Maltreatment 1997: Reports from the States to the National Child Abuse and Neglect Data System*. Washington, DC: U.S. Government Printing Office, 1999.

U.S. Department of Health and Human Services. *Child Maltreatment 1996: Reports from the States to the National Child Abuse and Neglect Data System.*Washington, DC: U.S. Government Printing Office, 1998.

U.S. Department of Health and Human Services NCoCAaN. *Third National Incidence Study of Child Abuse and Neglect: Final Report (NIS-3)*. Washington, DC: U.S. Government Printing Office, 1996.

Van der Kolk, B.A. "The body keeps score: Memory and the evolving psychobiology of postraumatic stress." *Harvard Review of Psychiatry* 1 (1994):253–265.

Watkins, B., and Bentovim, A. "Male children and adolescents as victims: A review of current knowledge." Pp 56–75 in *Male Victims of Sexual Assault* (2nd ed.) edited by Mezey, G., Oxford: Oxford University Press, 2000.

WHO, *Report of the Consultation on Child Abuse Prevention*. Geneva, World Health Organization (document WHO/HSC/PVI/99.1), March 29–31, 1999.

World Health Organization. *World Report on Violence and Health*. Washington, D.C.: U.S. Government Printing Office. accessed 10/3/2002: www5/who.int/violence_injury_prevention/main.cfm?s=0009.

Wind, T.W., and Silvern, L. "Parenting and family stress as mediators of the long-term effects of child abuse." *Child Abuse and Neglect* 18 (1994):439–453.

Wolfe, D.A., Wekerle, C., Reitzel-Jaffe, D., and Lefebvre, L. "Factors associated with abusive relationships among maltreated and nonmaltreated youth." *Development and Psychopathology* 10 (1998):61–85.

Wurtele, S.K., and Owens, J.S. "Teaching personal safety skills to young children: An investigation of age and gender across five studies." *Child Abuse and Neglect* 21 (1997):805–814.

Zelenko, M.A., Huffman, L., Lock, J., Kennedy, O., and Steiner, H. "Poor adolescent expectant mothers: Can we assess their potential for child abuse?" The *Journal of Adolescent Health* 29 (2001):271–278.

Zlotnick, C., Mattia, J., and Zimmerman, M. "Clinical features of survivors of sexual abuse with major depression." *Child Abuse and Neglect* 25, no. 3 (2001):357–67.

Chapter Five

Resiliency in Conditions of War and Military Violence: Preconditions and Developmental Processes

Raija-Leena Punamäki

In physics and engineering, resiliency refers to the capacity of material to absorb energy when it is deformed elastically and then, upon unloading, to have this energy recovered. In botany, a resilient plant bends in wind but does not break or uproot. In fairy tales the resilient heroes face unimaginable obstacles and dangers but triumph over them with the help of their own virtue and magic powers.

In developmental science humans are defined as resilient when they successfully adapt despite adversity (Rutter, 1985), overcome hardships and trauma, achieve developmental competencies, and even blossom in harsh conditions (Masten and Coatsworth, 1998; Werner, 1993) and create life in adversity through dynamic developmental processes (Luthar, Cicchetti, and Becker, 2000; Masten and Coatsworth, 1998). War with its heroic images and humiliating calamities tells about resiliency and vulnerability. Analyzing child development and mental health in conditions of war and military violence evokes some fundamental questions of resilience: How do processes that enhance versus endanger resiliency differ historically, that is, in times of peace and war? How universal or culture bound are risk and protecting factors?

This chapter starts with a review of research on resiliency among children living in conditions of war and military violence, and it continues in analyzing the ways that sociopolitical realities are embedded in the cognitive-emotional processes enhancing resiliency.

IMPORTANCE OF RESILIENCY ENHANCING PROCESSES

A number of hallmark studies have sought the secrets of resilient children. They have analyzed characteristics of the children who are competent, maintain their mental health intact, and flourish in adversities created by poverty (Fergusson and Horwood, 2003), physical impairment (Werner and Smith, 1982), parental mental illness and depression (Anthony, 1974; Beardslee and Podorefsky, 1988), and family violence and maltreatment (Bolger and Patterson, 2003; Cicchetti et al., 1993).

The results have shown that sources of resilience emerge from the child (e.g., easy temperament, high intelligence, secure attachment, and high self-esteem) and family (e.g., high socioeconomic status, wise and loving parents in a happy marriage), as well as a community that includes social support and good peer relations and the world (e.g., recognition of human rights and fight for economic equality) (Masten and Coatsworth, 1998; Masten et al., 1999; Olsson et al., 2003).

Currently, rather than conceptualizing resiliency as an attribute or characteristic of a child, researchers analyze the elements and preconditions that make resiliency possible (Luthar et al., 2000; Rutter, 2000; Yates, Egeland, and Sroufe, 2003). Even more so, it is crucial to clarify the multilevel and complex mechanism and developmental processes by which children become competent, families secure, and societies supportive, even and especially in harsh times. Accordingly, I analyze cognitive, emotional, and symbolic processes that enable children to meet new challenges, stressors, and trauma in adaptive, creative, and securing ways.

For children, war means loss of security, humiliation of family members, and constant threat to life. War and military violence constitute institutionalized hate and fear, often too intense to comprehend and master. When trying to understand processes that can enhance resiliency in these extreme conditions, two issues are important: developmental timing and activation of earlier schemata and working models. Accordingly and finally, the chapter analyzes the mechanisms that are salient for resiliency development from infancy to adolescence and examines attachment styles of war victims as an example of dormant schemes from early development being activated in the face of trauma.

RESILIENCY OF CHILDREN IN WAR AND MILITARY VIOLENCE

Witnessing children fall victim to war is painful for adults. Maybe this is why our views of resiliency among war children have been split, emotionally loaded, and lacking empirical evidence. On the one hand, children in war zones have been described as invulnerable heroes who actively participate in meaningful and rewarding national struggles (Bracken, Giller, and Summerfield, 1995; Summerfield, 2001). On the other hand, they have been referred as "lost generations, traumatized and aggressive" (Marcal, 2003). Both extremes are unfounded.

The resiliency versus vulnerability of children in war conditions has been attributed to the child's characteristics, family relationships, and community values and support, which corresponds in part with resiliency research in peaceful societies.

The majority of empirical resiliency-related research concerns children in the Middle East (Israeli, Palestinian, Lebanese, and Kurdish) and the former Yugoslavia (Bosnian, Croatian, and Serbian). There is a lack of comparative research across different countries and cultures into possible culture-specific resiliency and protective factors in conditions of war and military violence. Also, studies on refugee families having experiences of persecution in Cambodia (Kinzie, 2001), Rwanda (Dyregrov et al., 2000), and the Middle East (Almqvist, 2000; Montgomery and Foldspang, 2005) significantly contribute to our understanding of child development and health in extreme conditions. South American colleagues have provided insightful theoretical and clinical work on mental health and family dynamics in conditions of military dictatorship in Chile, Argentina, El Salvador, and Guatemala (Aron et al., 1991; Becker et al., 1990; Kordon, Edelman, and Lagos, 1986). Finally, research on South African children who were suffering from and struggling against apartheid is valuable in understanding children's activity aimed at changing their own history (Daves, Tredoux, and Feinstein, 1989; Straker, 1992).

NATURE AND ACCUMULATION OF TRAUMA

The nature, meaning, and amount of traumatic events are of great importance for child mental health in war conditions. There is some evidence of trauma- and gender-specificity for the severity of any subsequent psychiatric distress. A follow-up study among Iraqi children revealed that scenes that involved strong sensory impressions such as the smell of dead bodies and voices of suffering people constituted a serious risk for intrusive post-traumatic stress disorder (PTSD) symptoms (Dyregrov et al., 2002).

Loss of family members and personal injuries are likely to increase depressive and other internalizing symptoms, especially among girls (Khamis, 1993; Miller, El-Masri, and Qouta, 2000). Because family signifies a protective shield for children, witnessing humiliation and violence toward family members can seriously harm children's well-being (Dybdahl, 2001; Macksoud and Aber, 1996).

Gender Differences

Gender differences are illustrative, however, in attempting to understand resiliency in war conditions. In a Palestinian study, boys and girls suffered differently from PTSD and depressive symptoms depending on whether they or their mothers were the main trauma victims in the family. Girls showed especially severe distress when their mothers were exposed, while boys showed severe distress when both they and their mothers were the victims (Qouta et al., 2005b). Similarly, women appraised events in which their family members were harmed and humiliated by military forces as more traumatic than when violence was targeted toward themselves (Punamaki, 1986). General stress research has also evidenced the significant role of human relations in determining girls' vulnerability. Economic hardship, for instance, directly affects boys' mental health, whereas girls are affected through deteriorated familial relationships such as marital conflict and punitive parenting (Conger and Elder, 1994; Solantaus et al., 2004).

The Threshold Effect Model

There is evidence that children are capable of coping with low levels of risk factors, but after a certain threshold of exposure their vulnerability to mental health and developmental problems dramatically increases (Sameroff, 1999). A replication of the threshold effect model among Palestinian children confirmed that psychological disorders were more probable when the family had had more than five traumatic experiences, including, for example, death and imprisonment of family members, destruction of home, and witnessing shooting (Garbarino and Kostelny, 1996). The threshold effect model contradicts the dose effect model substantiated among adult trauma victims that shows that a higher dosage of traumatic exposure invariably leads to higher psychological distress (Breslau, 1998).

Physical and Emotional Proximity of Events

Traumatic events differ according to their content, proximity, and frequency. War conditions involve both physical and emotional proximity of events; physical proximity refers to witnessing destruction, fighting, and injuries, and emotional proximity involves family members' and friends' deaths, injuries, and disappearances (Yehuda et al., 1994). Terr (1991) distinguished between type I and type II trauma exposures among children, both demanding different adaptation processes. Type I refers to a one-time, acute, and clear-cut extraordinary experience such as witnessing a killing or road accident, and type II trauma refers to chronic stress and adversities that are an endemic part of a child's life, for example, family violence or hunger. In conditions of war and military violence both types of traumas are present and multiple risk factors tend to accumulate. Destruction of home, for instance, symbolizes a deep loss of basic security and strangers intruding into the most intimate part of human life. The symbolic meaning of a trauma is important for mental health consequences, and resilience may be possible when a child is capable of creating counteracting and consoling meanings for the trauma.

Parents bringing up their children in conditions of war and violence seem to be well aware of the threshold effects working in their traumatized families. A Palestinian mother had her own explanation for her child's withdrawal symptoms:

> The brothers' detention was the last straw that broke the camel's back. When the soldiers shot D's schoolmate, she cried but joined the protests. As you know, the curfews were unbearable for the whole family. Yet, somehow she found always something to do, and she even consoled others. However, now she needs help for herself.*

The severe impact of accumulation of traumatic events in war can be attributed to biased and narrowed cognitive-emotional processing of repeated loss and horrors, conceptualized as a pathological grief (Horowitz, Bonanno, and Holen, 1993; Smith et al., 2002). A Lebanese female student described her difficulty to complete bereavement: "When my first friend died I cried so that I thought I die myself of suffocation, when the second friend died, I cried and did not want to wake up in the morning. But when the fifth and sixth died, there were no tears left in me anymore." Later she says, when remembering the war, "Tears were crystallized in me and I felt them aching wherever I turned my eyes and body."*

There is also an opposite view arguing that children can become habituated to danger and that accumulation of traumas neutralizes their provocative impact. Research on children in Northern Ireland has advocated the belief that when military violence is an integral part of children's life, it no longer affects their mental health (Cairns, 1989). However, the argument of habituation to trauma contradicts the evidence that earlier trauma exposure is one of the main predictors of maladaptive responses during new exposures to trauma. The risk of earlier trauma predicting psychiatric distress in later trauma has been substantiated among war veterans (Kulka et al., 1990) and child victims (Kilpatrick et al., 2000; Salmon and Bryant, 2002).

In conclusion, it is likely that some elements of war experiences are universally traumatic, such as threat to life (Smith et al., 2002), whereas other aspects of child resiliency greatly vary in times of peace and war and according to the meaning and interpretation that cultures and individuals attribute to them. For an analysis of resiliency we have to build a sophisticated matrix that involves children's interpretation and attributions of causes of war trauma, emotional processing of the threat and danger, and their participation.

UNDERSTANDING AND COPING WITH TRAUMA

Whatever magnitude the hardships are, humans always attempt to protect their psychological integrity, heal their wounds, and even prosper. According to coping research, people resist by either changing the world or changing themselves. The first alternative involves problem-focused coping strategies aimed at removing the hardships and dangers, and the second refers to emotion-focused coping strategies that work by manipulating painful feelings and soothing arousals. Victims of hardships can also bring back their safety by reappraising and reinterpreting their perceptions of the threat and danger (Lazarus, 2000; Lazarus and Folkman, 1984). All these coping strategies work on behavioral, emotional, and cognitive levels of functioning, and they can be active or passive (Compas et al., 2001; Kochenderfer-Ladd and Skinner, 2002). Researchers have examined which coping strategies are effective in protecting children's mental health in the face of war and military violence.

Controllability, Acuteness, and Severity of the Trauma

While active and problem-focused coping is generally considered adaptive and emotion-focused coping maladaptive (Aldwin and Sutton, 1996; Asarnow et al., 1999), there is evidence that coping effectiveness depends on controllability, acuteness, and severity of the trauma (Kanninen, 2002; Rutter, 2000). The criterion for coping effectiveness is the goodness of fit between coping strategies and environmental demands. Illustrative enough, Israeli researchers found that children's distractive and passive coping strategies were effective during the Iraqi missile attacks (Weisenberg et al., 1993), apparently because avoidance matched well with the uncontrollable situation. The goodness of fit may explain why coping strategies of apparently opposite nature can be effective; for instance, both passive withdrawal and active participation can work well in war conditions (Punamäki and Suleiman, 1990).

Active Participation in Political Struggle

Active participation in political struggle among war-traumatized children and adolescents is considered beneficial because it enhances social affiliation, feeling of control, ventilating of feelings, and purposeful activity (Straker, 1992). Baker (1990) substantiated that Palestinian boys who participated in the independence struggle were better adjusted than passive boys in the midst of military violence. A follow-up study in turn showed that political activity predicted good adjustment among Palestinian children only once the military violence and life threat were over (Punamäki et al., 2001).

Barber (2001) further specified that active participation in the intifada struggle had positive developmental outcomes only when adolescents enjoyed supportive and wise parenting. Regarding active participation in military struggle as a sign of resiliency is problematic, because it means life endangerment and adultlike responsibility before ample maturation. On the other hand, political activity even if life endangering symbolizes self-esteem, courage, self-efficacy, and empowerment (Baker, 1990). Clinical observations, however, tell also about the negative impact of collective demands for heroism and endurance in war conditions. For a shy, sensitive, and slow child the demands of political activity can be devastating.

Flexibility and Repertoire of Coping Strategies

As different coping is suitable to different conditions, it may be beneficial for children to have a flexible and rich repertoire of various coping strategies that match the complex demands of war trauma. The effectiveness of coping repertoire concurs with resiliency research that advocates flexible problem-solving skills together with creativity, humor, and intelligence, all incorporating repertoire (Luthar et al., 1993; Masten et al., 1999; Werner, 1993). Research among Kurdish children found, however, that the effectiveness of coping repertoire was "module specific" (Punamäki, Muhammed, and Abdulrahman, 2004). A wide cognitive coping repertoire was beneficial, i.e., it associated with low levels of psychological distress, especially PTSD symptoms.

In a wide repertoire of cognitive coping, children apply flexible shifts of thoughts, use innovative new ways of looking at painful issues, and attempt to transform the meaning of trauma. By contrast, wide behavioral and emotional repertoires negatively affected children's mental health, associating especially with high levels of sleeping difficulties and somatic symptoms. The maladaptive nature of a wide repertoire of behavioral coping may refer to a phenomenon in which children show intense activity in the face of trauma at the expense of more reflecting and integrating aspects of coping (Näätänen et al., 2002). The intense repertoire of emotional coping can refer to attempts to ventilate painful experiences, which, however, turned out to be unsuccessful.

Understanding Reasons for Trauma

The effectiveness of cognitive coping strategies lies also in sophisticated causal attributions of reasons and consequences of trauma and feeling of control. The importance of understanding and explaining reasons for trauma and hardships goes parallel with results concerning resilient children in other stressful conditions (Beardslee and Podorefsky, 1988; Luthar et al., 1993).

For instance, Beardslee and Podorefsky (1988) found that resilient children in depressive families typically had "high self-understanding" that involved awareness of real reasons behind parental illness and ability to separate their own feelings and activity from parents' difficulties. Also, their causal attributions for the illness were based on actual knowledge and not on the self-blame that was typical for vulnerable children.

Finding a meaning in life seems to be especially salient in conditions of war and military violence. Ideological and religious commitment helps adolescents make sense of trauma, gives them a feeling of belonging and controlling of their own future, and provides social support and shared ventilating of emotions. Therefore, ideological attributions and political commitment have been used as an explanation for resiliency among war children (Garbarino and Kostelny, 1996). Empirical evidence is scarce, however. Shalom, Benbenishty, and Solomon (2001) showed that Israeli officers who used coherent, specific, and realistic attributions for the reasons for their being traumatized were more protected from deteriorated mental health (indicated by lack of PTSD). A study among Israeli children found that ideological commitment indicated by patriotic involvement and glorification could protect mental health (low levels of anxiety and depression) from negative impact of traumatic experiences (Punamäki, 1996).

CHILD CHARACTERISTICS

Personality, temperament, and other individual differences have been little studied as potential resources for resiliency among children living in war and military violence. The reason may lie in early trauma research strongly relying on an S-R model of human functioning (S = overwhelming stimulus beyond normal human experience; R = prevalence of diagnosis of PTSD) that ignored possible psychological mediating and moderating factors and processes. Furthermore, the highly political character of the debate on children and war made researchers careful to focus on "individualistic" and "Western" approaches (Bracken et al., 1995; Summerfield, 2001).

It is a pity, because we can observe intriguing variation in how children in war conditions need and tolerate excitement, seek and avoid new experiences, require regularity, and interpret security. They further differ in either enjoying or being overloaded by social contacts, silences, and loneliness, even when facing such a universally traumatic scene as loss of a family member. One of the most profane characteristics of war is the constant arbitrariness and unexpectedness of events. Children with strong needs for rhythm and regularity may therefore suffer most, while novelty seekers are less vulnerable.

In air raids, we could observe how infants substantially differed in their ease of arousal and time required to calm down, and how their emotional expression differed in intensity, stability, and oscillation. Temperament research has conceptualized these different behavioral tendencies as biologically rooted and relatively stable cognitive-emotional and psychophysiological responses (Plomin et al., 2001; Rothbart et al., 2000) that explain the unique interacting styles with different environmental demands (Calkins and Johnson, 1998).

Temperament

The crucial question is in what conditions different temperament types endure and bloom, and where they suffer and fall ill, and why. The earlier conceptualization of easy and difficult temperament is not informative enough in analyzing individual differences in resilient ways of dealing with war dangers and life threat. More probably it is the unique goodness of fit between dangerous environment and individual threshold for excitement, the need for novelty, emotional intensity, stability, and regularity that predicts resiliency (Plomin, Asbury, and Dunn, 2001; Rothbart, 2000). Although resiliency cannot be reduced to individual child characteristics of activity, intelligence, and charm (Cicchetti and Garmezy, 1993; Egeland et al., 1993), personality research is informative in analyzing the preconditions to the resiliency-enhancing characteristics. It has revealed, for instance, that preconditions and correlates of optimism involve multilevel differences in a person's functioning on biological (genetics, psychophysiology, brain), motivational, and social levels (Räikkönen et al., 1999). In other words, understanding preconditions to resilience in conditions of war and violence requires a multilevel information processing model that reveals interplay of cultural, social, psychological, and biological issues and the goodness of fit between them (Cicchetti et al., 1993; Dodge et al., 1995).

Intelligence

There is a consensus that high intelligence helps children face adversities such as parental depression (Cicchetti, Rogosch, and Toth, 1998), violence, stress, and poverty (Fergusson and Horwood, 2003; Pagani at al., 1999; Radke-Yarrow and Brown, 1993). Corresponding research is lacking among war-traumatized children, except one study by Qouta et al. (1995) among Palestinian children. They found that although high IQ was directly associated with resourcefulness indicated by high self-esteem, it could not protect children's emotional well-being when facing military trauma during the first intifada.

A follow-up study in more peaceful times[1] revealed, however, that it was not IQ alone but rather a balance between intelligence and creativity that could protect children's mental health from long-term negative impact of military trauma (Punamäki et al., 2001). A further follow-up showed that good cognitive capacity in middle childhood characterized by accurate and speedy responses to stimuli predicted good mental health in adolescence, indicated by lack of PTSD (Qouta et al., 2005a). Also, mental flexibility as an indicator of cognitive competence was able to protect children's mental health from negative trauma impact (Qouta et al., 2001). The results closely correspond with conceptualization of cognitive complexity as a precondition for emotional competency (Saarni, 1999) and resiliency (Luthar and Cicchetti, 2000). The core elements in PTSD are fragmented and inadequate cognitive processes of appraisal, memory, attention, and interpretation of traumatic events (Brewin et al., 1996; Dunmore et al., 2001; Foa, 1989), which explains the vital role of children's cognitive capacity in surviving life-endangering conditions of war and military violence.

In order to maintain resiliency, war children "must pray all Gods" and invite a wide repertoire of imaginary, creative, symbolic, and emotional elements for protection. Yet similarly important is to have access to cognitive framing, intellectual analysis, and problem-solving skills in order to reshape painful experiences. In the same vein, cognitive-emotional therapies invite concrete and symbolic representations and enhance both emotional ventilating and cognitive framing (Foa et al., 1999).

FAMILY AS A STRONGHOLD

There is a consensus that presence of secure, loving, and mutually intimate human relationship can protect children in adversity and enhance resiliency. Good parenting, characterized by sensitivity in infancy, loving guidance in middle childhood, and adequate availability in adolescence is associated with successful child development in general (Belsky, 1984) and in adversity (Conger and Elder, 1994). Substantial evidence is available of loving family relationship and social support contributing to child resiliency in poverty, losses, and illness, and favorable outcomes include good childhood mental health, school achievements, and peer relationships (Cicchetti et al., 1993; Masten and Coatsworth, 1998; Prevatt, 2003). In the same vein, good parenting has been found to buffer childhood mental health from negative impact of war and violence (Barber, 2001) and to enhance the processes by which children can become resilient (Punamäki et al., 1997a).

The research by Barber (2001) among Palestinians showed that children and adolescents who perceived their parents as harsh were more likely to develop antisocial behavior following involvement in intifada activity, whereas parental acceptance could protect their mental health from negative impact of military violence. Garbarino and Kostelny (1996) also reported that Palestinian children from dysfunctional families were the most vulnerable to psychological distress when facing military violence.

Research has further shown that good parenting is important in promoting other protective processes in war conditions. Punamäki et al. (1997a) found that loving and nonpunitive parenting was associated with children's high creativity and cognitive competence, which in turn could protect their mental health. The results in war zones are, to some extent, similar to studies of children living in community violence. For instance, Timko and Moos (1996) suggest that support from family leads to children's greater social participation instead of violent action. According to O'Connor et al. (2002), parental support was associated with higher levels of self-reliance and greater expectations for the future among adolescents living in violent communities. Clear and optimistic future expectations in turn predict good recovery in extreme trauma among both young children (Terr, 1991; Wyman et al., 1993) and adolescents (Baldwin et al., 1993).

War with its violent atmosphere, losses, and ideological sacrifices gives, however, distinct features to a parent-child relationship, which uniquely shapes resiliency development. First, the way the mother responds to stress and life threat are decisive for a child's mental health, which in turn is a great burden to mothers. Second, the intergenerational trauma can create specific communication patterns between family members characterized by mutual concern, role confusion, and guilt feelings. Third, life endangerment can result in strict hierarchies of resiliency and vulnerability between family members.

Stress Symptoms in Mothers and Children

Israeli research showed high correlations between mothers' and children's PTSD symptoms, both during acute danger of bombardment and six and thirty months later (Laor et al., 1997; Laor et al., 2001). Similarly, mothers' depression was associated with children's distress in Lebanese families (Bryce et al., 1989) and maternal mental health problems with children's distress in Palestinian families (Punamäki, 1987; Qouta et al., 2005).

There is also some evidence of dyadic symptom expression, indicating similarity between mothers' and children's psychological distress in war and life threat. A community sample among Bosnian war victims revealed that when mothers show PTSD symptoms, especially avoidance, it was likely that their children also suffer from the same symptoms (Smith et al., 2002). In Palestinian families significant associations were found between mothers' depressive and children's internalizing symptoms, and between mothers' hostile and children's externalizing symptoms (Qouta et al., 2005). Yehuda, Halligan, and Bierer (2001) evidenced genetic and physiological vulnerability to PTSD in a sample of second-generation Holocaust survivors. PTSD was present only in children who had at least one parent with chronic PTSD (Yehuda et al., 1994).

Although strong associations have been found between mothers' and children's psychological distress in war conditions, there is reason to be cautious about any causal links. Characteristic to life threat is that both parents and children intensively worry about each others' security, and similarities between maternal and child mental health reflect that concern (Garbarino and Kostelny, 1996; Punamäki, 1987).

It seems sometimes as if all women raising children in war zones have read their Freud and Burlingham (1943), who observed during the London air raids in World War II that "children do not only develop fears which belong to their own age and stage of development, but they also share the fear reactions of their mothers." Mothers are highly aware of the impossibility of their task of acting as a buffer between children's mental health and external danger and horror. The discrepancy between will and reality causes feelings of guilt and distress, as a Palestinian mother of four and prisoner's wife described. "I can never forgive myself that I let my children live [a] similar childhood to my own: refugee, humiliation and submission."*

In life danger young children are tuned according to the mother's emotional responses. They need parents' guidance and support in attempting to make sense of violence and danger. Foremost they seek cues about their mother's capability to protect them, and they feel highly vulnerable if her psychological state of mind communicates failure in protection. There is evidence that children's mental health is at special risk if the mother cannot control her frightening mental images (Laor et al., 1997) and there is fear in her eyes (Carlson, 1998). Mothers' negative emotionality, ambivalent feelings, and guilt interfere with their own and their children's emotional processing of traumatic experience and prevent sharing and support in the family (Laor et al., 2001; Yule, 2002). Optimally, the caregiver appears calm and reassuring without minimizing the importance of trauma and child distress. Laor and her colleagues (1997; 2001) showed that Israeli mothers' high capacity to form secure object relations and mature defense style predicted children's good psychological adjustment after missile attacks.

Some narratives of survivors give us an idea about the ways sensitive and loving parenting can function as a kind of inoculation against distress and despair in the face of trauma. A young Palestinian man analyzed reasons for his endurance in harsh prison conditions: "When the pain was overwhelming, I imagined my mother walking in our garden, I smelled the trees, touched the warm earth, listened to her voice . . . and this brought me back to my senses."* His example tells how re-creating a consoling image of the mother-child relationship could protect him in extreme trauma in adulthood.

A second example is a child's nocturnal dream collected in a dream diary as part of a dream study among Kurdish and Palestinian children (Punamäki, 1998b; Punamäki et al., 2005). The presence versus absence of maternal and paternal protection was a prominent theme in their dream reports, which reflects children's need to trust in parental omnipotence to save them from danger.

> I dreamt that the soldiers came to our neighbor's house and broke the door to take their son. I switched the light on, the soldiers came to our house and asked me why I switched on the light. I was frightened [of] them and trembling. They spank me on my face. I shouted for my mother. She took me from them and said, "He is but a little boy." I woke up terrified and worried and kept awake till morning.

Three-Generational Transmission of Trauma

In contemporary wars we meet families in which parents or grandparents have also been persecuted and possibly traumatized in earlier wars. Three-generational transmission of trauma can occur in Israeli, Kurdish, and Palestinian families and two-generation in Serbian, Croatian, and Bosnian families. The research on Holocaust survivors indicates that parental trauma does not form a general risk for psychiatric disorders in the second generation (Favaro et al., 1999; Levav et al., 1998), but offspring are more vulnerable to difficulties in intimate relationships (Bar-on et al., 1998; Sagi et al., 2002) and developmental crises in adolescence (Yehuda et al., 1994). Parental war trauma can activate children's vulnerability when they themselves are exposed to traumatic stress. Israeli researchers showed that exposure to compact trauma made offspring of Holocaust survivors more vulnerable to PTSD than other soldiers during the Lebanon war (Solomon, Kotler, and Mikulincer, 1988).

Conditions That May Break Intergenerational Transmission

It is important to seek the preconditions that can break intergenerational transmission of trauma on the next generation in conditions of continuous war and atrocities. Evidence confirms that breaking the transmission is possible and can be attributed to positive changes in family communication, high quality early mothering, and successful therapy. The dysfunctional communication in traumatized families is characterized by a knowing/not-knowing dilemma, where parents keep silent about their traumatic experiences in order to protect their children's innocence.

Children sense, however, their parents' anxiety and create horrifying images about their suffering that are based on the fragmented information. Left in a conspiracy of silence, family members feel pity for each other and attempt to protect each others' secrets (Lichtman, 1984). Research on child abuse suggests that mothers' dissociative states of mind in early interaction form a serious risk for intergenerational transmission (Schuengel, Bakermans-Kranenburg, and van Ijzendoorn, 1999). The first contact and interaction between mother and child is communicated through eyes, and therefore maternal fear and dissociation are especially traumatic in infancy (Egeland et al., 1996; Kretchmar and Jacobvitz, 2002).

Differences in Vulnerability among Family Members

Observations of families exposed to violence and atrocities suggest that family members differ in their vulnerability and resiliency. According to the family systems theory, members of a family respond to trauma and threat as a system where each member's behavior, emotional expression, and cognitive strategies serve a meaningful role in maintaining the family's integrity and well-being (Minuchin, 1974; Watzlawick, Beavin, and Jackson, 1967).

The differences in sibling resilience are also due to their unique perceptions and experiences with parents and peers (Plomin, Asbury, and Dunn, 2001). In families of torture victims, for instance, children adopt functional roles that differ in the lines of resiliency and vulnerability: one sibling may be the "symptom carrier" who shows vulnerability and expresses pain, another is the "family psychologist" who takes care of, consoles, and encourages suffering members, and the third is the "sunshine" and savior child who makes others forget and compensates for the losses.

Distinct Roles and Hierarchy between Family Members

It seems that severe trauma strengthens the distinct roles and hierarchy between family members. The metaphor of a ship in a storm applies to persecuted families where members take on distinct responsibilities and show a clear emotional share of work in resiliency and vulnerability (Punamäki, 1987; Punamäki et al., in press). Refugee families provide examples of how the strict hierarchy serves them well in life-threatening situations, whereas cemented roles and inflexible hierarchy may turn out to be problematic when resettling in a safer environment. Typically, the refugee child who was resilient in dangerous home country continues to take responsibility by learning more quickly the language and guiding parents in their new country (Almqvist, 2000).

There is some evidence that siblings respond differently to adversities such as parental depression (Moser and Jacob, 2002), marital conflict (Cummings, 2000), and alcohol abuse (interview data). War trauma and threat can both encourage support between siblings and invite dysfunctional characteristics such as scapegoating, isolation, and extreme dependency between family members (Garbarino and Kostelny, 1996; Hobfoll et al., 1991). Few studies have empirically examined symmetries and asymmetries in psychological distress and resources in war-traumatized families. Punamäki et al. (in press) revealed compensatory dynamics within spousal and between parental and sibling subsystems. For instance, if mothers reported high levels of psychological distress, older children reported low or vice versa, and if the mother was highly resilient, the father showed low resilience or vice versa.

SECURITY OF ATTACHMENT IN INSECURE CONDITIONS

Secure attachment is considered a resiliency factor (Fonagy et al., 1996), apparently due to evidence that it predicts social and cognitive competence (Belsky, 1996; De Rosnay and Harris, 2000), adequate emotional regulation, and good mental health (Contreras et al., 2000) both in preschool and adolescent years. Bowlby (1973) suggested that secure attachment is an armament against future stressors and adversities, and research has substantiated that feeling security against the odds works among adults (Mikulincer et al., 1999) and to some extent among children (Muller, Sicoli, and Lemieux, 2000).

However, the original function of each attachment style, created in early unique mother-child interaction, is to maintain emotional balance in the moments of danger and threats (Crittenden, 2000, 1997). Avoidant children, who cannot trust the caregiver to be available and sensitive to their needs, learn to trust in themselves and dismiss emotional affiliation. Ambivalent children, whose caregiver is arbitrarily available, deal with their insecurity by clinging to the caregiver and being emotionally preoccupied about the presence of potentially protective adults.

These two types of insecure children have thus solved in different ways the problem of a caregiver being incapable of providing safety and soothing their arousal: the avoidant children deny their need for affection and overcontrol, deactivate, and falsify their emotions, whereas ambivalent children escalate their need for affection and undercontrol their emotions (Crittenden, 2000; Main, 1996). The early learned working models of the safety of the world, worthiness of oneself, and availability of human care reactivate when the grown child faces traumatic events later in life (Bowlby, 1973; Crittenden, 1997). Attachment theory thus provides a compelling explanation for the great individual differences that are found among trauma victims.

The general hypothesis that secure attachment makes people resilient and insecure style makes them vulnerable may be too simple to capture the complex person-trauma interaction that is characteristic to war and military violence. Our research among war victims (survivors of human-rights abuse) gives an example by showing that the protective function of attachment style depended on the nature of the stress, i.e., whether it involved cruelty in interpersonal encounter (Kanninen, Punamaki, and Qouta, 2003). The results concur with Crittenden (1997), who suggests that due to the unique early learning experiences each attachment pattern provides a strategy (working model) that is the most adaptive solution to certain types of problems and threats.

Our results substantiated that victims with secure attachment style were protected from psychiatric distress when exposed to general traumatic stress, while both insecure-avoidant and insecure-preoccupied victims were vulnerable. However, when the trauma involved provocative and malevolent interpersonal relations, the secure victims showed vulnerability and inability to cope well, whereas insecure-preoccupied survivors were more resilient. The deceptiveness and unpredictability of torture and ill treatment were in accordance with the preoccupied victims' early working models expecting arbitrary and bad deeds from other humans and danger from the environment. The emotional numbness and disregard for human relations that is typical of dismissing individuals' working models provide them with protection in traumatic stress by distancing them emotionally.

Traumatic events apparently communicate different meanings to secure and insecure people. The basic premises of trauma requiring victims to fundamentally revise their models of reality, themselves, worldview, and other people (Horowitz, 1979; Janoff-Bulman, 1989) may be valid only or especially among secure individuals. This revision process is unique for each attachment style and the mismatch versus match between attachment-specific earlier working models and current traumatic reality explains the possibility for resiliency. Cruelty by fellow humans that is the core of war violence is a shattering experience for secure persons who perceive themselves as worthy of protection, other people as trustworthy, and the world as predictable and safe. Whereas human cruelty is matching with the lessons that preoccupied people have learned early in life: the world is an unsafe place and no good deeds can be expected from people. The lack of mismatch between their earlier schemata and current traumatic experiences could protect their mental health. Thus in conditions of war and military violence the secure attachment style cannot be considered a resiliency factor as such, but rather the match or mismatch between current traumatic experiences and the attachment-specific working models is decisive for each attachment style to enhance resiliency.

Exposure to trauma and danger activates the attachment-related working models that were originally learned to guarantee the child's safety and survival in the face of threat and danger (Bowlby, 1980). In war conditions we can observe how securely and insecurely attached children show unique ways of interpreting and evaluating the danger, regulating emotions, and seeking refugee. However, research is available only on adults' attachment-specific processes of maintaining psychological integrity and emotional balance in war danger. It confirms that victims with different attachment styles uniquely process their trauma-related emotions, cope with hardships, defend their psychological integrity, and benefit from therapy (Kanninen, Salo, and Punamäki, 2000; Mikulincer, Florian, and Weller, 1993; Mikulincer et al., 1999).

Mikulincer and his research group (1993, 1999) showed that individuals with a secure attachment style were protected from serious mental health problems when exposed to traumatic stress, while insecure persons were vulnerable. They also detected attachment-specific symptom expression: ambivalent (preoccupied) individuals responded typically with depression and avoidant (dismissing) behavior by somatization. Their results confirmed that exposure to danger and trauma triggers the attachment-related working model: insecure persons were especially vulnerable when living in dangerous areas, while attachment-specific differences were less salient in safer conditions (Mikulincer et al., 1999).

Another study showed that only among secure persons was exposure to war trauma associated with post-traumatic growth, defined as trauma-evoked positive changes involving deepening appreciation of life, and growing affiliation with others and spirituality (Tedeschi and Calhoun, 1996). By contrast, among insecure-preoccupied men, trauma exposure increased negative emotions (Salo, Punamäki, and Qouta, 2006)

Concerning emotions, Kanninen, Qouta, and Punamäki (2003) showed attachment-specific processing of traumatic experiences. Among insecure-dismissing survivors, the process was biased toward cognitive and rational responses and deactivation of emotions, whereas among insecure-preoccupied survivors the biases were toward intensification and overactivation of emotional responses. Insecure-preoccupied men also responded to traumatic memories by an intense behavioral urge to act, which may indicate their dependency upon procedural rather than upon semantic models to regulate emotions.

By contrast, secure victims showed moderate and balanced levels of both affective and cognitive responses to traumatic memories. In Crittenden's (1997) terms, insecure-avoidant survivors trusted cognitions and distrusted emotions, while insecure-preoccupied survivors distrusted cognitive information and relied predominantly on affective responses. Secure people in turn had access to both emotional and cognitive domains of their traumatic experiences. The insecure trauma victims thus segregate affective and episodic schemata from cognitive and semantic ones.

We may hypothesize that this segregation explains insecure people's greater vulnerability, because disintegration and fragmentation in processing of traumatic experience are the core characteristics of PTSD and dissociation symptoms. The resiliency of secure individuals may in turn be explained by their access to both emotional expression and cognitive framing of trauma and by their capability to achieve balance and integration between them.

The function of children's attachment behavior is to protect their psychological integrity in an adverse and unsafe environment. In infancy that behavior is highly visible when children seek their mothers for safety and soothing. Later in development attachment behavior is largely dormant and is especially activated in the face of dangers and threats. A constantly activated attachment behavior is burdening to a growing child, and a precondition to resilient development is the release of attachment behavior by finding an inner safe place. Adults, especially parents and teachers, are in a core position to create the safe place despite external dangers and insecurity. Building resiliency among children in war must therefore start by strengthening parents' resources to act as a psychological security zone. Sadly enough, the illusion of private safety seems to be the secret of resilient development.

MECHANISMS AND PROCESSES THAT ENHANCE RESILIENCY: WHAT, HOW, WHEN, AND WHY

It is vital to understand preconditions and processes that help children to resist and to maintain their sanity in the midst of war and violence. The metaphor of a struggle between sons of darkness and sons of light may illustrate war children's constant effort to balance between resilience and vulnerability. It is important to realize that simultaneously with traumatic impact counterforces are also activated to protect the child's psyche from pain and disintegration. They involve emotional, cognitive, symbolic, and neurophysiological processes that differ in their degree of voluntary and automatic nature. Table 5.1 summarizes underlying mechanisms and processes that can either promote resiliency or make children more vulnerable in war conditions.

Table 5.1. Impact of Traumatic Experience on Cognitive, Emotional, and Symbolic Processes and Ways of Promoting Resiliency

Processes	Trauma Impact	Promotion of Resiliency
Cognitive		
• Attention	• Excessive vigilance for threat and danger • Automatic activation without cognitive feedback • Generalization of threat to neutral cues	• Training for recognizing own automatized processes • Discriminatory analysis of safety versus nonsafety
• Memory	• Trauma scene does not fade, long duration • Vivid and intensive as if happening here and now • Sensory, kinesthetic, and behavioral dominate • Involuntary, arbitrary cues evoke • No verbal access and difficult to share	• Working with traumatic memories on all modalities: verbal, kinesthetic, sensory • Inviting narrative stories: play, theater, bibliotherapy, sociodrama
• Attribution and explanation models	• Expecting people to be harming and bad • Perceiving environment as globally unsafe • External causes and helplessness • Black and white worldview	• Peace education: analysis of similarities and differences between enemies, sharing memories • Reconciliation: forgiveness, justice, and future views • Empowerment, self-efficacy, and agency
• Problem solving	• Narrowing range of alternatives • Diminishing flexibility due to danger • Problems of concentration	• Enrichment programs: creative tasks, integrating cognitive and emotional domains of development

(continued)

Table 5.1. *(continued)*

Processes	Trauma Impact	Promotion of Resiliency
Emotions		
• Emotion experience	• Lack of synchrony between appraisal, feeling states, behavioral and physiology of emotions • Domination of behavioral urge to act at the expense of more reflecting emotions • Difficulty to name psychophysiological states	• Story telling, drawing, and communicating emotions • Recognition and training of bodily expression
• Emotion recognition and discrimination	• Emotion recognition biased to fear and anger • Diminished discrimination of nuances in other's feeling states	• Using emotional ladder to name and evaluate own feelings' valence and intensity
• Emotion expression	• Numbing or overwhelming feelings • Negative valence • Narrowed repertoire: fear and anger dominate	• Animate and inanimate feeling expression • Imaginary world of emotions
Symbolic processes		
• Dreaming	• Fragmented and nonnarrative reports • Realistic and lack of symbolism • Negative persecution themes • Lack of emotions	• Encouraging dream recall: keeping a dream diary • Guided dramatization of dreams: different endings, introducing of feeling repertoire, control, and condolence
• Playing and fairy tales	• Repetitive themes of persecution • Lack of narrative and integrative solutions • Contents involve helplessness and hate	• Introducing different themes, problem solutions, role change, and meta-analysis of own play • Alternative, emotionally loaded, and multiple outcomes

EMOTIONS: EXPERIENCE, RECOGNITION, AND REGULATION

Clinical experience shows that emotions are curiously either too overwhelmingly present or strangely absent among war-traumatized children. Some children respond to trauma and horrors with intense feelings of sadness and rage, their emotional states escalate, and they are difficult to soothe. On the contrary, other children respond with rational coolness and soon seem to have forgotten the frightening scenes. Sometimes their emotionless behavior is mistakenly interpreted as resiliency. Emotions serve a primary adaptive function, and both the absent and overloaded emotions communicate risks for child mental health and development (Cacioppo and Gardner, 1999; Diener and Mangelsdorf, 1999). The observations among children concur with research on adult trauma survivors who show distorted and biased emotional processing, resulting in both escalation and numbing of emotions (Litz et al., 2000; Näätänen et al., 2002)

Emotions constitute a comprehensive and integrated experience that functions on multiple levels: cognitive, meta, affective, behavioral, and psychophysiological (Frijda, Kuipers, and terSchure, 1989). To illustrate the multilevel emotional processing in the face of violence and life danger, I quote an eleven-year-old Palestinian boy's responses to military violence, depicted in a Picture test measuring coping strategies (Punamäki and Suleiman, 1990). On the cognitive level one can appraise the threat and danger as manageable or horrific and oneself as strong or helpless. The boy's response illustrates an attempt at control and strength: "I do not fear you and your weapons, because we have our [just] struggle and this is not your country." On a meta-level he is observing and reflecting his emotions and comparing them to those evoked by similar earlier events: "This is our life as long the soldiers are here. We have succeeded also earlier. Do not despair my friend."

Feeling states differ in intensity and positive-negative valence. The boy's feeling states involve high intensity of anger and sadness and low intensity of fear, surprise, and joy: "Mother, mother, do not cry, I do not fear and we will have happiness to come." The behavioral urges to act involve bodily felt emotional reactions: "My blood is boiling." "I feel like hitting the soldier." "I feel like disappearing from the earth." The psychophysiological level of emotional function can include extreme autonomic responses to cues that are reminiscent of trauma and neuroanatomical consequences of decreased hippocampal volume, indicating loss of integrated memories and activation of amygdalae and sensory areas of brain. These changes concur with the vividness of flashbacks of the trauma scenes (van der Kolk, 1997; Yehuda and McEwen, 2004).

Characteristic to a traumatic event is that it shatters the synchronized, integrated, and comprehensive emotional experience by inferring the multilevel functioning. Thus survivors not only experience intense negative emotions but their emotional experience is fragmented and intrusive, and feelings can oscillate between escalated and narrowed expressions (Litz et al., 2000; Thompson and Calkins, 1996). Their emotional experience tells about discrepancies between cognitive, affective, behavioral, and physiological domains and domination of one emotional level at the expense of others (Näätänen et al., 2002).

Impulsive behavior, for example, is common among war-traumatized adolescents, indicating that behavioral action readiness dominates their emotional processing at the expense of more reflective, manifold, and modulating aspects of emotions. War victims also show discrepancy between conscious (cognitive and meta levels) and automatic (psychophysiological) levels of emotional processing. They can report emotional numbness and deny their emotions but show strong physiological signs of distress. Similar dynamics have been evidenced in laboratory settings: children who numb and suppress their painful feelings show heightened levels of emotional arousals (Dozier and Kobak, 1992), and adults who repress negative feelings show high activation of psychophysiological responses (Greenberg, 1996).

During the first year of life infants are capable of recognizing the basic emotions and gradually toward toddlerhood they learn more complex emotions such as envy and guilt (Herba and Phillips, 2004; Pollak et al., 2000). Recognition of basic emotions of sadness, fear, anger, disgust, surprise, and joy systematically differs according to a child's age and experiences. Infants of depressive mothers recognized sadness more easily than joy, although in normal development recognition of positive emotions precedes the negative (Fox and Calkins, 2003).

Maltreated children show biased recognition of anger and fear and narrowed expression of emotions (Maughan and Cicchetti, 2002; Pollak et al., 2000) and face difficulties in understanding their own and others' feelings (Rogosch, Cicchetti, and Aber, 1995). Similarly, aggressive children more readily recognize angry and threatening emotional states in others, distort their perceptions toward negative expressions, and interpret others' initiatives as threatening and derogative (Chang et al., 2003; Dodge et al., 1995). The specific impact of adverse experiences on early automatic recognition and discriminating processes is an example of emotions serving the adaptive and life-protecting function.

The evidence that adversity can fundamentally impact the basic early processes of recognizing, discriminating, interpreting, and expression of emotions is important when promoting resiliency in war conditions. It is likely that in life-endangering conditions children become experts in recognizing and discriminating feelings of fear and cues of danger and threat. In optimal doses the accurate recognition of danger indicates survival skills, but there is a risk that vigilance for dangerous and aggressive cues generalizes to neutral situations (Brewinn et al., 2003). Research shows that deficiency in early emotion recognition can predict problems in emotion regulation, which in turn is a serious risk for psychological disorders such as aggression and depression (Eisenberg, 2000; Thompson and Calkins, 1996).

Distorted and biased emotion recognition can function as an underlying marker of mental health risks among war-traumatized children. Therefore interventions that aim at resiliency building include sessions where children are guided to recognize and discriminate their own and others' feelings, and apply a meta-analytic perspective to their own responses to traumatic scenes. Expressing a variety of trauma-related feelings using different modalities such as facial, kinesthetic, visual, and auditory is fundamental in resiliency building.

To conclude, emotional processes and mechanisms of promoting resilient development in war conditions include the following characteristics: First, resilient children can comprehensively and relatively quickly return to normal functioning after upsetting and horrifying experiences. This kind of elasticity is possible if children have access to both intense and moderate emotional states, with no tendencies of either numbing or escalating their feelings. Another precondition is a comprehensive, integrated, and coherent emotional experience that involves cognitive appraisal, meta-analysis, a repertoire of feeling states, and the behavioral urge to act, without discrepancies or domination of any level. Further, resiliency is possible when children show accurate and age-salient emotion recognition, discrimination, and interpretation, which contributes to the success of emotion regulation.

COGNITIVE: ATTENTION, INTERPRETATION, MEMORY, AND PROBLEM SOLVING

The core experience of a traumatized mind is biased attention and memory, distorted causal attribution, and deteriorated problem solving. Life threat, losses, and destruction constitute a severe developmental burden to children and adolescents living in war conditions. It is possible that biased and narrowed cognitive processes initially protected a child's psyche from overwhelming pain, but in the course of development the processes tend to lose their function and become counterproductive. For example, overvigilant attention to threatening cues serves survival in acute danger, but indicates psychopathology (arousal symptoms of PTSD) when prolonged and generalized to neutral cues. Basically, emotional and cognitive processes are children's friends, and in enhancing resiliency it is important to learn how, why, and when these processes turn out to be maladaptive, instead of protective.

Attention biases and distorted threat perceptions are underlying risk processes of PTSD. In avoidant symptoms the perception is narrowed and feelings numbed, whereas in intrusive symptoms perception is overactive, which makes the environment overwhelmingly dangerous, unreliable, and malevolent. Victims of childhood trauma continue to be highly vigilant for new threats and dangers, expect malevolent intentions from others, and show a shortened and pessimistic view of the future (Terr, 1991). War atrocities tax children's adaptive resources and can fundamentally change their basic philosophy of life toward hostile and split attributions and interpretations of the world, malevolent expectations about other humans, and helplessness of themselves (Horowitz, 1979; Janoff-Bulman, 1989). Resiliency is possible if these schemata are prevented from becoming stable, automatic, rigid, and generalized. Psychopathology is in turn likely if children apply trauma-specific schemata also to neutral and random cues in safer conditions.

Normal cognitive development forms a basis for resiliency characterized by flexible, rich, and accurate perceptions and interpretations of events. With age children learn to perceive and interpret social interactions more accurately, understand complex causal relationships between their own and others' behavior, and are more capable of understanding conflicting and nuanced information (Dodge and Price, 1994; Ronald, Spinath, and Plomin, 2002). The cognitive sophistication in turn increases their coping and problem-solving efficiency and enables extensive planning and repertoire of mental activities (Eisenberg, 2000). War propaganda and enmity can interfere with healthy cognitive development by introducing a simplified, fragmented, black-and-white worldview. Peace education and reconciliation between former enemies can thus serve as resiliency building, because they involve self-reflection of attention biases, reanalysis of causal attributions, novel experiences, changing misinterpretations, and sharing of painful memories (Sanson and Bretherton, 2001).

Remembering traumatic events differs from neutral memories in encoding, duration, recall, and in structure and possibility to be shared with others (Mechanic et al., 1998; van der Kolk and Fisher, 1995). Characteristic to traumatic memories are their long duration, vividness, involuntary recall, and nonverbal nature. While neutral memories fade away and can be accessed by conscious will, traumatic memories can stay alive from childhood to adulthood, often in a strangely vivid manner, as if they had happened yesterday. Normally people make efforts and work systematically to recall and remember, whereas traumatic memories return involuntarily, randomly, and intrusively. Neutral memories are narrative and can be verbally expressed and shared with others, whereas trauma scenes typically involve sensory and kinesthetic memories such as smell, voice, touch, and movement. Traumatic memories further arouse strong physical sensations and involve intense emotions.

These characteristics of traumatic memories can harm child development and mental health. Young children like to express their painful experiences in drawing and playing. However, if not combined with verbal access to painful and shameful scenes, the memories prevent children from further working through and sharing them with others. The intrusive and involuntary trauma memories are frightening to young children, who are sometimes more afraid of their memories than they were of the trauma itself (Yule, 2002), as a Somali boy of seven said: "The bombing is still going on in my head during the night."

Narrative techniques such as storytelling, fantasy, and role-play are common tools in interventions and preventions among war-traumatized children. Their effectiveness in enhancing resiliency lies in the possibility of changing maladaptive memory characteristics such as intrusiveness and nonverbalism into more integrated memory. They also enhance children's belief in the ability to exercise control over painful events and possibility of change. Understanding and accepting trauma as a part of one's personal history, indicated by integrated autobiographic memory, is crucial in recovery. Resilient cognitive processes in war conditions involve optimally vigilant appraisal and accurate interpretation of dangers, and flexible responses to them. Through these responses war seems more controllable and less threatening.

SYMBOLIC PROCESSES: DREAMING, PLAYING, AND FANTASY

Symbolic processes such as dreaming, playing, and fantasy are important when attempting to understand child resiliency in conditions of war and violence. They constitute a kind of natural healing process that an evolutionarily wise psyche provides children in order to help them to master overwhelming and horrifying images of trauma (Hartmann, 1995; Revonsuo, 2000). This view emphasizing the resilience-enhancing dream function differs from conceptualization that equates bad dreams and repetitious play with symptoms and dysfunction.

Researchers have tried to find out what kind of dreams can protect mental health in exposure to traumatic events and thus serve the underlying mechanism of resiliency. There is some evidence that dreams incorporating diversity of feelings and complete, bizarre, and symbolic narratives can protect children's mental health in war conditions in the Middle East (Punamäki, 1997b). By contrast, war trauma was associated with psychological distress among children whose dreams incorporated mundane, fragmented, and concrete elements (Punamäki, 1998). Clinical studies confirm that trauma exposed children whose dreams incorporate narrative scenes of trauma, such as a burning accident or parental abuse, show better adjustment than children who did not report dreams with relevant trauma-related themes (Barrett, 1996). Similarly, adult studies show that beneficial dreams incorporate complete narratives and intense emotional (Hartmann, 1996), symbolic, and metaphoric scenes of the painful experience (Barrett, 1996; Cartwright, 1996). Table 5.2 gives examples of resilient and vulnerable dreams among Palestinian children. They reported them by using a 7-night dream diary (Punamäki, 1998a). The scoring criteria for beneficial and at-risk dream characteristics are highlighted.

What is striking is that the protective and beneficial dream characteristics are the reverse of those that are common among war-traumatized children. Research shows that dreams of traumatized children are less dreamlike, i.e., they are less condensed, symbolic, and bizarre and involve fewer narratives and shifts in time and space than dreams of nontraumatized children. Trauma-related dreams are negative, incorporate vivid and realistic replications of the horrifying scenes, and involve threatening and persecuting themes and anxious and hostile emotions (Nader, 1996; Punamäki, 1998a; Terr, 1991).

Dreams of Palestinian and Kurdish children exposed to severe war trauma were highly concrete and realistic, replicating the violent scenes in a fragmented and nonnarrative way and ending in horrifying scenes without solution. High level of trauma was also associated with lack of symbolism and absence of emotional expression involving both positive and negative emotions (Punamäki, 1998b; Punamäki et al., 2005).

War and military violence thus constitute a vicious circle or a trap for child development, which subsequently interferes with possibilities for resiliency. The more the exposed children are in need of healing powers of dreaming, the more the very trauma strips these kinds of dreams from them.

Dreaming can be healing because it enables trauma victims to process the waking-time painful and provocative emotions and horrifying scenes in a safer, condensed, and unreal dream reality, which serves as mood regulation process (Cartwright et al., 1998; Kramer, 1993; Punamäki, 1999). The dreaming mind works intensively until the repetitious, vivid, horrifying, and concrete dreams fade and are replaced by emotionally loaded and symbolic themes (Barrett, 1996; Revonsuo, 2000).

Timing, rhythm, and duration of psychological responses matter for resiliency. The changes in children's dreams after traumatic experiences illustrate how they attempt to integrate and neutralize the painful memories

Table 5.2. Examples of Resilience-Enhancing and Vulnerable Dreams and Criteria

Resiliency-Enhancing Dream	Vulnerable Dream	Criteria
Last night I dreamed that I went to my uncle to hunt. I hunted a small bird, my uncle hunted two birds. *We went back to the house and we were happy. My uncle said the next day that he want to go to the market to sell the birds with the high price.* My uncle went and sold the birds and came back happy. The next day I went to see my bird, I found it very sick, between death and life. I let it go free.	I saw in my dream that the occupying soldiers [had] my brother in the street and beating him with baton. Till his bones were crushed from the severe beating. When I saw him *I started screaming hoping that my family would go out and to defend him. But nobody answered me because nobody could hear me.* I went to the soldiers . . . and they were all the time beating me. As to get rid of me. But I refused until I was taken from them and taken to the hospital. I came back to my house, and my family was waiting [for] me, but they didn't know what had happened.	• *Availability versus absence of family support* • *Problem solving versus nonending*
I dreamed this night that the soldiers entered my home and start to search. My brothers became very frightened and my father was standing and looking calm.		
I dreamed that my mother went to the market and bought me a big watch. I was very happy. I carried the watch in the street. A car of soldiers passed by and I couldn't find a stone to throw on the car; so I throw the watch and it was broken.	I dreamed that I was playing football with my friends, I fell into the ground and injured my head. The blood came out, so I woke up frightened.	• *Complete narrative versus fragmentation*
	I dreamed at night that I fell down into a hole.	
	I dreamed at night that I was imprisoned and was crying very much.	
I went to the sea and catch a fish and it was dead. Then, suddenly it moves and bites me. For that I went home and *asked my father to come with me every day to the sea and to kill the fish that I catch.*	I dreamed that I was going to school. The soldiers faced me. So, I became *frightened and waked up from my sleep.*	• *Persecution versus success theme*

(continued)

Table 5.2. *(continued)*

Resiliency-Enhancing Dream	Vulnerable Dream	Criteria
I dreamed at night that the soldiers ran after me and caught me. They took me to their prison center. The children ran after them throwing stones. My mother was shouting and throwing stones toward them, too. The soldier shot her and the ambulance took her to the hospital. *My mother was very sad and crying.* Then the soldiers let me go home. My mother *became very happy and left* the hospital and gave sweets to the neighbors.	I dreamed that a black snake bit me while sitting under a tree in the school. I stood after it had bitten me and killed it, and it was throwing her poison on me from her tongue.	• *Multiple emotions versus lack of emotions*
	I dreamed that my father came out of the prison and that my mother bought for me and my brothers shoes, pencils, erasers, rulers and we went to the sea. We were very happy, but the shoes were soon torn. I cleaned them and returned them to the place where Mother had bought them.	• *Symbolic versus realistic content*

(continued)

I was at my grandfather's house. I went with my cousins to play. We went with my cousins to play. We dug in the ground, money came out from the ground. We dug, silver came out. We dug and gold game out. People gathered around us. We quarrelled with them. We told them: "These money and gold belong to us. You don't have anything from it, because we are the ones who found it."

Last night I went to my aunt's house in the camp, on my bike, while I was walking, I saw the army soldiers beating youngsters and so youngsters were throwing them with stones. While I was looking at them they came and hit me and took my bike and broke my bike. And left me. So I went to my house instead of going to my aunt's house.

and gain physiological and psychological balance. Immediately after trauma children's dreams replicate the original trauma scene in a concrete and very visual, auditory, and kinesthetic, fashion (Nader, 1996; Terr, 1991). Gradually dreams involve an increasingly symbolic, disguised, and narrative course of traumatic events, which indicates a successful healing process allowing neutralization and disguising of painful memories. The changes toward symbolic and narrative characteristics can function as a marker for an underlying mechanism for resilient development in war conditions.

Traumatic experiences severely burden children's integrative dreaming processes, because frightening and shocking emotions and provocative visual images do not match with earlier memory networks. The dreaming mind is attempting to give the trauma scene new mnemonic and narrative structure so that it could concur with the mind's similar previous experiences (Hartmann, 1995). The reframing is apparently successful among resilient dreamers, whereas failed processing of traumatic images results in PTSD. The intrusive images of the trauma scene, nightmares, and vigilance for dangers are typical among trauma victims (Breslau, 1998), which indicates that the integrative process, like dreaming, is broken down, and the original trauma scene intrudes into daily life as continual fragmented memories and incomprehensible fears.

DEVELOPMENT OF RESILIENCY

The classics of resiliency research focused on biological prenatal and perinatal risk factors combined with socioeconomic adversity (Garmezy, 1990; Werner, 1993) and mental illness (Anthony, 1974; Hammen, 2003). The results provide good examples of how child resiliency versus vulnerability are a function of multiple pathways evolving and integrating biological, social, and psychological domains (Cicchetti and Garmezy, 1993; Egeland et al., 1993; Sameroff, 1999). They also succinctly illustrate various mechanisms through which resiliency versus vulnerability factors accumulate and are activated, strengthened, or neutralized by other factors. Contemporary research on prenatal and perinatal predictors of child development can be fruitful to analysis of early biological and psychological determinants of resiliency (Field et al., 2004; Miceli et al., 1998; O'Connor et al., 2002).

Evidence is growing that high maternal stress and anxiety during pregnancy negatively affect child development, both directly and through medical complications. Prenatal depressive symptoms are associated with premature gestation, difficult labor, and birth complications, and stress during pregnancy is associated with premature birth and low birth weight (Hoffman and Hatch, 2000; Kurki et al., 2000). These neonatal vulnerabilities in turn predict insecurity in parent-child interaction (Sajaniemi et al., 2001) and problems in children's cognitive and emotional development (Bradley et al., 1994).

There are sad reasons for the importance of pre-, peri-, and postnatal risk factors affecting child resiliency in contemporary wars and military violence. For mothers living in war conditions anxiety equates with threat to life and excessive fear for child security, and depression-related losses often carry with them horrifying images and intrusive memories.

In contemporary wars civilians, that is, women and children, are increasingly the target of military violence and victims of atrocities. Human-rights organizations have reported that warfare has been deliberately targeted toward pregnant women and women with young children during the wars and military conflicts in the Balkans, Middle East, and Africa (Marcal, 2003; UNICEF, 2004). In order to enhance children's resiliency in war conditions, it is vital to provide mental health services for pregnant women and mother-infant dyads. A Palestinian mother expressed the importance of early interventions succinctly by saying: "You trust too much on biology, when you think that we can protect our children. It is right to help preschoolers and school children, but . . . when you are pregnant you feel the most vulnerable and your anxiety heightens because we are two."* As it happens in developmental science, the mothers are teaching the professionals.

There is no agreement on how the age of the child affects the resiliency versus vulnerability among war victims. On the one hand, younger children are expected to be at especially high risk because they lack sophisticated cognitive strategies to conceptualize and master the danger, and on the other hand, they are expected to be protected because of the very same reason of not grasping the serious consequences of trauma (Landau and Litwin, 2000; Lynch and Cicchetti, 1998; Pfefferbaum, 1997). However, it is more likely that each developmental age provides children unique protecting resources, on one hand, and makes them vulnerable, on the other (Masten and Coatsworth, 1998).

Table 5.3 shows the salient and age-specific resources and vulnerabilities among infants, toddlers and preschoolers, school-age children, and adolescents. The argument is that resiliency building should be tailored to increase the age-specific strengths, to decrease age-specific risks, and seek balance between them.

Table 5.3. Strengths and Resources versus Vulnerabilities and Risk on Social, Emotional, and Cognitive Domains According to Developmental Age and Salient Developmental Tasks

Developmentally Salient Tasks	Strengths and Resources	Vulnerabilities and Risks
Infancy		
• Social: parent-infant relationship	• Secure attachment: trust in available care and benevolence, and self-worth	• Distrust in available care: emotional withdrawal or clinging to others
• Emotional: recognition and attuning	• Recognition and expression of positive emotions	• Negative and intensive emotional arousal
		• Fear and anger dominate
• Cognitive: exploring environment	• Sensomotor coordination and focused attention	• Distrust in predictability of event
		• Fear prevents exploring and curiosity

Integration as a precondition of resiliency: attachment security, emotional attuning, and soothing, procedural experience of causality between own and mother's behavior.

Toddler and preschool age		
• Social: expanding of family relationship	• Attachment to siblings and extended family	• Regressive clinging to others as a result of trauma
		• Sibling rivalry for security
• Emotional: regulation of emotions and theory of mind	• Complex emotions emerge and are learned: guilt, shame, envy, jealousy	• Difficulty in emotion regulation: escalation of fear and aggression
	• Balanced theory of mind: understanding own or others' feeling > development of empathy	• Difficulty in empathy development: recognizing own and others' feelings
• Cognitive: language, memory, causality, and symbolism	• Learning rules and causal relations	• Regression in language development: mutism
	• Vocabulary and syntactic repertoire increases	• Traumatic memory: nonverbal and kinesthetic
		• Symbolic development: Difficulties in separating between reality and fantasy

Integration as a precondition of resiliency: Comprehensive theory of mind and adequate emotion regulation enable social participation and play, which further facilitate rich vocabulary and high-quality symbolization.

Middle childhood

Domain	Competencies	Problems
Social: peer relations and friendship	• Reciprocal friendship and sharing with peers • Feeling of belonging • Balance between family and peer relations	• Adultlike commitment in adverse conditions • Peer rejection, discrimination, and bullying • Inability to share emotions, lack of friends
Emotional: emotional recognition	• Recognition of nuanced and multiple emotions: high emotional intelligence • Understanding complex and conflicting motives	• Narrow or biased emotional repertoire • Selective empathy • Non-normative aggression
Cognitive: sophisticated causal explanation, advanced problem solving	• Sophisticated problem solving and high IQ • Good academic performance • Peer acceptance and feeling of belonging • Moral development from concrete to abstract	• Splitting between good and bad • Fear shadows reasoning capacity • Concentration problems

Integration as a precondition of resiliency: Feeling of self-competence, security in peer relationships, and increasing reliance on friends without losing trust in parental relationship.

Adolescence

Domain	Competencies	Problems
Social: intimate relationship and romantic partnership	• Constructing own identity and worldview • Experience of intimacy, caring, and sharing • Distancing from parents	• Traumatic scenes interfere with intimate relationship • Distrust in human virtue • Disregard for dangers and life threat • Concern and dependency on family relationships
Emotional: sharing and expressing feelings	• Adaptation of own emotional expression style • Exploring multiple emotions	• Strong oscillations between mood states • Impulsive behavior: emotions acted out, lack of nuanced feelings and evaluations
Cognitive: worldview, moral issues, attribution discrepancies	• Ability of abstract reasoning and thinking • Multilevel and conflicting decision and planning • Moral development reaches universal and nonrelativist stage	• Appraisal of own future narrowed and unrealistically pessimistic • Difficulty in making decisions and concrete demands for survival • Distorted belief in one's invulnerability

Integration as a precondition of resiliency: Identity emerging on social, emotional, and cognitive domains, increasing commitment and responsibility, selective intimacy, and trust in future competence.

Infancy

In infancy the development task is to find a balance between needs for security and curiosity. A sensitive mother provides the infant a safe place for training emotions, exploring the environment, and training sensomotor and cognitive capabilities. In this dyadic interaction the child learns causality between personal initiative and maternal responses, which serve the basic representations of oneself, the world, and other people (Crittenden, 1997). The age-salient resiliency is building on attachment security, experience of being soothed, and procedural causal interpretation of predictability of mother's behavior.

Toddlers

In their extending family relations toddlers learn to regulate and adequately express emotions and master complex feelings of shame, guilt, and jealousy (Thompson and Calkins, 1996). Toddlers gain understanding of their own and others' beliefs, behavior, and emotions and learn about causality between thinking and behaving (Saarni, 1999; Steelman et al., 2002). The emotional-cognitive sophistication forms in turn precondition for prosocial and empathetic behavior (Eisenberg, 2000). To separate fantasy from reality is a core developmental task in toddlers that is achieved through intensive imagination, fantasy, and symbolic play. Preconditions for resilient development are smooth integration of inner capabilities of emotional and cognitive achievements and familial and social demands, indicated by emotion regulation and multimodal expressiveness, rich vocabulary, and high quality of symbolization.

Middle Childhood

In middle childhood peer relations become important, serving as a mirror of identity, self-esteem, and confirmation of competencies and worthiness (Deater-Deckard, 2001; Hymel, Bowker, and Woody, 1993). Cognitive development is intense and enables sophisticated problem solving and nuanced communication. More comprehensive understanding and recognition of complex and conflicting emotions in others enable social skills to develop and mark transition to adolescence (Shipman, Zeman, and Stegall, 2001). Resilient development in middle childhood is a function of good friendships and peer relations, investment in cognitive advances, and emotional complex learning.

Adolescence

Adolescents' main tasks are planning for the future, creating intimate relationships, and committing to one's worldview, morality, and identity. Adolescents have strong beliefs in their own invulnerability, general justice, and their own capability to change the world. Their cognitive resources allow increasingly sophisticated and abstract thinking and dealing with conflicting moral and human problems and complex cause and effect. On the other hand, emotionally and socially, young people tend to experience themselves as unsure, and their emotions oscillate intensely (Davison and Susman, 2001). Adolescents maintain their resiliency if it is possible for them to have an impact on society and their own lives. Resilience-enhancing conditions involve also latitude for moral analyses and decisions, the possibility of gaining intimacy, and balance between independence and a feeling of belonging.

Research on developmental transitions can be valuable in understanding the developmental preconditions for resiliency. In the Piagetian sense, during a transition from one stage to the next, the developing mind is more porous, elastic, and in movement and thus more receptive to new experiences and challenges. The increasing knowledge about developmental spurts gives substance to the claim that transitions provide both challenges and risks for children, and timing of resiliency building is therefore of great importance. In resiliency building, transitions are vital because they enable formation of qualitatively new cognitive, emotional, and social activities. For example, brain development makes possible problem solving and memorizing, and cognitive recognition of one's own and others' complex emotional and motivational processes concur with prosocial and regulative development (Kagan, 2003).

There is clinical evidence that in extremely traumatic conditions children can regress to their earlier developmental stage. Freud and Burlingham (1943) described how excessive external destruction and fear made it difficult for toddlers to regulate their aggressive impulses, and they were therefore at risk for regression to early dependency. Children who simultaneously face demands of both developmental transitions and traumatic stress are especially vulnerable to developmental regression. We have observed how toddlers can lose their new-learned vocabulary, which can lead to temporal mutism in extreme trauma. Bedwetting is another serious problem in war-torn areas, and mothers attribute it to fear and arousal, which interfere with developmental achievements. Preschoolers face difficulties in controlling their aggressive behavior, which is one of their main tasks in emotional regulation before school age. Clinging to parents and an obsession about their safety in middle childhood can also be interpreted as regression to earlier stages of development.

Children in war have been described as a generation growing up too fast, referring to the age-inadequate and adultlike burdens due to the nearness of death and active participation in national struggle. The best-known images of adolescent activists, called either freedom fighters or terrorists, are from Northern Ireland, South Africa, and Palestine, whereas child soldiers in some

Asian and African conflicts are less gloriously portrayed. We lack knowledge whether and how cognitive and emotional processes would speed up as a consequence of adultlike experiences. Armies recruiting minors for the military argue that in some cultures (e.g., hot climates) children grow up earlier, which is shown in their hormonal maturation. Argumentation cannot, however, focus only on timing of maturation processes but should involve also moral issues.

Threat to life is an indispensable part of participation in national struggle, and according to our understanding, it is too heavy a developmental burden for children of any age. On the other hand, participation is glorified and believed to bring meaningfulness into traumatized children's lives. The dilemma between national demands and life threat, sometimes called "a conflict between horror and heroism" (Punamäki and Suleiman, 1990), is expressed by a Palestinian adolescent telling about his imprisonment: "I was but a child when they put me into a confinement cell, accused of throwing stones with other kids and resisting occupation. I was so proud that they took me for a fighter . . . and in the nights I wept."*

The phenomenon parallels concern that resilient children should not be considered invulnerable saviors of family pride, fulfillment of parents' failed dreams, and invincible heroes of their community but rather flexible and creative human beings struggling for balance and survival (Luthar et al., 2000; Rutter 2000). Constant strength and responsibility form a risk of being biased toward cognitive and behavioral strengths, at the cost of more repertoires of emotional and personality development. Research evidences that in high-risk conditions children seldom show resiliency in all developmental domains. They, for instance, show good school achievement but suffer from loneliness and emotional distress (Luthar et al., 1993; Radke-Yarrow and Brown, 1993).

CONCLUSION

Conceptualizing resilience as a victory of protective factors over the vulnerability seems to be inspired by Sleeping Beauty's developmental paths:

> At last the queen had a daughter. There was a very fine christening; and the princess had for her godmothers all the fairies they could find in the whole kingdom. They found seven and every one of them gave her a gift, as was the custom of fairies in those days. . . . The youngest fairy gave for her gift that she should be the most beautiful person in the world; the next, that she should have the wit of an angel; the third, that she should have a wonderful grace in everything she did; and the fourth, that she should dance perfectly well. . . . But they saw come into the hall a very old fairy, whom they had not invited, because it

was above fifty years since she had been out of a certain tower, and she was believed to be dead or captured (Lang, 1889).

The invited fairies brought the child protective factors, while the uninvited fairy brought Sleeping Beauty a vulnerability factor. Wisely, activation of the early childhood vulnerability was timed to concur with the transition period from girlhood to womanhood: "On her eighteenth birthday, the princess will die." The solution that a stubborn and curious prince will neutralize the curse on the dormant potentials of Beauty also accords with the beneficial role of social and intimate human relationship predicting survival, empowerment, and resilience.

The criticism of resiliency research goes along the lines of warning against listing favorable "fairies" and waiting for the "black fate to be activated" by an unfortunate event (e.g., Fonagy et al., 1996; Rutter, 2000). Research has been atheoretical, intuitively exploring child-, family-, and society-related explanations (Fonagy et al., 1996). One may also argue that the initial wondering of why some children stay sane, competent, and blossom even in extreme adverse conditions implicitly relies on an S-R relationship between subject and environment. The question of why all those exposed to high levels of childhood adversity do not become ill is based on the implicit assumption that the human mind is a reflection of outside reality: If we live with snakes, we become a snake; if we witness aggression, we become aggressive. Similarly, the early research on resilience assumed that constitutional risks inevitably predict developmental and mental health problems.

Research on protective and risk factors involved a kind of implicit othernesses in viewing children living in war and military violence. Until the Balkan wars in the 1990s and the September 11, 2001, terrorist attacks, the majority of modern wars were fought in places other than Europe and North America. It was expressed in definition of trauma as an event outside of normal experience (DSM-III), whereas currently trauma involves characteristics such as "threat to life and feeling of intensive helplessness" (DSM-IV) and can happen to any of us anywhere on the globe.

Early research on resiliency to some extent ignored the basics of developmental science that emphasize the activity, subjectivity, and agency of children making sense of and affecting their environment and ignored the mediated and multilevel nature of mechanisms associating child development and adversities. On a philosophical level, both deeply religious people and evolutionists would argue that hardships, threat, and adversities are part of our life, and all of us are programmed for survival either by phylogenetic inheritance or divine goodwill. It does not, however, silence the voice of human rights and peace activists reminding us that war and injustice are created by humans and therefore are removed by humans.

NOTES

*Citations are from research fieldwork and clinical interviews in the Gaza Community Mental Health Program.

1. The study took place during the governing period of the Palestinian Authority (PA) after the Oslo Agreement, signed between Israel and the PLO in Washington in 1993. During this time the nighttime curfew that had lasted for six years was suspended and a substantial number of political prisoners from the Palestinian areas of West Bank and Gaza Strip were released.

REFERENCES

Aldwin, C.M., and Sutton, K.J. (1996). The development of coping. Resources in adulthood. *Journal of Personality* 64:837–871.

Almqvist, K. (2000). Parent-child interaction and coping strategies in refugee children. In L.V. Willigen (Ed.), *Health Hazards of Organized Violence in Children (ii): Coping and Protective Factors* (pp. 53–68). Utrecht: Pharos.

Anthony, E.J. (1974). The syndrome of the psychologically invulnerable child. In E.J.A.C. Kopernick (Ed.), *The Child and His Family: Vol 3. Children at Psychiatric risk* (pp. 529–544). New York: Wiley.

Aron, A., Corne, S., Fursland, A., and Zelwer, B. (1991). The gender-specific terror of El Salvador and Guatemala. *Women's Studies International Forum* 14.

Asarnow, J., Glynn, S., Pynoos, R.S., Nahum, J., Guthrie, D., Cantwell, D.P., et al. (1999). When the earth stops shaking: Earthquake sequlae among children diagnosed for pre-earthquake psychopathology. *Journal of the American Academy of Child and Adolescent Psychiatry* 38:1016–1023.

Baker, A. (1990). The psychological impact of the Intifada on Palestinian children in the occupied West Bank and Gaza: An exploratory study. *American Journal of Orthopsychiatry* 60:496–505.

Baldwin, A.I., Baldwin, C.P., Kasser, T., Zax, M., Sameroff, A., and Seifer, R. (1993). Contextual risk and resiliency during late adolescence. *Development and Psychopathology* 5:741–761.

Barber, B.K. (2001). Political violence, social integration, and youth functioning: Palestinian youth from the Intifada. *Journal of Community Psychology* 29:259–280.

Bar-on, D., Eland, J., Kleber, R.J., Krell, R., Moore, Y., Sagi, A., Soriano, E., Suedfeld, P., van der Velden, P.G., and van Ijzendoorn, M.H. (1998). Multigenerational perspectives on coping with the Holocaust experience: An attachment perspective for understanding the developmental sequence of trauma across generations. *International Journal of Behavioral Development* 22.

Barrett, D. (1996). *Trauma and Dreams*. (pp. 1–6) Cambridge, Mass: Harvard University Press.

Beardslee, W.R., and Podorefsky, D. (1988). Resilient adolescents whose parents have serious affective and other psychiatric disorders: The importance of self-understanding and relationships. *American Journal of Psychiatry* 145:63–69.

Becker, D., Lira, E., Castillo, M.I., Comez, E., and Kovalskys, J. (1990). Political repression in Chile: The challenge of social reparation. *Journal of Social Issues* 46: 133–149.

Belsky, J. (1984). The determinants of parenting: A process model. *Child Development* 55:83–96.

Belsky, J., Spritz, B., and Crnic, K. (1996). Infant attachment security and affective-cognitive information processing at age 3. *Psychological Science* 7:111–114.

Bolger, K.E., and Patterson, C.J. (2003). Sequelae of child maltreatment. In S.S. Luthar (Ed.), *Resilience and Vulnerability. Adaptation in the Context of Childhood Adversities* (pp. 156–181). New York: Cambridge University Press.

Bowlby, J. (1973). *Attachment and Loss: Separation, Anxiety and Anger.* New York: Basic Books.

Bowlby, J. (1980). *Attachment and Loss: Sadness and Depression.* New York: Basic Books.

Bracken, P., Giller, J.M., and Summerfield, D. (1995). Psychological responses to war and atrocity: The limitation of current concepts. *Social Science and Medicine* 40:1073–1082.

Bradley, R.H., Whiteside, L., Mundfrom, D.J., Casey, P.H., Kelleher, K.J., and Pope, S.K. (1994). Early indications of resilience and their relation to experiences in the home environments of low birthweight, premature children living in poverty. *Child Development* 65:346–360.

Breslau, N. (1998). Epidemiology of trauma and posttraumatic stress disorder. In R. Yehuda (Ed.), *Psychological trauma* (Vol. 17, pp. 1–29). Washington, DC: American Psychiatric Press.

Brewin, C.R., Dalgeish, T., and Joseph, S. (1996). A dual representation theory of posttraumatic stress disorder. *Psychological Review* 103:670–686.

Brewin, C.R., and Holmes, E.A. (2003). Psychological theories of posttraumatic stress disorder. *Clinical Psychology Review* 23:339–376.

Bryce, J.W., Walker, N., Ghorayeb, F., and Kanj, M. (1989). Life experiences, response styles and mental health among mothers and children in Beirut, Lebanon. *Social Science and Medicine* 28:685–695.

Cacioppo, J.T., and Gardner, W.L. (1999). Emotion. *Annual Review of Psychology* 50: 191–214.

Cairns, E., and Wilson, R. (1989). Mental health aspects of political violence in Northern Ireland. *International Journal of Mental Health* 18:38–56.

Calkins, S.D., and Johnson, M.C. (1998). Toddler regulation of distress to frustrating events: Temperamental and maternal correlations. *Infant Behavior and Development* 21:379–395.

Carlson, E. (1998). A prospective longitudinal study of attachment disorganization/disorientation. *Child Development* 69:1107–1128.

Cartwright, R.D. (1996). Dreams and adaptation to divorce. In D. Barrett (Ed.), *Trauma and Dreams* (pp. 179–185). Cambridge, MA: Harvard University Press.

Cartwright, R., Luten, A., Young, M., Mercer, P., and Bears, M. (1998). Role of REM sleep and dream affect in overnight mood regulation: A study of normal volunteers. *Psychiatry Research* 81:1–8.

Chang, L., Schwartz, D., Dodge, K., and McBride-Chang, C. (2003). Harsh parenting in relation to child emotion regulation and aggression. *Journal of Family Psychology* 17:598–606.

Cicchetti, D., and Garmezy, N. (1993). Prospects and promises in the study of resiliency. *Development and Psychopathology* 5:497–502.

Cicchetti, D., Rogosch, F.A., Lynch, M., and Holt, K.D. (1993). Resilience in maltreated children: Process leading to adaptive outcome. *Development and Psychopathology* 5:629–647.

Cicchetti, D., Rogosch, F.A., and Toth, S. (1998). Maternal depressive disorder and contextual risk: Contribution to the development of attachment insecurity and behavioral problems in toddlerhood. *Development and Psychopathology* 10:283–300.

Compas, B.E., Connor-Smith, J.K., Salzman, H., Harding, B., Thomsen, A., and Wadsworth, M.E. (2001). Coping with stress during childhood and adolescence: Problems, progress, and potential in theory and research. *Psychological Bulletin* 127:87–127.

Conger, R.D., and Elder, G.H.J. (1994). *Families in Troubled Times: Adapting to Change in Rural America*. New York: Aldine De Gruyter.

Contreras, J., Kerns, K., Weimer, B., Gentzler, A., and Tornich, P. (2000). Emotion regulation as a mediator of associations between mother-child attachment and peer relationships in middle childhood. *Journal of Family Psychology* 14:111–124.

Crittenden, P. (2000). Attachment and psychopathology. In R.M.S. Goldberg and J. Kerr (Ed.), *Attachment Theory: Social, Developmental, and Clinical Perspectives*. Hillsdale, NJ: Analytic Press.

Crittenden, P.M. (1997). Toward an integrative theory of trauma: A dynamic-maturational approach. In D.C.S. Toth (Ed.), *The Rochester Symposium on Developmental Psychopathology, Vol. 10. Risk, Trauma, and Mental Processes* (pp. 34–84). Rochester, NY: University of Rochester Press.

Cummings, E.M., Davies, P.T., and Campbell, S.B. (2000). *Developmental Psychopathology and Family Process Theory, Research and Clinical Implications*. New York: Guilford Press.

Daves, A., Tredoux, C., and Feinstein, A. (1989). Political violence in South Africa: Some effects on children with violent destruction of their community. *International Journal of Mental Health* 18:24–30.

Davison, K.K., and Susman, E.J. (2001). Are hormone levels and cognitive ability related during early adolescence? *International Journal of Behavioral Development* 25:416–428.

De Rosnay, M., and Harris, P.L. (2000). Individual differences in children's understanding of emotion: The roles of attachment and languange. *Attachment and Human Development* 4:39–54.

Deater-Deckard, K. (2001). Annotation: Recent research examining the role of peer relationships in the development of psychopathology. *Journal of Child Psychology and Psychiatry* 42:565–579.

Diener, M.L., and Mangelsdorf, S.C. (1999). Behavioral strategies for emotion regulation in toddlers: Associations with maternal involvement and emotional expressions. *Infant Behavior and Development* 22:569–583.

Dodge, K.A., Pettit, G.S., Bates, J.E., and Valente, E. (1995). Social information-processing patterns partially mediate the effect of early physical abuse on later conduct problems. *Journal of Abnormal Psychology* 104:632–643.

Dodge, K.A., and Price, J.M. (1994). On the relation between social information processing and socially competent behavior in early school-aged children. *Child Development* 65:1385–1397.

Dozier, M., and Kobak, R. (1992). Psychophysiology in attachment interviews: Converging evidence for deactivating strategies. *Child Development* 63:1473–1480.

Dunmore, E., Clark, D.M., and Ehlers, A. (2001). A prospective investigation of the role of cognitive factors in persistent posttraumatic stress disorder (PTSD) after physical or sexual assault. *Behaviour Research and Therapy* 39:1063–1084.

Dybdahl, R. (2001). Children and mothers in war: An outcome study of a psychosocial intervention program. *Child Development* 72:1214–1230.

Dyregrov, A., Gjestad, R., and Raundalen, M. (2002). Children exposed to warfare: A longitudinal study. *Journal of Traumatic Stress* 15:59–68.

Dyregrov, A., Gupta, L., Gjestad, R., and Mukanoheli, E. (2000). Trauma exposure and psychological reactions to genocide among Rwandan children. *Journal of Traumatic Stress* 13:3–21.

Egeland, B., and Susman-Stillman, A. (1996). Dissociation as a mediator of child abuse across generations. *Child Abuse and Neglect* 20:1123–1132.

Egeland, B., Carlson, E., and Stroufe, L.A. (1993). Resilience as a process. *Development and Psychopathology* 5:517–528.

Eisenberg, N. (2000). Emotion, regulation, and moral development. *Annual Review of Psychology* 51:665–697.

Favaro, A., Rodella, F.C., Colombo, G., and Santonastaso, P. (1999). Post-traumatic stress disorder and major depression among Italian Nazi concentration camp survivors: A controlled study 50 years later. *Psychological Medicine* 29:87–95.

Fergusson, D. M., and Horwood, L. J. (2003). Childhood adversity. Results of a 21-year study. In S. S. Luthar (Ed.), *Resilience and Vulnerability. Adaptation in the Context of Childhood Adversities* (pp. 130–155). New York: Cambridge University Press.

Field, T., Diego, M., Dieter, J., Hernandez-Reif, M., Schanberg, S., Kuhn, C., et al. (2004). Prenatal depression effects on the fetus and the newborn. *Infant Behavior and Development* 27:216–229.

Foa, E.B., Dancu, C.V., Hembree, E.A., Jaycox, L.H., Meadows, E.A., and Street, G.P. (1999). A comparison of exposure therapy, stress inoculation training, and their combination for reducing posttraumatic stress disorder in female assault victims. *Journal of Consulting and Clinical Psychology* 67:194–200.

Foa, E.B., Steketee, G., and Rothbaum, B.O. (1989). Behavioral/cognitive conceptualisation of post-traumatic stress disorder. *Behavior Therapy* 20:155–176.

Fonagy, P., Steele, M., Steele, H., Higgitt, A., and Target, M. (1996). The Emanuel Miller Memorial Lecture 1992: The theory and practice of resilience. *Journal of Child Psychology and Psychiatry and Allied Disciplines* 35:231–257.

Fox, N., and Calkins, S. (2003). The development of self-control of emotion: Intrinsic and extrinsic influences. *Motivation and Emotion* 27:7–26.

Freud, A., and Burlingham, D.T. (1943). *War and Children.* New York: Medical War Books, Ernest Willard.

Frijda, N., Kuipers, P., and terSchure, L. (1989). Relations between emotion, appraisal and emotional action readiness. *Journal of Personality and Social Psychology* 57:212–228.

Garbarino, J., and Kostelny, K. (1996). The effects of political violence on Palestinian children's behavior problems: A risk accumulation model. *Child Development* 67:33–45.

Garmezy, N. (1990). Resiliency and vulnerability to adverse developmental outcomes associated with poverty. *American Behavioral Scientist* 34:416–430.

Greenberg, L.S. (1996). Allowing and accepting of emotional experience. In B.Z.R.D. Kavanaugh, and S. Fein (Ed.), *Emotion: Interdisciplinary Perspectives* (pp. 315–336). Mahwah, NJ: Lawrence Erlbaum.

Hammen, C. (2003). Risk and protective factors for children of depressed parents. In S.S. Luthar (Ed.), *Resilience and Vulnerability. Adaptation in the Context of Childhood Adversities* (pp. 50–75). New York: Cambridge University Press.

Hartmann, E. (1995). Making connections in a safe place: Is dreaming psychotherapy? *Dreaming* 5:213–228.

Hartmann, E. (1996). Who develops PTSD nightmares and who doesn't? In D. Barrett (Ed.), *Trauma and Dreams* (pp. 100–113). Cambridge, MA: Harvard University Press.

Herba, C., and Phillips, M. (2004). Annotation: Development of facial expression recognition from childhood to adolescence: Behavioural and neurological perspectives. *Journal of Child Psychology and Psychiatry* 45:1185–1198.

Hobfoll, S., Spielberger, C., Breznitz, S., Figley, C., Folkman, S., Lepper-Green, B., et al. (1991). War-related stress: Addressing the stress of war and other traumatic events. *American Psychologist* 46:848–855.

Hoffman, S., and Hatch, M.C. (2000). Depressive symptomatology during pregnancy: Evidence for an association with decreased fetal growth in pregnancies of lower social class women. *Journal of Health Psychology* 19:535–543.

Horowitz, M.J. (1979). Psychological response to serious life events. In V.H.D.M. Warburton (Ed.), *Human Stress and Cognition: An Information Processing Approach* (pp. 235–263). Chichester: John Wiley & Sons.

Horowitz, M. J., Bonanno, G. A., and Holen, A. (1993). Pathological grief: Diagnosis and explanation. *Psychosomatic Medicine* 55:260–273.

Hymel, S., Bowker, A., and Woody, E. (1993). Aggressive versus withdrawn unpopular children: Variations in peer and self-perceptions in multiple domains. *Child Development* 64:879–896.

Janoff-Bulman, R. (1989). Assumptive words and the stress of traumatic events: Application of the schema construct. *Social Cogniton*: 113–136.

Kagan, J. (2003). Biology, context, and developmental inquiry. *Annual Review of Psychology* 54:1–23.

Kanninen, K., Salo, J., and Punamäki, R.L. (2000). Attachment patterns and working alliance in trauma therapy for victims of political violence. *Psychotherapy Research* 10:435–449.

Kanninen, K., Punamäki, R.L., and Qouta, S. (2002). The relation of appraisal, coping efforts, and acuteness of trauma to PTS symptoms among former political prisoners. *Journal of Traumatic Stress* 15:245–253.

Kanninen, K, Punamäki, R.-L. (2003). Adult attachment and emotional responses to traumatic memories among Palestinian former political prisoners. *Traumatology* 9: 15–26.

Kanninen, K., Punamäki, R.-L., and Qouta, S. (2003). Personality and trauma: Adult attachment and posttraumatic distress among former political prisoners. *Peace and Conflict: Journal of Peace Psychology* 9:97–126.

Khamis, V. (1993). Post-traumatic stress disorder among the injured of the Intifada. *Journal of Traumatic Stress* 6:555–559.

Kilpatrick, D.G., Acierno, R., Schnurr, P., Resnick, H.S., Saunders, B.E., and Best, C.L. (2000). Risk factors for adolescent substance abuse and dependence: Data from a national sample. *Journal of Consulting and Clinical Psychology* 68:19–30.

Kinzie, J.D. (2001). Psychotherapy for massively traumatized refugees. *American Journal of Psychotherapy* 55:475–490.

Kochenderfer-Ladd, B., and Skinner, K. (2002). Children's coping strategies: Moderators of the effects of peer victimization? *Developmental Psychology* 38:267–278.

Kordon, D., Edelman, L., and Lagos, D. (1986). *About the Experiences of the Orientation Groups with Relatives of Missing Persons*. Buenos Aires: Group of Psychological Assistance to Mothers of Plaza de Mayo.

Kramer, M. (1993). The selective mood regulatory function of dreaming: An update and revision. In A. Moffitt and M. Kramer (Eds.), *The Functions of Dreaming. SUNY Series in Dream Studies* (pp. 139–195). Albany, NY: State University of New York Press.

Kretchmar, M.D., and Jacobvitz, D.B. (2002). Observing mother-child relationships across generations: Boundary patterns, attachment, and the transmission of caregiving. *Family Process* 41:351–374.

Kulka, R.A., Schlenger, W.E., Fairbank, J.A., Hough, R.L., Jordan, B.K., and Marmar, C.R. (1990). *Trauma and the Vietnam War Generation*. New York: Brunner/Mazel.

Kurki, T., Hiilesmaa, V., Raitasalo, R., Mattila, H., and Ylikorkala, O. (2000). Depression and anxiety in early pregnancy and risk for preeclampsia. *Obstetrics and Gynecology* 95:487–490.

Landau, R., and Litwin, H. (2000). The effects of extreme early stress in very old age. *Journal of Trauma Stress* 13:473–483.

Lang, A. (1889). *The Blue Fairy Book*. (pp. 54–63). London: Longmans, Green, and Company. [Originally from Perrault, Charles. (1697). *Histoires ou contes du temps passé, avec des moralitez*. Paris.]

Laor, N., Wolmer, L., and Cohen, D.J. (2001). Mothers' functioning and children's symptoms 5 years after a Scud missile attack. *The American Journal of Psychiatry* 158:1020–1026.

Laor, N., Wolmer, L., Mayes, L.C., Gershon, A., Weizman, R., and Cohen, D.J. (1997). Israeli preschools under Scuds: A 30-month follow-up. *Journal of American Academy of Child and Adolescent Psychiatry* 36:349–356.

Lazarus, R.S. (2000). Towards better research on stress and coping. *American Psychologist* 55:665–673.

Lazarus, R.S., and Folkman, S. (1984). *Stress, Appraisal, and Coping*. New York: Springer.

Levav, I., Kohn, R., and Schwartz, S. (1998). The psychiatric after-effects of the Holocaust on the second generation. *Psychological Medicine* 28:755–760.

Lichtman, H. (1984). Parental communication of Holocaust experiences and personality characteristics among second-generation survivors. *Journal of Clinical Psychology* 40:914–924.

Litz, B.T., Orsillo, S.M., Kaloupek, D., and Weathers, F. (2000). Emotional processing in posttraumatic stress disorder. *Journal of Abnormal Psychology* 109:26–39.

Luthar, S.S., and Cicchetti, D. (2000). The construct of resilience: Implications for intervention and social policy. *Development and Psychopathology* 12:555–598.

Luthar, S.S., Cicchetti, D., and Becker, B. (2000). The construct of resilience: A critical evaluation and guidelines for future work. *Child Development* 71:543–562.

Luthar, S.S., Doernberger, C.H., and Ziegler, E. (1993). Resilience is not a unidimensional construct: Insights from a prospective study of inner-city adolescents. *Development and Psychopathology* 5:703–717.

Lynch, M., and Cicchetti, D. (1998). Trauma, mental representation, and the organization of memory for mother-referent material. *Development and Psychopathology* 10:739–759.

Macksoud, M., and Aber, J. (1996). The war experiences and psychosocial development of children in Lebanon. *Child Development* 67:70–88.

Main, M. (1996). Introduction to the special section on attachment and psychopathology: An overview of the field of attachment. *Journal of Consulting and Clinical Psychology* 64:237–243.

Marcal, G. (2003). *Impact of Armed Conflict on Children: A Review of Progress Since the 1996 United Nations Report on the Impact of Armed Conflict on Children.* New York: UNICEF.

Masten, A.S., and Coatsworth, J.D. (1998). The development of competence in favorable and unfavorable environments: Lessons from research on successful children. *American Psychologist* 53:205–220.

Masten, A.S., Hubbard, J.J., Gest, S.D., Tellegen, A., Garmezy, N., and Ramirez, M. (1999). Competence in the context of adversity: Pathways to resilience and maladaption from childhood to late adolescence. *Development and Psychopathology* 11:143–169.

Maughan, A., and Cicchetti, D. (2002). Impact on child maltreatment and interadult violence on children's emotion regulation abilities and socioemotional adjustment. *Child Development* 73:1525–1542.

Mechanic, M.B., Resick, P.A., and Griffin, M.G. (1998). A comparison of normal forgetting, psychopathology, and information-processing models of reported amnesia for recent sexual trauma. *Journal of Consulting and Clinical Psychology* 66: 948–957.

Miceli, P.J., Whitman, T.L., Borkowski, J.G., Braungart-Rieker, J., and Mitchell, D.W. (1998). Individual differences in infant information processing: The role of temperamental and maternal factors. *Infant Behavior and Development* 21:119–136.

Mikulincer, M., Florian, V., and Weller, A. (1993). Attachment styles, coping strategies, and posttraumatic psychological distress: The impact of the Gulf War in Israel. *Journal of Personality and Social Psychology* 64:817–826.

Mikulincer, M., Horesh, N., Eilati, I., and Kotler, M. (1999). The association between adult attachment style and mental health in extreme life-endangering conditions. *Personality and Individual Differences* 27:831–842.

Miller, T., El-Masri, M., and Qouta, S. (2000). *Health of Children in War Zones: Gaza Child Health Study.* Hamilton: Centre for Studies of Children at Risk.

Minuchin, S. (1974). *Families and Family Therapy.* Cambridge, MA: Harvard University Press.

Montgomery, E., and Foldspang, A. (2005). Seeking asylum in Denmark: Refugee children's mental health and exposure to violence. *European Journal of Public Health* 15:233–237.

Moser, R.P., and Jacob, T. (2002). Parental and sibling effects in adolescent outcomes. *Psychological Reports* 91:463–480.

Muller, R.T., Sicoli, L.A., and Lemieux, K.E. (2000). Relationship between attachment style and posttraumatic stress symptomalogy among adults who report the experience of childhood abuse. *Journal of Traumatic Stress* 13:321–332.

Näätänen, P., Kanninen, K., Qouta, S., and Punamäki, R.-L. (2002). Trauma-related emotional patterns and their association with post-traumatic and somatic symptoms. *Anxiety, Stress and Coping: An International Journal* 15:75–94.

Nader, K. (1996). Children's traumatic dreams. In D. Barrett (Ed.), *Trauma and Dreams* (pp. 9–24). Cambridge, MA: Harvard University Press.

O'Connor, T.G., Heron, J., Glover, V., and the ALSPAC. (2002). Antenatal anxiety predicts child behavioral/emotional problems independently of postnatal depression. *Journal of the American Academy of Child and Adolescent Psychiatry* 41:1470–1477.

Olsson, C.A., Bond, L., Burns, J.M., Vella-Brodrick, D.A., and Sawyer, S.M. (2003). Adolescent resilience: A concept analysis. *Journal of Adolescence* 26:1–11.

Pagani, L., Boulerice, B., Vitaro, F., and Trebley, R.E. (1999). Effects of poverty on academic failure and delinquency in boys: A change and process model approach. *Journal of Child Psychology and Psychiatry* 40:1209–1219.

Pfefferbaum, B. (1997). Posttraumatic stress disorder in children. A review of the past 10 years. *Journal of the American Academy of Child and Adolescent Psychiatry* 36:1503–1511.

Plomin, R., Asbury, K., and Dunn, J. (2001). Why are children in the same family so different? Nonshared environment a decade later. *Canadian Journal of Psychiatry* 46:225–233.

Plomin, R., DeFries, J.C., McClearn, G.E., and McGuffin, P. (2001). *Behavior Genetics.* New York: Worth.

Pollak, S.D., Cicchetti, D., Hornung, K., and Reed, A. (2000). Recognizing emotion in faces: Developmental effects of child abuse and neglect. *Developmental Psychology* 36:679–688.

Prevatt, F.F. (2003). The contribution of parenting practices in a risk and resiliency model of children's adjustment. *British Journal of Developmental Psychology* 21:469–480.

Punamaki, R.L. (1986). Stress among Palestinian women under military occupation: Women's appraisal of stressors, their coping modes, and their mental health. *International Journal of Psychology* 21:445–462.

Punamäki, R.-L. (1987). Psychological stress of Palestinian mothers and their children in conditions of political violence. *The Quarterly Newsletter of the Laboratory of Comparative Human Cognition* 9.

Punamäki, R.-L. (1996). Can ideological commitment protect children's psychological well-being in political violence? *Child Development* 67:55–69.

Punamäki, R.-L. (1998a). The role of dreams in protecting psychological well-being in traumatic conditions. *International Journal of Behavioral Development* 22:559–588.

Punamäki, R.-L. (1998b). Correspondence between waking-time coping and dream content. *Journal of Mental Imagery* 22:147–164.

Punamäki, R.-L. (1999). The relationship of dream content and changes in daytime mood in traumatized vs. non-traumatized children. *Dreaming: Journal of the Association for the Study of Dreams* 9:213–233.

Punamäki, R.-L. (2002). The uninvited guest of war enters childhood: Developmental and personality aspects of war and military violence. *Traumatology* 8:30–54.

Punamäki, R.-L., and Abdulrahman, H.A. (2004). Impact of traumatic events on coping strategies and their effectiveness among Kurdish children. *International Journal of Developmental Behavior* 28:59–70.

Punamäki, R.-L. Ismail, Jelal Ali, K., and Nuutinen. (2005). Trauma, dreaming and psychological distress among Kurdish children. *Journal of Dreaming* 16.

Punamäki, R.-L., Jelal Ali, K., and Nuutinen, J. (2005). Trauma, dreaming and psychological distress among Kurdish children. *Dreaming* 17:20–28.

Punamäki, R.-L., Qouta, S., and El Sarraj, E. (1997a). Models of traumatic experiences and children's psychological adjustment: The role of perceived parenting, children's resources and activity. *Child Development* 68:718–728.

Punamäki, R.-L., Qouta, S., and El Sarrah, E. (1997b). Relationships between traumatic events, children's gender and political activity, and pereception of parenting styles. *International Journal of Developmental Behavior* 21:91–109.

Punamäki, R.-L., Qouta, S. and El Sarraj, E. (2001). Resiliency factors predicting psychological adjustment after political violence among Palestinian children. *International Journal of Behavioral Development* 25:256–267.

Punamäki, R.-L., Qouta, S., Montgomery, E., and El Sarraj, E. (in press). Psychological distress and resources among siblings with parents exposed to traumatic events. *International Journal of Developmental Behavior.*

Punamäki, R.-L., and Suleiman, R. (1990). Predictors and effectiveness of coping with political violence among Palestinian children. *British Journal of Social Psychology* 29:67–77.

Qouta, S., Punamäki, R.-L., and El Sarraj, E. (1995). Relations between traumatic experiences, activity and cognitive and emotional responses among Palestinian children. *International Journal of Psychology* 30:289–304.

Qouta, S., Punamaki, R.-L., and El Sarraj, E. (2001). Mental flexibility as resiliency factor in traumatic stress. *International Journal of Psychology* 36:1–7.

Qouta, S., Punamäki, R.-L. and El Sarraj, E. (2005a). Predictors of psychological distress and positive resources among palestinian adolescents: Trauma, child, and mothering characteristics. *Child Abuse and Neglect* 23.

Qouta, S., Punamäki, R.-L., and El Sarraj, E. (2005b). Mother-child expression of psychological distress in war trauma. *Clinical Child Psychology and Psychiatry* 10:135–156.

Radke-Yarrow, M., and Brown, E. (1993). Resilience and vulnerability in children of multiple-risk families. *Development and Psychopathology* 5:581–592.

Räikkönen, K., Matthews, K.A., Flory, J.D.O., J.K., and Gump, B.B. (1999). Effects of optimism, pessimism and trait anxiety on ambulatory blood pressure and mood during everyday life. *Journal of Personality and Social Psychology* 76:104–113.

Raine, A., Brennan, P., and Mednick, S.A. (1994). Birth complications combined with early maternal rejection at age 1 year predispose to violent crime at age 18 years. *Archives of General Psychiatry* 51:984–988.

Revonsuo, A. (2000). The reinterpretation of dreams: An evolutionary hypothesis of the function of dreaming. *Behavioral and Brain Sciences* 23:877–901; discussion 904–1121.

Rogosch, F., Cicchetti, D., and Aber, J.L. (1995). The role of child maltreatment in early deviations in cognitive and affective processing abilities and later peer relationship problems. *Development and Psychopathology* 7:591–609.

Ronald, A., Spinath, F.M., and Plomin, R. (2002). The aetiology of high cognitive ability in early childhood. *High Ability Studies* 13:103–114.

Rothbart, M.K., Ahadi, S.A., and Evans, D.E. (2000). Temperament and personality: Origins and outcomes. *Journal of Personality and Social Psychology* 78:122–135.

Rutter, M. (1985). Resiliency in the face of adversity: Protective factors and resistance to psychiatric disorder. *British Journal of Psychiatry* 147:598–611.

Rutter, M. (2000). Resiliency reconsidered: Conceptual consideration, empirical findings and policy implications. In J.P.S.S. Meisels (Ed.), *Handbook of Childhood Intervention* (pp. 651–683). Cambridge: Cambridge University Press.

Saarni, C. (1999). *The Development of Emotional Competence. The Guilford Series on Social and Emotional Development.* New York: Guilford Press.

Sagi, A. V.I., Marinus and H., Joels, T., Scharf, M. (2002). Disorganized reasoning in Holocaust. *American Journal of Orthopsychiatry* 72:194–203.

Sajaniemi, N., Hakamies-Blomqvist, L., Katainen, S., and Wendt, L. (2001). Early cognitive and behavioral predictors of later performance: A follow-up study of elbw children from ages 2 to 4. *Early Childhood Research Quarterly* 16:343–361.

Salmon, K., and Bryant, R.A. (2002). Posttraumatic stress disorder in children—the influence of developmental factors. *Clinical Psychology Review* 22:163–188.

Salo, J., Punamäki, R.-L., and Qouta, S. (in press). The role of adult attachment in the association between experiences and post-traumatic growth among former political prisoners. *Anxiety, Stress and Coping: An International Journal.*

Sameroff, A.J. (1999). Ecological perspectives on developmental risks. In J.D. Osofsky, and H.E. Fitzgerald (Ed.), *Waimh Handbook of Infant Mental Health: Vol. 4. Infant Mental Health Groups at Risk* (pp. 223–248). New York: Wiley.

Sanson, A., and Bretherton, D. (2001). Conflict resolution: Theoretical and practical issues. In R.V. Wagner, D.J. Christie, and D.D. Winter (Ed.), *Peace, Conflict, and Violence. Peace Psychology for the 21st Century* (pp. 193–209). NJ: Prentice Hall.

Schuengel, C., Bakermans-Kranenburg, M.J., and van Ijzendoorn, M.H. (1999). Frightening maternal behavior linking unresolved loss and disorganized infant attachment. *Journal of Consulting and Clinical Psychology* 67:54–63.

Shalom, D., Benbenishty, R., Solomon, Z. (1995). Mental health officers' causal explanations of combat stress reaction. *Journal of Traumatic Stress* 259–269.

Shipman, K., Zeman, J., and Stegall, S. (2001). Regulating emotionally expressive behaviour: Implications of goals and social partner from middle childhood to adolescence. *Child Study Journal* 31:249–268.

Smith, P., Perrin, S., Yule, W., Hacam, B., and Stuvland, R. (2002). War exposure among children from Bosnia-Hercegovina: Psychological adjustment in a community sample. *Journal of Traumatic Stress* 15:147–157.

Solantaus, T., Leinonen, J. and Punamäki, R.-L. (2004). Children's mental health in times of economic recession: Replication and extension of the family economic stress model in Finland. *Developmental Psychology* 40:412–429.

Solomon, Z., Kotler, M., and Mikulincer, M. (1988). Compact-related posttraumatic stress disorder among second generation Holocaust survivors: Preliminary findings. *American Journal of Psychiatry* 145:865–868.

Steelman, L.M., Assel, M.A., Swank, P.R., Smith, K.E., and Landry, S.H. (2002). Early maternal warm responsiveness as a predictor of child social skills: Direct and indirect paths of influence over time. *Applied Developmental Psychology* 23:135–156.

Straker, G., with Moosa, F., Becker, R. and Nkwale. (1992). *Faces in the Revolution. The Psychological Effects of Violence on Township Youth in South Africa.* Cape Town: David Philip.

Summerfield, D. (2001). The invention of PTSD and the social usefulness of a psychiatric category. *British Medical Journal* 322:95–99.

Tedeschi, R.G., and Calhoun, L.G. (1996). The posttraumatic growth inventory: Measuring the positive legacy of trauma. *Journal of Traumatic Stress* 9:455–471.

Terr, L. (1991). Childhood traumas: An outline and overview. *American Journal of Psychiatry*.

Thompson, R.A., and Calkins, S.D. (1996). The double-edged sword: Emotional regulation for children at risk. *Development and Psychopathology* 8:163–182.

Timko, C. and Moos, R. (1996). The mutual influence of family support and youth adaptation. In G. Pierce, B. Sarason, and I. Sarason, (eds.) *Handbook of Social Support and the Family*, pp. 289–310. New York: Plenum.

UNICEF. (2004). *State of the World's Children.* New York: Oxford University Press.

van der Kolk, B.A. (1997). The psychobiology of posttraumatic stress disorder. *Journal of Clinical Psychiatry* 58:16–24.

Van der Kolk, B.A., and Fisher, R. (1995). Dissociation and fragmented nature of traumatic memories: Overview and exploratory study. *Journal of Traumatic Stress* 8:505–525.

Watzlawick, P., Beavin, J. H., and Jackson, D. D. (1967). *Pragmatics of Human Communication.* New York: Wiley.

Weisenberg, M., Schwarzwald, J., Waysman, M., Solomon, Z., and Klingman, A. (1993). Coping of school-age children in the sealed room during Scud missile bombardment and postwar stress reactions. *Journal of Consulting and Clinical Psychology* 61:462–467.

Werner, E., and Smith, R. (1982). *Vulnerable but Invincible: A Longitudinal Study of Resilient Children and Youth.* New York: McGraw-Hill.

Werner, E.E. (1993). Risk, resilience, and recovery: Perspectives from the Kayai longitudinal study. *Development and Psychopathology* 5:503–515.

Wyman, P.A., Cowen, E.L., Work, W.C., and Kerley, J. (1993). The role of children's future expectations in self-system functioning and adjustment to life stress: A prospective study of urban at-risk children. *Development and Psychopathology* 5:649–661.

Yates, T.M., Egeland, B., and Sroufe, A. (2003). Rethinking resilience. A developmental process prospective. In S.S. Luthar (Ed.), *Resilience and Vulnerability. Adaptation in the Context of Childhood Adversities* (pp. 243–266). New York: Cambridge University Press.

Yehuda, R., Halligan, S.L., and Bierer, L.M. (2004). Relationship of parental trauma exposure and PTSD to PTSD, depressive and anxiety disorders in offspring. *Journal of Psychiatric Research* 35:261–270.

Yehuda, R., Kahana, B., Southwick, S.M., and Giller Jr., E.L. (1994). Depressive features in Holocaust survivors with post-traumatic stress disorder. *Journal of Traumatic Stress* 7:699–704.

Yehuda, R., and McEwen, B.S. (2004). Protective and damaging effects of the biobehavioral stress response: Cognitive, systemic and clinical aspects: ISPNE XXXIV meeting summary. *Psychoneuroendocrinology* 29:1212–1222.

Yule, W. (2002). Alleviating the effects of war and displacement on children. *Traumatology* 8:1–14.

Chapter Six

School Influences on Child and Adolescent Mental Health

Amira Seif el Din

Although the main focus of school is education, its effects on children's lives are considerably more extensive. The ethos of a particular school can be affected by the characteristics of the children who attend and their families. In turn children are influenced by the quality of teaching materials, by the school environment, and by teachers, especially those whose personal qualities can have considerable influence on the development of children and adolescents.

School is the social and educational institution with the strongest effect on a child's life, as almost all children attend at some time during their lives. It can be a stress factor if the quality of teaching is suboptimal, but at the same time it can act as a safety net, protecting children from the hazards that affect their learning, development, and psychosocial well-being (Hendren et al., 1994).

The school environment is important. This includes the physical environment: school and class size, pupil-teacher ratio, extracurricular activities, and child interaction. There is evidence that positive outcomes can result from good teaching and from the use of praise in the classroom (Rutter et al., 1979). Teachers actively involved in mental health programs can reach generations of children. Those receiving training in developmental principles can become adept at identifying mental health problems in school-age children (Seif el Din, 1990a).

School is of course an important part of most children's lives: for eleven years they are expected to spend much of their time in the classroom. Until recently there has been in countries such as England comparatively little academic interest in whether some schools are more successful than others in helping children to develop their full potential. However, most parents are concerned with the quality of education their children receive, assuming that the school, its formal curriculum, and its general ethos will all have important effects on personality development as well as on academic attainment (Rutter,

1998). In contrast, in developing countries great interest is directed at the quantity of educational materials. Parents and school staff are not fully aware of the children's developmental stages and needs and do not give these due consideration (Seif el Din, 2001).

This may result in increasing the number of school dropouts, as illustrated in an Egyptian national survey, which showed that one-quarter of boys and one-third of girls ages ten–nineteen were out of school (Ibrahim et al., 1999).

A comprehensive mental health program should be part of a comprehensive school health program and include health instruction at all grade levels; easily accessible health services; and a healthy, nurturing, and safe environment, in addition to ongoing dialogue with families and community organizations (Young and Williams, 1989).

EMOTIONAL PROBLEMS IN SCHOOL CHILDREN AND ADOLESCENTS

Anxiety disorder is one of the most common psychiatric conditions in school children and adolescents. Epidemiological studies in the United States indicate that the prevalence of anxiety disorders is between 5% and 15% (Costello and Angold, 1995). In developing countries the figures are similar. In Attia et al.'s (1988) study, 17% of high school students reported high scores on Taylor's anxiety scale, the level of anxiety being related to age. Retrospective and prospective studies indicate that anxiety disorders have an early onset, run a chronic and fluctuating course into adulthood, and predict adult psychopathology, including anxiety disorders, major depression, and suicide attempts (Achenbach et al., 1995; Pine et al., 1998).

Depressive disorders among adolescents are comparatively commonplace. A number of studies report lifetime prevalence rates of 15% to 20% (Birmaher et al., 1996). In a study carried out in Egypt by Abou Nazel et al. (1991), 10.25% of a large sample ($n = 1,561$) of middle school children had high levels of depressive symptoms on the Children Depression Inventory (CDI) questionnaire. In India Joshi (2005) reported major depression in 4.7% of younger children and 20.8% of middle and high school young people. In addition, they noted that the total suicide rate had almost doubled between 1947 and 1991, in both sexes. Depressive symptoms at a young age increase the probability of later depression (Birmaher et al., 1996). Even so-called subsyndromal depression is a serious risk factor for depressive episodes in youth or later in life (Lewinsohn et al., 2000).

Clarke et al. (1995, 1999) have identified cognitive behavioral treatment as the most effective therapy for anxious and depressed children and adolescents as well as prevention in high-risk groups. Nevertheless, Shochet et al. (2001)

have argued that being included in prevention programs might in itself be a source of stigmatization for adolescents. They argue that this is a main reason for recruitment difficulties and the high dropout rates of these programs. These authors therefore advocate universally applied programs that include all students, independent of their actual risk for anxiety or depression. They recommend the establishment of prevention programs within the context of regular school classes. Ginsburg and Drake (2002) also support the school setting because it can provide mental health services for students who might not otherwise have access to services. Moreover, many anxiety-provoking situations experienced by adolescents are associated with school (e.g., problems with peers, academic performance). The school setting may provide opportunities for young people to practice new coping skills and engage in exposure exercises, thereby increasing the generalizability of skills learned in therapy to real-life situations. Finally, a school-based intervention can provide students with ongoing peer support, something not readily available in clinic settings.

The use in developing countries of cognitive behavior therapy (CBT) to manage anxiety and depressive disorders has generated great interest. Its effectiveness in the school setting has been shown by Habib and Seif el Din (2005) in a study of middle school children with depressive symptoms. This approach is a welcome alternative to psychopharmacological therapy, as the latter is expensive and carries a stigma.

SUICIDE AND SCHOOL

The school environment by its very nature can cause stress and strain for children, through, for example, the stress surrounding examinations, low self-esteem in cases of failure, and depression in cases of bullying (Mohit and Seif el Din, 1998). Suicide among adolescents is sometimes ascribed to pressure to achieve academically. Academic failure is particularly painful for adolescents whose families place heavy emphasis on academic achievement and success. Some adolescents may choose suicide over failure (Hussain and Vandiver, 1984; Cohen et al., 1995).

According to WHO statistics, suicide in Arab countries is very low in comparison to other parts of the world (Appleby et al., 1999). However, a study of middle schools by Seif el Din (1990b) showed that suicidal thoughts were common among those with high CDI-measured depressive scores: 80% of them reported having had such thoughts at times and 25% reported at least one suicide attempt.

The data highlight the importance for school and classroom teachers to become involved in the lives of adolescent and their families. The teacher may be a confidant for an adolescent under stress or the first to know about his or her problem.

School can be a source of relief for anxiety and isolation, partly because school attendance is compulsory. Programs that increase and extend interactions between troubled students and their peers and teachers could help the students establish meaningful social interactions and reduce suicide threats and attempts.

The following considerations may be helpful to teachers in assisting potentially suicidal students:

• Listening is of paramount importance.
• The threat of suicide should be taken seriously, not viewed as merely an expression of adolescent manipulation or attention seeking.
• The degree of urgency will vary, and the teacher will have to rely on his or her own judgment.
• The teacher and school can serve as a knowledgeable resource and assist the adolescent and his or her parents in obtaining professional help (Hussain and Vandiver, 1984; Cohen et al., 1995).

SOMATOFORM COMPLAINTS, EMOTIONAL PROBLEMS, AND SCHOOL REFUSAL

Livingston et al. (1988) among other authors have documented how somatic complaints can be associated with anxiety disorders, major depression, and psychosis. In their study, severity of depression was positively correlated with frequency of somatic complaints.

The most common childhood somatic complaints include headache, stomachache, musculoskeletal pain, back pain, dizziness, and fatigue (Campo and Fritsch, 1994; Garber et al., 1991). The epidemiological literature indicates that 10% to 30% of children and adolescents report weekly or frequent headaches (Egger et al., 1999). Recurrent abdominal pain is one of the most frequent somatic complaints in children, occurring in about 10% of primary and secondary school populations (Apley and Naish, 1958). It has been reported that children with mental health problems complain to the pediatrician about problems of the digestive tract more frequently than about any other symptoms complex.

In East Africa hysteria with conversion symptoms is found especially in school girls between ages twelve and seventeen, with the following symptoms: paralysis, aphonia, and multiple vague symptoms (Swift and Asuni, 1975). The prevalence of somatoform disorder in India is between 5% and 10%, rates increasing with the approach of puberty and females predominating. There may be an association with low academic achievement (Malhotra, 2005).

Few studies have evaluated the relationship between specific anxiety disorders and associated somatic symptoms. Both separation anxiety disorder and panic disorder involve physical symptoms according to DSM-IV diagnostic criteria (1994), and not surprisingly they are associated with high levels of somatic complaints (Last, 1991; Livingston et al., 1988). A study of outpatient children and adolescents with anxiety disorders found that those who reported more somatic complaints were more likely to be older and have refused to attend school (Last, 1991).

Studies of school refusal have not looked at links between school attendance, somatic complaints, and psychiatric illness (e.g., anxiety and depressive disorders). Nevertheless, it seems plausible that school absence rates will be related to the severity of somatization, anxiety, and depression. It is important to clarify this because school absence can have substantial adverse consequences for the adolescent, including loss of peer relationships and academic difficulties (Bernstein et al., 1997).

School refusal is recognized through the presence of strong emotional reactions preventing the child from going to school, even though both parents and child are convinced of the necessity of school attendance. Symptoms such as emotional distress, somatization, erroneous and dysfunctional thoughts, subjective experience of anxiety, and significant avoidance reactions can be present.

Last and Strauss (1990) studied a sample of sixty-three school-refusing children. They found that there were two primary diagnostic subgroups: separation anxiety and phobia. Last et al. (1987) compared children with separation anxiety disorder and children with phobic symptoms regarding school. Understandably, children with school phobia were more likely than those with separation anxiety disorder to avoid school (100% versus 73%). When they compared children with separation anxiety disorder who exhibited school avoidance with those who did not, there were no significant differences between the groups on demographic characteristics, concurrent disorders, or symptom measures (Martin et al., 1999).

ROLE OF SCHOOL IN CRISES

There is increasing awareness of the effects of stressful and traumatic events on children and adolescents. Particular characteristics of the stressors are most likely important as mediators and include stressor intensity and duration, the degree of injury or life threat, the loss of family members, and the disruption of the continuity of community, school, and family (Newman 1976; Pynoos et al., 1987). Regressive behavior, episodic aggression, psychophysiological disturbances, guilt, grief reaction, changes in school performance, and depressive and anxiety symptoms can be seen in children exposed to stressors (Chimienti et al., 1989; Dyregrov et al., 1987; Shaw and Harris, 1989). Latency-age children (ages six–eleven) may have attention problems, and their schoolwork may suffer. Signs of anxiety include school avoidance, somatic complaints (e.g., headache and stomachache), irrational fears, and sleep problems (Nader et al., 1990; Pynoos et al., 1987; Terr et al., 1999).

The role of school is to identify children at risk and to conduct school-based interventions to treat post-traumatic stress disorder (PTSD) and other psychiatric symptoms. This has received empirical support in the literature (La Greca et al., 1996; Swenson et al., 1996; Vernberg et al., 1996). La Greca et al. (1994) developed a school-based intervention manual to help children cope after Hurricane Andrew. This has been distributed to schools internationally and has been used in other disasters, including the Oklahoma City bombing. Vernberg (2000) and Storm et al. (1994) developed a manualized treatment program for use following traumatic Australian bush fires.

SCHOOL-BASED EFFORTS TO PREVENT AND TREAT PTSD

School-based prevention and treatment efforts are effective for traumatized children or those at risk for trauma. They provide access to children in a developmentally appropriate environment that encourages normality and minimizes stigma. School is also a setting in which PTSD and associated symptoms are likely to emerge. For example, intrusive thoughts and difficulty concentrating are likely to interfere with the child's academic performance and social adaptation. Therefore consultation around the effects of trauma and the recovery process may be both necessary and useful.

School-based programs include (1) curricular interventions addressing traumatizing events and stress responses; (2) opportunities for disclosure and discussion; (3) small-group activities; (4) projective techniques such as play, artwork, and storytelling; and (5) formal and informal opportunities for assessing psychological response, correcting misperceptions and fears, and encouraging normalization and recovery. Pynoos and Nader (1993), however, caution that the goals of school-based interventions must be appropriate for the setting. For example, the classroom is an excellent place in which to identify at-risk children and to normalize recovery, but it is not the place to discuss revenge fantasies. It is imperative that school-based programs do not supplant efforts to identify and refer children in need of more intensive individual work (Pfefferbaum, 1997).

Terr (1981) in her work with psychic trauma in kidnapped children found that symptoms such as fear of recurrence and of other traumas might not be observed for up to a year after the trauma. She reported reduction in symptoms for many who received brief counseling. Galante and Foa (1986) provided long-term counseling to Italian children exposed to a devastating earthquake. Though useful, this was not fully effective in relieving long-lasting symptoms.

Schools are the second-most important natural environment for children. Rehabilitating work in this environment and using the school's own resources ought therefore to be a priority for any postdisaster relief program. For this to be successful, child mental health professionals need to provide teachers with clinical knowledge translated into effective classroom didactic materials (Wolmer et al., 2003), as well as social theory particularly formulated and adapted to school activities (Laor and Wolmer, 2002).

Postdisaster support in school may influence the development of PTSD after disasters (Udwin et al., 2000), since school-based screening allows clinicians to identify and treat children exhibiting the most severe post-traumatic symptoms (Chemtob et al., 2002). School-based intervention models may include small-group programs for high-risk or agitated children who need additional attention and class activation programs with or without the presence of the teacher (Klingman, 1993). This is intended to minimize stigma, teach normal reactions to stress, and reinforce the expectation that children will soon resume their roles as students (Pfefferbaum, 1997).

To implement teacher-mediated interventions where teachers become true partners, mental health consultants need to genuinely address three issues: Why intervene? Why intervene in school? Why intervene through teachers? (Caffo et al., 2004).

BEHAVIORAL PROBLEMS IN SCHOOL

Attention-deficit/hyperactivity disorder (ADHD) is a heterogeneous disorder of childhood onset that affects 2% to 14% of school-age children (Costello et al., 1996; Wolraich et al., 1996). ADHD is one of the leading causes of academic underachievement in school and of disruptive behaviors. It is readily recognized, being based on overt and salient behaviors including overactivity, impulsiveness, and inattentiveness. These problems are recognized in children in most cultures (Taylor, 2004).

Several studies around the world have studied childhood ADHD. In Brazil an ADHD outpatient and school program identified a prevalence of 6% in a sample of young adolescents and high levels of comorbidity with other disruptive behavior disorders (47.8% with conduct or oppositional behavior disorders; Rohde et al., 1999). A Ukrainian study found a prevalence of ADHD among children ages ten to twelve of 19.8%, a much higher rate than in the United States. Ukrainian children with ADHD symptoms were rated as more hyperactive, oppositional, and aggressive by both parents and teachers than non-ADHD youngsters (Gadow et al., 2000). ADHD has received little attention in the scientific literature of the Arab world. In an epidemiological study of mental health problems among school-age children in Al-Ain (United Arab Emirates), however, Eapen et al. (1998) found a weighted prevalence of ADHD of 0.46%. In Egypt a large number of these children are referred to psychiatric clinics for assessment because of scholastic underachievement in elementary school; hyperactivity and attention deficit symptoms are significantly more often encountered among underachievers than among average children.

Since ADHD has an effect on school progress, school-based interventions have become increasingly common and can be effective. These interventions should target academic performance, but classroom behavior and peer relationships are also important. The most appropriate classroom environment is probably a well-structured classroom, with the child placed in the front of the room, close to the teacher, where he or she may be less easily distracted and more able to focus. The use of contingency management and daily teacher-completed report cards of the child's progress in targeted areas are hallmarks of this type of intervention (Braswell and Bloomquist, 1994).

Incentives and tangible rewards, reprimands, and time-out in the classroom setting can be used in school as well as in the home (Cantwell, 1996; Jensen et al., 2004). The school can play a crucial role in a concerted effort to improve the child's poor impulse and anger control and social skills, targeting the child's entry into the school group, the development of conversational skills, and problem-solving skills (Cantwell, 1996).

VIOLENCE AND SCHOOL

Child maltreatment—including overt physical abuse, sexual abuse, neglect, and emotional abuse—is considered an important risk factor for the development of aggressive behavior in young people (Garbarino, 1995). In Egypt, corporal punishment in schools has been banned since 1971. Nevertheless, a substantial proportion of boys (79.96%) and girls (61.53%) have been noted to incur corporal punishment at the hand of their teachers (Youssef and Attia, 1998).

Aggressive behavior was found in a study to be nearly 2.5 times higher among children and adolescents subjected to corporal punishment in school

(Odd Ratios [OR] = 2.65) and even higher among those who were subjected to this form of punishment by their caregivers (OR = 3.58; Youssef et al., 1999). Thus both individual and group violence can be a consequence of the trauma experienced by young people themselves (Widom, 1989, 1995), and the use of appropriate discipline may have a central role in violence prevention (Stone, 1996a, 1996b). Kachur et al. (1996) conducted a nationwide survey of violent deaths in U.S. schools during 1992. They identified 105 deaths occurring in communities of all sizes across twenty-five states. Homicide was the predominant cause of death (81%), usually involving firearms (77%).

School can address a broad range of behaviors, skills, communication patterns, and attitudes, and school policies may be developed to prevent and control violence. In all countries, the school system could be a most efficient and systematic means of reaching large sections of the population, including young people and school staff as well as family members (WHO, 1999).

In many developing countries the school is an ideal setting for health-promotion activities, with school structure, resources, and staff all contributing. Health services of some form or another are provided for students in almost every country. Many have some type of school health program and thus the potential for developing a school and health integrated approach to violence prevention (WHO, 1996). Early intervention can be less expensive and more effective than trying to change established patterns of violence among older children.

Olweus (1993) described an interesting national intervention campaign in Norway, a school program to reduce aggressive behavior and bullying. Instead of teaching individual children to cope with bullying by aggressive peers, a national campaign was developed and successfully implemented to reduce bullying throughout the entire school system. The intervention consisted of workshops for teachers and parents, booklets, videos, problem-solving and social skills training for students, all conveying the firm, nonaggressive message that bullying would not be tolerated.

Olweus followed up four cohorts of 600–700 pupils each and found that frequency of bullying decreased by 50% or more during the two years following the campaign. Researchers also noted reduced rates in antisocial behavior such as theft, vandalism, and truancy. Findings were consistent among boys and girls and across all grades. The effects of the intervention were more significant after two years than after one year.

In another study, a violence-prevention curriculum was used in more than 10,000 elementary schools in the United States and Canada. Grossman et al. (1996) observed 588 students in the classroom, playground, and cafeteria settings and concluded that the curriculum had led to a moderate decrease in physically aggressive behavior and to an increase in prosocial behavior in school.

A review of evidence of school effectiveness shows that democratically organized schools are effective in "fostering the democratic values which are conducive to the non-violent resolution of conflict" (UNESCO, 1997)

INTEGRATING VIOLENCE PREVENTION INTO A HEALTH-PROMOTING SCHOOL PROGRAM

"To educate the child of today is to prevent the criminal or the violent abuser of tomorrow" (Guerra de Macedo, 1994). To achieve this, it is necessary to train school staff to deal with aggression (WHO, 1999):

• Instill an understanding of the nature and types of local violence.
• Develop staff skills in conflict resolution, intergroup relations skills, and classroom management.
• Demonstrate the teaching methods being taught and provide a chance to practice these methods and receive feedback.
• Provide knowledge and skills to respond to student disclosure of all types of violence.
• Encourage and empower teachers to shape the teaching process within their own schools and classrooms, and provide adequate opportunities for them to share in decision making.
• Demonstrate strategies for integrating these concepts and skills into social studies, language, art, and other core academic subjects.
• Train teachers to recognize symptoms associated with abuse and trauma.

Children who are or have been victims of violence or show aggressive or disruptive behavior in school have a particular need for support and intervention. It is important to identify these children in order to provide them with services, evaluate their progress, and continue to monitor them. Schools have a role to play in this process, even where resources are scarce. In a health-promoting school, health services will work in a coordinated partnership with students, school personnel, families, and community members (WHO, 1999).

SCHOOLS' ROLE IN RELATION TO ADOLESCENT RISK-TAKING BEHAVIOR

Risk-taking behaviors, including tobacco, substance and alcohol use and abuse, reckless driving, risky sexual behavior, and delinquency are serious threats for high school students.

Fergusson et al. (1996) and Obot et al. (2000) have reported associations between early onset (i.e., prior to age fifteen) risk-taking behaviors and school dropout. Akabawi (2001) described, among high school students in Egypt, a profile of first-time use of any drug (including tobacco) at age fourteen, use of light alcoholic beverages and smoking cannabis at age seventeen, and use of synthetic hypnosedative drugs at age eighteen.

Among school students in India Mohan et al. (1985, 1987) found use of alcohol to be highest (4%–13%), followed by tobacco (3%–6%), and minor tranquilizers (1%–4%). A recent rise in opiate use in schoolchildren has been reported (Kalra 1997, 1998).

There have been active initiatives to prevent adolescent risk-taking behavior through school-based prevention programs. This can lead trained teachers to show increased confidence in their ability to identify students with substance abuse problems (Kantor et al., 1992). A national, school-based organization of students against driving drunk aims to prevent students from driving after drinking (Windle et al., 1996).

While school-based programs addressing alcohol and substance abuse are usually concerned with prevention, student assistance programs tend to also provide aftercare counseling or groups for high-risk youth (Fleisch, 1991).

A school-based program in Chandigarh, India, was launched to reduce tobacco use among young people by teaching students not only about the dangers of tobacco use but also life skills, refusing skills, and media literacy to resist the influence of tobacco marketers and peers. It included ensuring that sports activities conducted at school were tobacco free, helping to discriminate among messages on the health impact of tobacco, teachers and other staff avoiding using tobacco in front of students, and making sure that children had access to adequate opportunities to participate in sports to help them avoid developing a tobacco habit, a possible "royal path" to other drug dependencies (Malhotra et al., 2005).

DROPPING OUT OF SCHOOL

School dropout is of course a major concern for schools (Mattison, 1999). It is a worldwide problem, especially significant in developing countries. Recently, the United Nations Children's Fund (UNICEF) document "State of the World's Children 2005" noted that 121 million primary school-age children are out of school worldwide (UNICEF, 2005). In Brazil, though 95% of children have access to school, only 58% complete the eighth grade (UNICEF, 1999). The school dropout rate is an important indicator of the educational condition of a country (Kominski, 1990) and predicts future problems in the child (Berg et al., 1993).

Most studies have focused on student factors associated with dropping out rather than on school factors such as adequacy of facilities, leadership, and teacher characteristics (Rumberger, 1987). Such variables must, however, be important, since dropout rates do vary among schools. There is some evidence that dropout rates may be lower in schools with an ethos emphasizing academic pursuits, an orderly environment, active faculty interaction with students, and reduced differences in students in demographic and academic backgrounds. This is consistent with findings by Rutter et al. (1979) on the effect of school variables on children.

In developing countries, the school environment has a clear potential to help decrease school dropout rates. Two studies carried out in public primary schools in Brazil and Egypt revealed that improvements in the school environment were linked to a decrease in school dropout rates (Graeff-Martins et al., 2005; Seif el Din et al., 2005).

To achieve this, school staff and in particular school counselors should attempt to (1) promote daily school attendance; (2) encourage parental participation in school learning activities; (3) provide strong and consistent school leadership; (4) which is clearly and widely spelled out and disseminated across classrooms; (5) help students establish and progress toward personally meaningful career goals; (6) place high priority on school resources for early elementary grades; (7) assist students in developing effective learning and study skills; and (8) establish a school climate where achievement is respected and rewarded (Walz, 1987).

LIFE SKILLS EDUCATION WITHIN THE SCHOOL SETTING

Skills-based health education is an approach to creating and maintaining healthy lifestyles and conditions through the development of knowledge, attitudes, and especially skills, using a variety of learning experiences and with an emphasis on participatory methods. Life skills are abilities for adaptive and positive behavior that enable individuals to deal effectively with the demands and challenges of everyday life (WHO, 1994).

Life skills are a group of psychosocial competencies and interpersonal skills that help people make informed decisions, solve problems, think critically and creatively, communicate effectively, build healthy relationships, empathize with others, and cope with and manage their lives in a healthy and productive manner. Life skills may be directed toward personal actions or actions toward others, as well as toward actions to change the surrounding environment to make it conducive to health (WHO, 2001).

WHY IS LIFE SKILL EDUCATION IN
THE SCHOOL SETTING IMPORTANT?

Life skills education is highly relevant to the daily needs of young people. When it is part of the school curriculum, the indications are that it can help prevent mental health problems. For children ages six to fifteen the school setting is critical in helping to build skills and habits. Children are developing the ability to think abstractly, to understand consequences, to relate to their peers in new ways, and to solve problems alongside the experience of increasing independence from their parents and the development of greater control over their own lives (WHO, 2001). Evaluative studies of life skill programs suggest that they can help improve teacher and pupil relationships (Parsons et al., 1988) and improve academic performance (Weissberg et al., 1989). Other positive effects include improved school attendance (Zabin et al., 1986), less bullying and school dropout, fewer referrals to specialist support services, and better relationships between children and their parents (WHO, 1977).

Life skills have been taught in many schools around the world. Some initiatives are in use in just a few schools in some countries, but in other developing and developed countries, life skills school programs have been introduced in a large proportion of schools across different age groups (Malhotra et al., 2005; Seif el Din et al., 1993; Weissberg et al., 1989).

Student acquisition of skills is based on learning through active participation, through brainstorming and role-play. Brainstorming is a creative technique for generating ideas and suggestions on a particular subject. It can be a helpful technique for the life skill teacher to learn how much students understand a particular subject and how they describe it in their own terms. Role-play can be of considerable value for dealing with sensitive issues that may cause anxiety in real-life encounters.

Life skills lessons should also include homework assignments, to encourage pupils to extend their understanding and extension of life skills to their own lives at home and in their communities (WHO, 1997).

To enhance the effectiveness of a multifaceted school approach of this kind, educational, health, and social welfare systems coupled with the support of relevant nongovernmental organizations (NGOs) must all intervene to promote, prevent, and intervene early. Several active programs in developed and developing countries are now attesting to the importance of an interagency school approach in national programs that reproduce the Norway experience described earlier (Olweus, 1993; Malhotra et al., 2005; Seif el Din et al., 1993).

CHILDREN LEARN WHAT THEY LIVE

If children live with hostility
They learn to fight
If children live with ridicule
They learn to be shy
If children live with shame
They learn to feel guilty
If children live with encouragement
They learn to be patient
If children live with praise
They learn to appreciate
If children live with fairness
They learn to be just
If children live with security
They learn to have faith
If children live with acceptance and friendship
They learn to find love in the world

REFERENCES

Abou Nazel, M., Fahmy, S., Younis, I., and Seif el Din, A. (1991). A study of depression among Alexandria preparatory school adolescents. *Journal of Egyptian Public Health* Association 66 (5):649–674.

Achenbach, T., Howell, C., McConaughy, S., and Stranger, C. (1995). Six-year predictors of problems in a national sample of youth, I: Cross-informant syndromes. *Journal of the American Academy of Child and Adolescent Psychiatry* 34:336–347.

Akabawi, A. (2001). *Drug abuse in the Arab world: A country profile of Egypt.* In *Images in Psychiatry, An Arab Perspective.* ed. Ahmed Okasha and Mario Maj. WPA series, pp. 143–150.

Apley, J., and Naisf, N. (1958). Recurrent abdominal pains: A field survey of 1,000 schoolchildren. *Arch Dis Child* 8:165–170.

Appleby, L., Shaw, J., and Amos, T. (1999). Suicide within 12 months of contact with mental health services: National clinical survey. *British Medical Journal* 318:1235–1239.

Attia, M., Seif el Din, A., Sherbini, A., Kamel, M., and El Kerdany, I. (1988). Study of anxiety among secondary school children in Alexandria. *Bulletin of HIPH* 18 (4):695–708.

Berg, I., Butler, A., Franklin, J., Hayes, H., Lucas, C., and Sims, R. (1993). DSM-III-R disorders, social factors, and management of school attendance problems in the normal population. *Journal of Child Psychology and Psychiatry* 34:1187–1192.

Bernstein, G.A., Massie, E.D., Thuras, P.D., Perwien, A.R., Borchardt, C.M., and Crosby, R.D. (1997). Somatic symptoms in anxious-depressed school refusers. *Journal of the American Academy of Child and Adolescent Psychiatry* 36:661–668.

Birmaher, B., Rayan, N.D., Williamson, D.E., et al. (1996). Childhood and adolescent depression: A review of the past 10 years. Part I. *Journal of the American Academy of Child and Adolescent Psychiatry* 35:1427–1439.

Braswell, J., and Bloomquist, M. (1994). *Cognitive Behavior Therapy of ADHD*. New York: Guilford Press.

Caffo, E., Forresi, B., Belaisa, C., Nicolais, G., et al. (2004). *Innovative Interventions in the Community. Facilitating Pathways. Care, Treatment and Prevention in Child and Adolescent Mental Health*. ed. Remschmidt Belfer. Goodyer. Berlin: Springer Medizin Verlag.

Campo, J.V., and Fritsch, S.L. (1994). Somatization in children and adolescents. *Journal of the American Academy of Child and Adolescent Psychiatry* 33:1223–1235.

Cantwell, D. (1996). Attention deficit disorder: A review of the past 10 years. *Journal of the American Academy of Child and Adolescent Psychiatry* 35:978–987.

Chemtob, C.M., Nakashima, J.P., and Hamada, R.S. (2002). Psychosocial intervention for post-disaster trauma symptoms in elementary school children. *Archives of Pediatric and Adolescent Medicine* 156:211–216.

Chimienti, G., Nasr, J.A. and Khalifeh, I. (1989). Children's reactions to war-related stress: Affective symptoms and behavior problems. *Social Psychiatry and Psychiatric Epidemiology* 24:282–287.

Clarke, G.N., Hawkins, W., Murphy, M., Sheeber, L., Lewinsohn, P.M., and Seeley, J.R. (1995). Targeted prevention of unipolar depressive disorder in an at-risk sample of high school adolescents: A randomized trial of a group cognitive intervention. *Journal of the American Academy of Child and Adolescent Psychiatry* 34:312–321.

Clarke, G.N., Rohde, P., Lewinsohn, P.M., Hops, H., and Seely, J.R. (1999). Cognitive behavioral treatment of adolescent depression: Efficacy of acute group treatment and booster sessions. *Journal of the American Academy of Child and Adolescent Psychiatry* 38:272–279.

Cohen, Y., Spirito, A., and Brown, L. (1995). *Handbook of Adolescent Health Risk Behavior. Suicide and Suicidal Behavior*. Ed. DiClemente, R.J., Hansen, W.B., and Ponton, L. New York: Plenum Press, pp. 193–224.

Costello, E., and Angold, A. (1995). Epidemiology in anxiety disorders in children and adolescents. In *Anxiety Disorders in Children and Adolescents*, March, J., ed. New York: Guilford, pp. 109–124.

Costello, E.J., Angold, A., Burns, B.J., et al. (1996). The Great Smoky Mountains study of youth: Goals, design, methods, and the prevalence of DSM-III-R disorders. *Archives of General Psychiatry* 53:1129–1136.

Dyregrov, A., Raundalen, M., Lwanga, J. and Mugisha, C. (1987). *Children and War*. Paper presented at the Annual Meeting of the Society for Traumatic Stress Studies, October, Baltimore, Maryland.

Eapen, V., Al Gazali, L., Bin-Otman, S., and Abou Saleh, M. (1998). Mental health problems among school children in United Arab Emirates: Prevalence and risk factors. *Journal of the American Academy of Child and Adolescent Psychiatry* 37:880–886.

Egger, H.L., Costello, J., Erkanli, A., and Angold, A. (1999). Somatic complaints and psychopathology in children and adolescents: Stomach aches, musculoskeletal pains and headache. *Journal of the American Academy of Child and Adolescent Psychiatry* 38:852–860.

Fergusson, O.M., Lynskey, M.T., and Horwod, L.J. (1996). The short-term consequences of early onset cannabis use. *Journal of Abnormal Child Psychology.* 24 (4):499–512.

Fleisch, B. (1991). *Approaches in the Treatment of Adolescents with Emotional and Substance Abuse Problems.* Rockville, MD: U.S. Department of Health and Human Services.

Gadow, K.D., Molan, E.E., Lichter, L., Carlson, G.A., Parinan, Golovakia E., Sprafkin, J., and Bromet, E.J. (2000). Comparison of attention-deficit hyperactivity disorder sympotom subtypes in Ukranian schoolchildren. *Journal of the Medical Academy of Child and Adolescent Pyschiatry* 39:1520–1527.

Galante, R., and Foa, D. (1986). An epidemiological study of psychic trauma and treatment effectiveness for children after a natural disaster. *Journal of the American Academy of Child and Adolescent Psychiatry* 25:357–363.

Garbarino, J. (1995). *Raising Children in a Socially Toxic Environment.* San Francisco: Jossey-Bass.

Garber, J., Walker, L.S., and Zeman, J. (1991). Somatization symptom in a community sample of children and adolescents: Further validation of the children's somatization inventory. *Psychological Assessment* 3:588–595.

Ginsburg, G., and Drake, K. (2002). School-based treatment for anxious African-American adolescents: A controlled pilot study. *Journal of the American Academy of Child and Adolescent Psychiatry* 41:768–775.

Graeff-Martins, A., Oswald, S., Kieling, C.H., and Rohde, L. (2005). *What Can We Learn from a Comprehensive Intervention to Reduce School Drop-out in a Public School in a Developing Country? Who can benefit from this intervention?* XIII WPA Congress in Cairo, September.

Grossman, D.C., Neckerman, K.J., Koepsell, T.D., Liu, P.Y., Asher, K.N., Beland, K., et al. (1996). Effectiveness of a violence prevention curriculum among children in elementary school: A randomized controlled trial. *Journal of the American Medical Association* 227 (20):1506–1611.

Guerra de Macedo, C. (1994). *Society, Violence and Health: A New Agenda for Democracy.* Keynote Address. Society, Violence, and Health: Memoirs of the Inter-American Conference on Society, Violence, and Health, November 16–17, 1994.

Habib, D., and Seif el Din, A. (2005). Impact of cognitive behavior therapy on children with depressive symptoms. Accepted for publication at WHO, *EMRO Journal* (in press).

Hassen, E. (1999). *Epidemiological study of scholastic under achievement among primary school children in Alexandria: Prevalence and causes.* Thesis submitted faculty of Nursing. Alexandria. University.

Hendren, R., Birrell Weisen, R., and Orley, J. (1994). *Mental Health Programmes in Schools.* Division of Mental Health. World Health Organization. Geneva.

Hussain, S., and Vandiver T. (1984). *Suicide in Children and Adolescents.* ed. SP New York: Medical and Scientific Books, pp. 164–172.

Ibrahim, B., Sallam, S., El Tawili, S., Gibaly, O. and Sahn, F. (1999). *Transitions to Adulthood.* A National Survey of Egyptian Adolescents. New York: Population Council.

Jensen, P., So, C., Bauermeister, J., Murray, L., and Hoagwood, K. (2004). *Cognitive Behavioral Manual for Children and Adolescents*. Presidential Program of XIII WPA.

Joshi, P.T. (2005). Mood disorders in children and adolescents. *Mental Disorders in Children and Adolescents: Needs and Strategies for Intervention*. Delhi-Bagalore: CBS Publishers & Distributor, pp. 48–60.

Kachur, S.P., Stennies, G.M., Powell, K.E., et al. (1996). School associated violent deaths in the United States 1992 to 1994. *Journal of the American Medical Association* 275:1729–1733.

Kalra, R.M. (1997). *Drug Addiction in Schools*. New Delhi: Vikas Publishing.

Kalra, R.M. (1998). *Education and Prevention of Drug Abuse Among School Children*. In Drug Demand Reduction Report (ed. Ray, R.), pp. 195–198. New Delhi: UNDCP Regional Office for South Asia.

Kantor, G.K., Caudill, B.D., and Ungerleider, S. (1992). Project impact: Teaching the teachers to intervene in student substance abuse problems. *Journal of Alcohol and Drug Education* 38 (1):11–29.

Klingman, A. (1993). School-based interventions following a disaster. In Saylor, C.F. (ed), *Children and Disaster*. New York: Plenum Press, pp. 187–210.

Kominski, R. (1990). Estimating the national high school dropout rate. *Demography* 27:303–11.

La Greca, A.M., Silverman, W.K., Vernberg, E.M., and Prinstein, M.J. (1996). Symptoms of posttraumatic stress after Hurricane Andrew: A prospective study, *Journal of Consulting and Clinical Psychology* 64:712–723.

La Greca, A.M., Vernberg, E.M., Silverman, W.K., Vogal, A., and Prinstein, M.J. (1994). *Helping Children Cope with Natural Disaster: A Manual for School Personnel*. Miami, FL. Available at www.psy.miami.edu/child/childclinical/helpingchildrencope .phtml.

Laor, N., and Wolmer, L. (2002). *Children Exposed to Disaster: The Role of the Mental Health Professional* In Lewis, M. (ed), *Text-book of Child and Adolescent Psychiatry*, 3rd ed. Baltimore: Williams and Wilkins, pp. 925–937.

Last, C.G. (1991). Somatic complaints in anxiety disordered children. *Journal of Anxiety Disorders* 5:125–138.

Last, C.G., Francis, G., Hersen, M., Kazdin, A.E., and Strauss, C.C. (1987). Separation anxiety and school phobia: A comparison using DSM-III criteria. *American Journal of Psychiatry* 144:653–657.

Last, C.G., and Strauss, C.C. (1990). School refusal in anxiety disordered children and adolescents. *Journal of the American Academy of Child and Adolescent Psychiatry* 29:31–35.

Lewinsohn, P.M., Solomon, A., Seeley, J.R., and Zeiss, A. (2000). Clinical implications of "subthreshold" depressive symptoms. *Journal of Abnormal Child Psychology* 109:345–351.

Livingston, R., Taylor, J.L., and Crawfold, S.L. (1988). A study of somatic complaints and psychiatric diagnosis in children. *Journal of the American Academy of Child and Adolescent Psychiatry* 27:185–187.

Malhotra, S., Sharan, P., Gupta, N., and Malhotra, A. (2005). *Mental Disorders in Children and Adolescents: Need and Strategies for Intervention*. Delhi: CBS Publishers & Distributors, pp. 71–81.

Martin, C., Carbol, J., Bouvard, M.P., Lepine, J.P., and Simeoni, C.M. (1999). Anxiety and depressive disorders in fathers and mothers of anxious school-refusing children. *Journal of the American Academy of Child and Adolescent Psychiatry* 38:916–922.

Mattison, R. (2000). School consultation: A review of research on issues unique to the school environment. *Journal of the American Academy of Child and Adolescent Psychiatry* 39(4):402–413.

Mohan, D., Sethi, H.S., and Tongue, E. (1985). *Current Research in Drug Abuse in India* Series II. New Delhi: Jay Pee Brothers.

Mohan, D., Sundaram, K., and Ray, R. (1987). *Multicentered Study of Drug Abuse among University Students.* Report submitted to Ministry of Health and Family Welfare, Govt. of India.

Mohit, A., and Seif el Din, A. (1998). *Mental Health Promotion for Schoolchildren. A Manual for Schoolteachers and School Health Workers.* World Health Organization. EMRO. Alexandria, Egypt.

Nader, K., Pynoos, R., Fairbanks, L., and Frederick, C. (1990). Children's reactions one year after a sniper attack at their school. *American Journal of Psychiatry* 147: 1526–1530.

Newman, J. (1976). Children of disaster: Clinical observations at Buffalo Creek. *American Journal of Psychiatry* 133:306–312.

Obot, I.S., and Anthony, J.C. (2000). *School Drop-out and Injecting Drug Use in a National Sample of White Non-Hispanic American Adults.*

Olweus, D. (1993). *Bullying at School: What We Know and What We Can Do.* Oxford: Blackwell Publishers.

Parsons, C., Hunter, D., and Warne, Y. (1988). *Skills for Adolescence: An Analysis of Project Material, Training and Implementation.* Christ Church College, Evaluation Unit. Canterbury, UK.

Pfefferbaum, B. (1997). Posttraumatic stress disorder in children: A review of the past 10 years. *American Journal of Child and Adolescent Psychiatry* 36:1503–1511.

Pepler, D.J., and Slaby, R. (1996). Theoretical and developmental perspectives on youth and violence. In Eron, L.D., Gentry, J.H., and Schlegel, P. (eds). *Reason to Hope: A Pychosocial Perspective on Violence and Youth.* Washington, DC: American Psychological Association.

Pine, D., Cohen, P., Gurley, D., Brook. J., and Ma, Y. (1998). The risk for early-adulthood anxiety and depressive disorders in adolescents with anxiety and depressive disorders. *Archives of General Psychiatry* 55:56–64.

Pynoos, R.S., and Nader, K. (1993). Issues in the treatment of posttraumatic stress in children and adolescents. In *International Handbook of Traumatic Stress Syndromes*, Wilson, J.P., and Raphael, B., eds. New York: Plenum, pp. 535–549.

Pynoos, R., Frederick, C., Nader, K., et al. (1987). Life threat and post traumatic stress in school age children. *Archives of General Psychiatry* 44:1057–1063.

Rohde, L. A., Biederman, J., Busnello, E. A., et al. (1999). ADHD in a school sample of Brazilian adolescents: A study of prevalence, comorbid conditions and impairments. *Journal of the American Academy of Child and Adolescent Psychiatry* 38:716–722.

Rohde, L.A. (2002). ADHD in Brazil: The DSM-IV criteria in a culturally different population. *Journal of the American Academy of Child and Adolescent Psychiatry* 41:1131–1133.

Rumberger, R. W. (1987). High school dropout: A review of issues and evidence. *Rev Educ Res* 57:101–121.

Rumberger, R.W., and Larson, K.A. (1998). Student mobility and the increased risk of high school dropout. *American Journal of Education* 107 (1):1–35.

Rutter, M. (1998). *Developmental Psychiatry* ed. American Psychiatric Press, Inc. Washington, DC, 2005, p. 67.

Rutter, M., Maughan, B., Mortimore, P., and Ouston, J. (1979). *Fifteen Thousand Hours*. London: Open Books.

Seif el Din, A. (1990a). Evaluation of the training program for professionals working with school children in Alexandria. *Journal of Pediatrics* 4 (1):61–68.

Seif el Din, A. (1990b). Clinical assessment of high scorers on a depressives inventory among school children in Alexandria. *Journal of Pediatrics* 4 (3):333–344.

Seif el Din, A. (2001). An Arab perspective. In *Child Psychiatry in the Arab World*. Ed. Ahmed Okasha and Mario Maj. WPA. Pp. 151–166.

Seif el Din, A., Moustafa, T., Mohet, A., Abou Nazel, M., and Koura, M. (1993). *A Multisectoral Approach to School Mental Health*. Alexandria, Egypt. Part II. *Health Services Journal of the Eastern Mediterranean Region*. World Health Organization Vol. 7, 2.

Seif el Din, A., Azzer, M., and Habib, D. (2005). *Comprehensive Program for Prevention of School Drop-out in an Egyptian Public School*. XIII WPA Congress in Cairo, September 2005.

Shaw, J. and Harris, J. (1989). A prevention intervention program for children of war in Mozambique, presented to the annual meeting of the *Journal of the American Academy of Child and Adolescent Psychiatry,* October, New York.

Shochet, I.M., Dadds, M.R., Holland, D., Whiterfield, K., Harnett, P.H., and Osgarby, S.M. (2001). The efficacy of a universal school-based program to prevent adolescent depression. *Journal of Clinical Child Psychology* 30:303–315.

Stone, L.A. (1996a). Humpty Dumpty. *Journal of the American Academy of Child and Adolescent Psychiatry* 35:273–278.

Stone, L.A. (1996b). Violence, an epidemic. International Child Health: *A Digest of Current information; International Pediatric Association with UNISEF and World Health Organization* 7:53–57.

Storm, V., McDermott, B., and Finlayson, D. (1994). *The Bushfire and Me*. Newtown, Australia: VBD Publications.

Swenson, C.C., Saylor, C.F., Powell, M.P., Stokes, S.J., Foster, K.Y., and Belter, R.W. (1996). Impact of a natural disaster on preschool children: Adjustment 14 months after a hurricane. The *American Journal of Orthopsychiatry* 66:122–130.

Swift, C.R., and Asuni, T. (1975). *Mental Health and Disease in Africa*. ed. Churchill Livingstone, London and New York, pp. 103–114.

Taylor, E. (2004). *Early Detection and Prevention of Attention Deficit/Hyperactivity Disorders*. Facilitating Pathways. Care, Treatment and Prevention in Child and Adolescent Mental Health. Ed. Remschmidt, Belfer, Goodyer. Springer Berlin, N.Y.

Terr, L.C. (1981). "Forbidden games": Post traumatic child's play. *Journal of the American Academy of Child and Adolescent* Psychiatry 20:741–760.

Terr, L.C., Bloch, D.A., Michel, B.A., Shi, H., Reinhardt, J.A., and Metayer, S. (1999). Children's symptoms in the wake of *Challenger*. A field study of distant-traumatic effects and an outline of related conditions. *American Journal of Psychiatry* 156: 1536–1544.

Udwin, O., Boyle, S., Yule, W., Bolton, D., and O'Rayan, D. (2000). Risk factors for long-term psychological effects of a disaster experienced in adolescence: Predictors of posttraumatic stress disorder. *Journal of Child Psychology and Psychiatry* 41:969–979.

UNESCO. (1997). *School Effectiveness and Education for Democracy and Nonviolence.* Harber, C. Paris: UNESCO.

UNICEF (United Nation Children's Fund). (2005). The State of the World's Children 2005. Full text. Access online at: www.unicef.org.

Vernberg, E.M. (2000). Intervention approaches following disasters. In *Helping Children Cope with Disasters and Terrorism*, La Greca, A.M., Silverman, W.K., Vernberg, E.M., Roberts, M.C., eds. Washington, DC: American Psychological Association, pp. 55–72.

Vernberg, E.M., La Greca, A.M., Silverman, W.K., and Prinstein, M.J. (1996). Predictors of child's post-disaster functioning Hurricane Andrew. *Journal of Abnormal Psychology* 105:237–248.

Walz, G.R. (1987). Combating the school dropout problem: Proactive strategies for school counselors. Access online at www.edrs.com/members/ericfac.cfm?an ED287112

Weissberg, R.P., Caplan, M.Z., and Sivo, P.J. (1989). A new conceptual framework for establishing school-based social competence promotion programs. In Bond, L.A., and Compas, B.E. (eds), *Primary Prevention and Promotion in Schools*. Newbury Park, CA: Sage.

Weissman, M.M., Wolk, S., Goldstein, R.B., et al. (1999). Depressed adolescents grown up. *Journal of the American Medical Association* 281:1707–1713.

WHO (World Health Organization). (1977). Life skill education for children and adolescents in schools. Program on Mental Health. WHO/MNH/933 Rev. 1, WHO, Geneva.

WHO (World Health Organization). (1994). *Mental Health Programmes in Schools.* Ed. Hendren, R., Weisen, B., and Orley, J. Division of Mental Health. Geneva.

WHO (World Health Organization). (1996). *The Status of School Health.* Prepared for WHO/HQ HEP Unit by Education Development Center, Inc., Newton, MA.

WHO (World Health Organization). (1997). *Life Skills Education in Schools.* Program on Mental Health. World Health Organization. Geneva.

WHO (World Health Organization). (1999). *WHO Information Series on School Health: Local Action: Creating Health-Promoting Schools.* Prepublished draft. Geneva: World Health Organization.

WHO (World Health Organization). (2001). Skills for health. Skills-based health education including life skills: An important component of a child-friendly/health promoting school. Information Series on School Health. Document (9), WHO, Geneva.

Widom, C.S. (1989). The cycle of violence. *Science* 244:160–166.

Widom, C.S. (1995). *Victims of Childhood Sexual Abuse: Later Criminal Consequences.* National Institute of Justice: Research in brief. March. Washington, DC: U.S. Department of Justice.

Windle, M., Shope, J.T., and Bukstein, O. (1996). *Alcohol Use.Handbook of Adolescent Health Risk Behavior*. ed. DiClemente, R.J., Hansen, W., and Ponton, L. New York: Plenum Press, pp. 115–159.

Wolmer, L., Laor, N., and Yazgan, Y. (2003). Implementating relief programs in schools after disasters: The teacher as clinical resource. *Child and Adolescent Psychiatric clinics of North America* 12:363–381.

Wolraich, M.L., Hannah, J.N., Pinnock, T.Y., Baumgaettel, A., and Brown, J. (1996). Comparison of diagnostic criteria for attention-deficit hyperactivity disorder in a country-wide sample. *Journal of the American Academy of Child and Adolescent Psychiatry* 35:319–324.

Young, I., and Williams, T. (1989). *The Healthy School*. Edinburgh: Scottish Health Education Group.

Youssef, R. and Attia, M. (1998). Child abuse and neglect: Its perception by those who work with children. *J EMRO*, World Health Organization Vol. 4, No. 2:276–292.

Youssef, R., Attia, M., and Kamel, M. (1999). Violence among school children in Alexandria. *J EMRO*, World Health Organization Vol. 5, No. 2:282–298.

Zabin, L.S., Hirsch, M.B., Smith, E.A., Streett, R., and Hardy, J.B. (1986). Evaluation of a pregnancy prevention program for urban teens. *Family Planning Perspectives* 18:119–126.

Index

About the Editors and Contributors

Myron Belfer is professor of psychiatry and a child and adolescent psychiatrist in the Department of Social Medicine at Harvard Medical School. He is cochair of the International Child Mental Health Program sponsored by Children's Hospital, Boston and the Department of Social Medicine. He served as senior adviser for child and adolescent mental health in the Department of Mental Health and Substance Abuse at the World Health Organization in Geneva from 2000 to 2005. He trained in adult and child psychiatry at Harvard Medical School–affiliated programs and has a Master's in public administration from the John F. Kennedy School of Government at Harvard University. He is president of the International Association for Child and Adolescent Psychiatry and Allied Professions, and cochair of the International Relations Committee of the American Academy of Child and Adolescent Psychiatry.

Ernesto Caffo is professor of child psychiatry at the University of Modena and Reggio Emilia. He is currently president of the European Society for Child and Adolescent Psychiatry (ESCAP) and vice-president of the International Association for Child and Adolescent Psychiatry and Allied Professions (IACAPAP). He is president of Telefono Azzurro, an Italian helpline engaged in child abuse prevention and promotion of children's rights. He is also director of Tetto Azzurro, a center for diagnosis and treatment of abused and neglected children in Rome. He has been researching child abuse and neglect for many years and has published extensively on these subjects as well as on developmental psychopathology, traumatic stress, and autism. He is involved in national and international research projects.

Martine Flament is a child and adolescent psychiatrist. She received an M.D. from the University of Paris V and a Ph.D. from the University of Paris VI. She obtained her research training at the child psychiatry branch of the National Institute of Mental Health in the United States. Then she was a researcher at the National Institute of Health and Medical Research (INSERM) in France. Currently, Dr. Flament is the director of the Youth Unit at the University of Ottawa Institute of Mental Health Research (IMHR), and professor in the Department of Psychiatry and the School of Psychology at the University of Ottawa.

Barbara Forresi is a psychologist. She received her doctorate in psychobiology at the University of Modena and Reggio Emilia. Her clinical and research interests are traumatic events and their impact on children and adolescent adjustment.

M. Elena Garralda is professor of child and adolescent psychiatry at Imperial College, London. Her clinical and research interests include the interface between physical and mental health problems and medical help-seeking in children and adolescents. With Professor Martine Flament, she is coeditor of the IACAPAP (International Association for Child and Adolescent Psychiatry and Allied Professions) book series.

Ian M. Goodyer is professor of child and adolescent psychiatry at the University of Cambridge. He is director of the Emotion Development and Mood Disorders Research Group in the Developmental Psychiatry Section of the Department of Psychiatry. His research interests are in the development of depressive disorders and the role of emotion in behavioral development. He has published widely on the role of social, psychological, and hormonal factors in the onset, course, and outcome of clinical depression. His current research is investigating the role of emotion in behavioral development, risk, and resilience processes for psychiatric disorders during adolescence and the treatment of depression in young people.

Johannes Hebebrand is head of the Department of Child and Adolescent Psychiatry at the University of Duisburg-Essen. His main research interests pertain to the genetics of obesity, eating disorders, and attention deficit/hyperactivity disorder.

Anke Hinney is head of the Molecular Genetic Laboratory at the Department of Child and Adolescent Psychiatry at the University of Duisburg-Essen. Her main research interests are the genetics of obesity, eating disorder, and attention deficit/hyperactivity disorder.

Luisa Strik Lievers is a child psychiatrist and Ph.D. student at the University of L'Aquila, Italy. Her clinical and research interests are in preschoolers' psychopathology and family dynamics.

Thomas G. O'Connor is associate professor of psychiatry and of psychology, and director of the Laboratory for the Prevention of Mental Disorders at the University of Rochester. His research focuses on family factors in children's development and the long-term effects of early stress exposure on development.

Raija-Leena Punamäki is a psychologist and professor at the University of Tampere, Finland. Her research has focused on child development and mental health in conditions of war and military violence. The specific topics are resiliency, symbolic processes such as dreaming and playing, family dynamics, and adult attachment in traumatic conditions. In cooperation with the Gaza Community Mental Health Program, she specializes in rehabilitation of victims of human rights abuse, preventive interventions with schoolchildren, and mother-infant interaction at risk.

Kathrin Reichwald is a research scientist in a group with Johannes Hebebrand and Anke Hinney. Her main interest is the analysis of sequence variations in genes contributing to early-onset extreme obesity.

Benno Graf Schimmelmann works in the Department of Child and Adolescent Psychiatry at the University of Duisburg-Essen. His main research interests are the genetics of ADHD, early-onset psychosis, and psychopharmacology.

Stephen B. C. Scott is reader in child health and behavior and consultant child and adolescent psychiatrist in the Department of Child and Adolescent Psychiatry and the Institute of Psychiatry in London. He has conducted several randomized controlled studies of parenting intervention and is a leading researcher in this area in Europe.

Amira Seif el Din is professor and chairperson of the Community Medicine Department, Alexandria University, Egypt. She is also president of EMACA-PAP. Her research focuses mainly on school mental health and epidemiology of child psychiatric problems in the Arab world.